Dfl. 57,60

Fluctuations and growth in a near full employment economy

Fluctuations and growth in a near full employment economy

A quarterly econometric
analysis of the Netherlands

W. DRIEHUIS

Foreword by C.A. van den Beld,
Director of the Central Planning Bureau, The Hague,
Professor of economics,
Netherlands School of Economics, Rotterdam

Rotterdam University Press/1972

HC 325
.D7

Copyright © 1972 by Universitaire Pers Rotterdam
No part of this book may be reproduced in any form, by print, photoprint, microfilm or any other means without written permission from the publisher.
Printed in Belgium
ISBN: 90 237 2244 2

to the memory of my mother,
to my father,
to tineke

Foreword

The first macro-economic models for the Netherlands' economy were built in the nineteen thirties when Professor J. Tinbergen started on his epoch making work. After 1945 the Central Planning Bureau continued along similar, but more advanced lines. As a matter of fact these models are indispensable for the forecasting of economic developments and as an instrument for the preparation of macro-economic policy, both short and medium term.

However, as these models were all annual models, there always was a gap, viz. the developments during the year could not be analysed. This gap has now been filled by Dr. Driehuis' exhaustive quarterly analysis of the Netherlands' economy. With the Central Planning Bureau's know-how of annual models at his disposal Dr. Driehuis made a highly original contribution to model building. This originality emerges from the theoretical bases on which the quarterly model is built, the causalities which have been found and the treatment of the lag structures.

In addition to its theoretical merits Dr. Driehuis' treatise is of a great practical value. As a more exact valuation of the business cycle has now become available the development of the Netherlands' economy will be more readily recognizable. It may well be that forecasting errors will diminish and the preparation of macro-economic policy may thus come to rest on a more fundamental basis.

I have no doubt that this model will be an inspiration to further research. The author himself touches on the subject where he mentions a new task "... possibly leading to an enlarged insight into 'Economic Policy in a Near-Full Employment Economy' ", (page 218), calling such a study both time consuming and ambitious. Whether this study will turn out to be as time consuming and as ambitious as was the construction of the quarterly model is still an open question.

C.A. van den Beld,
Director of the Central Planning Bureau, The Hague,
Professor of economics,
Netherlands School of Economics, Rotterdam

Acknowledgements

It has been my privilige to carry out the research, laid down in this book as a staff member of the Netherlands Central Planning Bureau. Not only did I have all the know-how compiled during 25 years of model building at my disposal, I was also in the happy position that I could discuss problems with a great number of specialist economists and econometricians. I am grateful that they were willing to give me the benefit of their knowledge and experience.

I was fortunate in finding Professor C.A. van den Beld, the director of the Central Planning Bureau, willing to discuss the study with me and I feel greatly indebted to him for his stimulating and helpful comments. The shortcomings which remain are, of course, my responsibility.

During the compilation of the whole project I have been extremely ably assisted by Mr. W.H. Winkler who looked after all the technical details; he has shared with me the pleasures and disappointments inherent in a project like this. I wish to thank him here for his excellent research assistance and the pleasant cooperation.

Messrs. J.T.N. van der Lem and H. den Hartog very kindly read through a great number of chapters and I am indebted to them for their valuable remarks. Mr. van der Lem was also a great help to me in analyzing the monetary phenomena. My thanks are also due to Messrs. R.J.A. den Haan and B.L. de Groot for assisting me in the analysis of foreign trade and wage determination and wage policy respectively.

My special appreciation goes to Dr. J.H.C. Lisman who in an earlier stage collected the data and greatly stimulated me to set out on this study. He followed it from the very beginning to the end, showing his interest and tending practical help whereever he could.

I also wish to thank the Computer Section and the Section of Applied

Mathematics of the Central Planning Bureau, who looked after the calculations and computer programming.

The often difficult task of preparing the typescript has been excellently dealt with by Miss A.C.J. Haagen, Miss I.B. Baas, Mrs. V.G.E. de Geus, Mrs. G. van de Pas and Miss J.F.V. Trienekens. I wish to thank them all here.

To Mr. H. van Oortmerssen for the drawings, and to Mr. F.P. Toet for the tables in chapters XIII-XV I also owe a debt of gratitude.

Finally, I would like to express thanks to my wife who, through a period of years, showed great forebearance. I realize that her passive task cannot always have been pleasant. Her moral assistance has been quite indispensable for me.

W. Driehuis

Contents

I.	INTRODUCTION	1
1.1.	General background	1
1.2.	Character of the model	3
1.3.	General outline	5

II.	GENERAL PROBLEMS OF SPECIFICATION AND ESTIMATION	7
2.1.	Introduction	7
2.2.	Sources of the data	7
2.3.	Seasonal adjustment	9
2.4.	Use of logarithms	11
2.5.	Estimation of the model equations	12
2.6.	Causes and types of lag structures	13
2.7.	Formalization of distributed lags	14
2.8.	Estimation of distributed lags	16
2.9.	Notation	24

III.	THE LABOUR MARKET	25
3.1.	Introduction	25
3.2.	Demand for labour theory	26
3.3.	Imperfect competition on markets for production factors	34
3.4.	Empirical results of demand for labour	37
3.5.	Supply of labour theory	42

XI

3.6.	Empirical results of labour supply	45
3.7.	The utilization rate of labour	48

IV.	INVESTMENT BEHAVIOUR OF ENTERPRISES	53
4.1.	Introduction	53
4.2.	Theory of investment for expansion	54
4.3.	Theory of investment for replacement and modernization	58
4.4.	Empirical results	61

V.	PRIVATE CONSUMPTION EXPENDITURES	65
5.1.	Introduction	65
5.2.	The role of incomes and prices	66
5.3.	The role of other variables	72
5.4.	Empirical results	74

VI.	INVENTORY FORMATION	78
6.1.	Introduction	78
6.2.	Theory of inventory formation	78
6.3.	Empirical results	82

VII.	EXPORTS AND IMPORTS OF GOODS AND SERVICES	85
7.1.	Introduction	85
7.2.	Exports of goods and services theory	86
7.3.	Empirical results of exports	88
7.4.	Imports of goods and services theory	95
7.5.	Empirical results of imports	97

VIII.	WAGE DETERMINATION AND WAGE POLICY	103
8.1.	Introduction	103
8.2.	A simple theory of wage determination	104

8.3.	The role of imperfect competition	105
8.4.	Institutional factors	106
8.5.	Wage drift	107
8.6.	The basic wage equation	109
8.7.	Empirical results: the whole period 1951:1–1968:4	112
8.8.	Short summary of wage policy in the Netherlands	115
8.9.	Empirical results: the period 1951:1–1954:3	117
8.10.	Empirical results: the period 1954:4–1959:2	120
8.11.	Empirical results: the period 1959:3–1962:4	123
8.12.	Empirical results: the period 1963:1–1968:4	125
8.13.	Conclusions	128

IX.	PRICE FORMATION	129
9.1.	Introduction	129
9.2.	Theory of price formation	129
9.3.	The price of private consumption	135
9.4.	The price of gross fixed investment in enterprises	138
9.5.	The price of autonomous expenditures	140
9.6.	The price of exports of manufactured goods	142
9.7.	The price of exports of services	145

X.	GOVERNMENT RECEIPTS AND EXPENDITURES	147
10.1.	Introduction	147
10.2.	Institutional aspects of taxation	148
10.3.	Wage and income tax	149
10.4.	Taxes on non-wage income	150
10.5.	Taxes on sales	151

XI.	MONETARY PHENOMENA	152
11.1.	Introduction	152
11.2.	Determinants of the interest rate	152
11.3.	Empirical results	158
11.4.	Theory of money supply	161
11.5.	Empirical results	165

XII.	THE COMPLETE MODEL	170

12.1. Introduction	170
12.2. Static and reduced version of the model	171
12.3. Working of the model	176
12.4. Classification of endogenous variables	177
12.5. Classification of exogenous variables	179
12.6. Target and instrument variables	180

XIII.	SHORT-TERM SIMULATIONS	184

13.1. Introduction	184
13.2. Simulation 1951:1–1952:4	186
13.3. Simulation 1953:1–1954:4	187
13.4. Simulation 1955:1–1956:4	187
13.5. Simulation 1957:1–1958:4	187
13.6. Simulation 1959:1–1960:4	187
13.7. Simulation 1961:1–1962:4	206
13.8. Simulation 1963:1–1964:4	206
13.9. Simulation 1965:1–1966:4	206
13.10. Simulation 1967:1–1968:4	207
13.11. Summary	207

XIV.	MEDIUM-TERM SIMULATIONS	209

14.1. Introduction	209
14.2. Simulation 1951:1–1955:4	211
14.3. Simulation 1955:1–1959:4	211
14.4. Simulation 1959:1–1963:4	213
14.5. Simulation 1963:1–1967:4	213
14.6. Summary	215

XV.	POLICY AND OTHER SIMULATIONS	218

15.1. Introduction	218
15.2. Short evaluation of the simulations	220
15.3. Conclusions	225

APPENDICES 226

Appendix A. Model equations	226
Appendix B. List of symbols	240
Appendix C. Derivation of quarterly figures from annual data	246
Appendix D. Seasonal adjustment of the data	248
Appendix E. Weighting schemes for exports	251
Appendix F. Weighting schemes for imports	253
Appendix G. Method of solution of the model	255

BIBLIOGRAPHY 258

INDEX 267

I. Introduction

1.1. GENERAL BACKGROUND

Since TINBERGEN (1936)[1] constructed the first econometric model of the Netherlands' economy, several other models have been developed for this country: the short term annual model constructed by VERDOORN (1967), the cyclical growth model developed by VAN DEN BELD (1968) and other models.[2] The Central Planning Bureau of the Netherlands has most of all used different versions of the short term forecasting model. This model therefore was, and still is, an important tool in the forecasting of the future development of the Netherlands' economy as well as in the assessment of short term effects of policy measures.[3]

This book describes the construction and application of a completely new econometric model for the Netherlands. This model, based on quarterly data, was designed to explain short term fluctuations and medium term growth of the Netherlands' economy over the period 1951-1965. The estimated parameters describing the causal relations between the relevant variables must be suited for forecasting purposes and for the evaluation of measures of economic policy. There are mainly three reasons for our undertaking of the analysis.

Each year, in January or February, the Central Planning Bureau publishes a set of forecasts concerning the economic situation of that year as prescribed

---

1. Throughout this book references to items in the bibliography will be made by means of a year in parentheses following the author's name.
2. See for instance VAN DEN BELD, VAN DE PAS and TJAN (1965), VAN DEN BELD (1967), MERKIES and VAN DE PAS (1969), SIEBRAND and HOOGLAND (1969), VAN DEN BELD and MIDDELHOEK (1971), KOOYMAN and MERKIES (1971) and DEN HARTOG and FRAENKEL (1972).
3. For a description of the planning procedure in the Netherlands and the role of the Central Planning Bureau, see ABERT (1969), ALBECK (1969) and VAN DEN BELD (1970).

by the Act of April 21, 1947. This Act says that the Bureau's task is to carry out all activities related with the preparation of a Central Economic Plan which shall at regular times be presented by the government. The Act defines the term plan as a 'balanced system of estimates and guidelines with regard to the Netherlands' economy.'

The Central Economic Plan has a preliminary version in September of the preceding year. This publication, the so-called Macro Economic Outlook, is presented to Parliament on the third Tuesday of September together with the budget proposals for the coming calendar year. It therefore has an important role in the drawing up of economic policy measures for the near future.

When these September forecasts are prepared in July and August very few statistical material is available, related to the first and sometimes to the second quarter of the year. The knowledge of economic developments within the base year is thus far from complete and must be supplemented with assessed data, preferably on a quarterly basis. The same argument holds as well with the preparation of the Central Economic Plan in October-November.

In both the Macro Economic Outlook and the Central Economic Plan the greater part of the forecasts and effects of policy measures is formulated in percentage changes in the variables with respect to the previous year. Sometimes the level form is used, for instance in the case of the balance of payments on current account and the number of unemployed. It is, however, evident that a meaningful interpretation of annual data makes knowledge of the development of the levels of the relevant economic variables within the years under consideration indispensable. For instance: the forecast of a positive percentage change in a certain variable may suggest a satisfactory development but is highly misleading from a point of view of interpretation when the development of that variable within the projection year is downward directed. Figure 1.1 illustrates this. Another example is the development of the balance of payments on current account during the years 1956 and 1957. Both years show a deficit of about 700 million guilders, but within these years the direction of change is quite opposite (see also figures 13.3 and 13.4).

Apart from the above there is another reason for undertaking a quarterly analysis of the Netherlands' economy. An econometric model based on annual data may explain and forecast economic developments in an acceptable way. But, the estimates of the time lags involved will be necessarily rough approximations when based on linear interpolation of annual data. It seems therefore preferable to consider the time shape of reactions within a year. In addition to this problem of the optimal estimation of the reaction

Figure 1.1. Comparison of an annual percentage change with quarterly data in level form

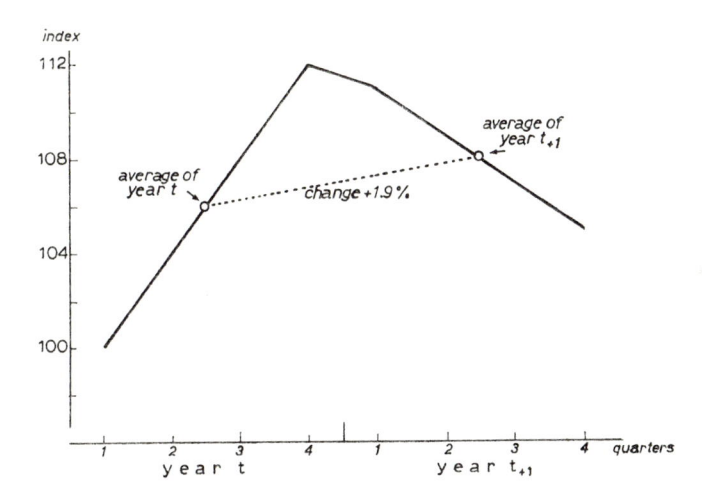

patterns the use of an annual model may have unpleasant consequences from an economic policy point of view. For an annual model may generate the cyclical turning points inadequately,[4] which may lead to wrong policy decisions, either as a result of bad timing or even as a wrong interpretation of the direction into which the economy moves.

In conclusion, an effort to increase the knowledge of the behaviour of the Netherlands' economy from quarterly data seems fully worth while. From an academic point of view it may be useful because the understanding of the working of the Netherlands' economy can probably be enlarged. From a practical point of view because forecasts of the economic development can presumably be improved and economic policy consequences better evaluated. Time and experience will show whether these ends have been reached.

1.2. CHARACTER OF THE MODEL

The estimation of the model equations is based upon quarterly data, enabling us to obtain specifications of a highly dynamic character and to consider short and long term patterns of reaction. Although the standard forecasting

---

4. For an evaluation of the capability of the short term annual model to forecast cyclical turning points, see VAN DEN BELD (1965), pp. 37–39.

period will involve eight quarters, the quarters of the current and the next year, the model includes some medium term elements like the substitution between labour and capital and it considers explicitly the influence of technological progress. It is therefore possible to use the model for the evaluation of the time path of the economy over a period of more than two years.

It will be understood that the estimation of the model parameters is conditional upon the economic development abroad and the economic policy measures actually taken during the sample period consisting of sixty quarters from 1951:1 to 1965:4. The estimations are also conditional upon structural elements of the economy like its open character and its operation near full employment with a high savings ratio. The open character of the economy becomes apparent from the fact that imports and exports of goods and services have a share of about 40–50% of Gross National Product. Near full employment follows from the low average unemployment rate of 1.7% over the observation period with the actual unemployment rate moderately fluctuating. The savings ratio of 20 percent of GNP is one of the highest of the industrialized world. There is no doubt that if this structure should change considerably in the future the model will not be suitable for forecasting the time path of the economy nor for an accurate evaluation of the effects of economic policy measures.

The equations, which collectively represent the complete quarterly model, have been estimated with special emphasis on three aspects, *viz.* theoretical consistency, analytical reliability for economic policy purposes and forecasting accuracy. All three aspects will come up for discussion in the course of this study. Nevertheless it may be useful to summarize some details in connection with these.

We will here confess to our ambition of building a model based on a number of hypotheses which we intend to maintain throughout the whole analysis. These hypotheses should be consistent from a theoretical point of view and at the same time they must be sufficiently realistic. In addition, there are a number of technical characteristics of the model which are worth while to know in advance. To allow the reader an easy judgement of the features and deficiencies of this study these hypotheses and technical aspects can be summed up as to include the following:

i. a Cobb Douglas production function with unconstrained returns to scale;
ii. predominantly imperfect competition on markets for production factors;
iii. predominantly imperfect competition on markets for products;
iv. the validity of the marginal productivity theory;

v.   profit maximizing behaviour of entrepreneurs;
vi. the use of the utilization rate of labour as an approximation for the utilization rate of capital;
vii. the predominant use of elasticities rather than marginal quota's;
viii. the predominant use of finite lag structures between dependent and independent volume variables, of finite lag structures between dependent price variables and independent volume variables and of infinite lag structures between both dependent volume and price variables and independent price variables;
ix. relationships of a largely recursive nature between the endogenous variables;
x.   the inclusion of both target and instrument variables;
xi. the estimation of equations by the method of ordinary least squares;
xii. the use of seasonally adjusted data; and finally
xiii. the aggregative character of the model.

The model is largely a demand model. Five equations represent the demand for the main expenditure categories *viz.* gross fixed business investment, private consumption, inventory formation, exports of goods and exports of services. The demand for production factors is represented by three equations, one for the demand for labour and one each for imports of goods and services. The supply side of the economy is taken into account by five equations explaining the prices of private consumption, gross fixed business investment, autonomous expenditures, exports of goods and exports of services. In addition, capacity (labour) utilization is determined with the help of a labour supply relationship. Income formation is represented by four wage equations, one for each distinguished period of wage policy, as well as by a balance equation from which non-wage income follows as a residual. Finally, monetary phenomena are considered by means of two equations, one for the rate of interest and one for the liquidity ratio. In total there are 68 endogenous variables.

1.3. GENERAL OUTLINE

This study falls into three main parts.
The first part treats introductory remarks and problems of a more technical nature (chapters I and II).
The second part analyses the reaction equations of the model (chapters III–XII). Chapter III, on the labour market, treats demand and supply of labour as well as the utilization rate of the labour force. Chapters IV–VI

analyse domestic expenditures: private consumption expenditures, investment behaviour of firms and inventory formation. Four important items of the current account of the balance of payments are discussed in chapter VII. These are exports and imports of goods and services in volume terms. A theory of wage determination is developed in chapter VIII and evaluated in the light of the changes in wage policy during the sample period. The result is that the model contains four wage equations, one for each separate period of wage policy. The price formation of both domestic and export prices is analyzed in chapter IX. Government receipts and expenditures require separate attention which is given in chapter X, while monetary phenomena in the form of the interest rate and the liquidity ratio are treated in chapter XI. Chapter XII considers the complete model and the results obtained.

The third part (chapters XIII–XV) is concerned with simulations. Chapters XIII and XIV give results of tests about the performance of the complete model for eight quarter and twenty quarter periods, both in and beyond the sample period. Ultimately, chapter XV is concerned with the time path of the economy under a restricted number of alternative domestic policies and circumstances abroad.

Furthermore seven appendices are added for more technical information as well as a bibliography and an index.

II. General problems of specification and estimation

2.1. INTRODUCTION

In the previous chapter we mentioned a number of theoretical and technical characteristics of this study. This chapter is devoted to a more comprehensive treatment of some technical problems, *viz.* those of specification and estimation of the model equations.

When the purposes and the economic policy requirements of a model are known, static specifications are obtained from theoretical reasoning. These specifications are then completed by introducing hypotheses of dynamic behaviour, such as the hypothesis of partial adjustment or the hypothesis of adaptive expectations. Especially in making a quarterly model the estimation of dynamic aspects of a sufficient number of relevant variables requires appropriate tools.

Our main tools to obtain results as meaningful and accurate as possible are:
i. the adjustment of the data for seasonal variation;
ii. the use of log-linear specifications, and
iii. the use of specific procedures for the estimation of time lags.

Before these methodological aspects are viewed in detail, some remarks have to be made on the sources of the data and their use.

2.2. SOURCES OF THE DATA

The construction of a quarterly econometric model of the Netherlands is complicated by a statistical problem. The Central Bureau of Statistics does not publish a consistent and complete quarterly picture of the Netherlands economy: there are no official quarterly national accounts except for the first quarter of 1949 up to the second quarter of 1952.[1]

The quarterly national accounts data used in this book have not been published, since they were compiled by the Central Planning Bureau for internal use only. A detailed description of the preparation of these quarterly figures is outside the scope of this study. A very brief summary may suffice here.

An important part of the required time series can be obtained from regularly published official data. The Central Bureau of Statistics publishes monthly data on private consumption, imports and exports of commodities and manufacturing production.[2] In addition, there is the quarterly publication of investment data, both for the private and the public sector. In most of these cases data are available in current and constant prices. Furthermore a number of time series needed has been compiled by the Central Planning Bureau on the basis of information from the Ministry of Finance and 'De Nederlandsche Bank.' In this way it is possible to estimate government consumption, imports and exports of services, factor incomes and net transfers to abroad.

Another portion of the required statistical material has been estimated from data on relevant final demand components. For example, quarterly figures of the production of the services and the building industry have been assessed with the help of elasticity coefficients found in a regression analysis of annual production data of these sectors and annual figures of appropriate final demand components.

Finally, a very small number of the time series has been derived from annual data by interpolation, such as the production of the agricultural sector[3] and a number of labour market data.

With the mentioned final demand components in constant prices known, as well as the production of enterprises and government, the closing item in the *constant prices* sphere, inventory formation, can be computed.

The resources and expenditures account in *current prices* is then balanced by subtracting imports, wage income, depreciation, indirect taxes less sub-

---

1. See Statistical and Econometric Studies of the CBS, Utrecht, 1952. New Series, 3rd Quarter 1952, pp. 127–154 (in Dutch).
2. Throughout this book we use the word production in the sense of gross value added in constant prices.
3. The production of the agricultural sector is about 10% of total production of enterprises. The applied procedure has therefore minor consequences for the fluctuations of total production.

sidies and net factor income from abroad, from total final demand in current prices. The residual is called non-wage income.

We already mentioned that only a relatively small part of the required quarterly national accounts data is obtained from interpolation and so is a number of other variables needed for the preparation of complete quarterly national accounts and for the construction of the model, especially labour market data (employment, labour supply, etc.).[4] In these cases the quarterly figures were derived from their annual totals by a method designed for this purpose, see BOOT, FEIBES and LISMAN (1967), which will be summarized in appendix C. It is to be noted that quarterly figures obtained from this method of interpolation are by definition not subject to seasonal fluctuations.

2.3. SEASONAL ADJUSTMENT

In quarterly models dummy variables are often introduced for the representation of seasonal fluctuations. We are thinking of the model of the United Kingdom constructed by KLEIN, BALL, HAZLEWOOD and VANDOME (1961), the model of Western Germany constructed by LÜDEKE (1969), the model of Canada constructed by OFFICER (1968) and a recent model of Japan developed by QUIRITANI and MARU (1970). On the other hand, quarterly models with seasonally adjusted data have been built especially for the United States economy, among which the Brookings Quarterly Econometric Model (1965) and the models constructed by LIEBENBERG, HIRSCH and POPKIN (1966), EVANS and KLEIN (1967), de LEEUW and GRAMLICH (1968) and HYMANS and SHAPIRO (1970).

The present econometric analysis of the Netherlands economy is based on seasonally adjusted data. On technical grounds quarterly data derived from annual time series by Lisman's method are by their very nature free of seasonal fluctuations. From the point of view of consistency this requires the other time series to be without seasonal variation as well. However there are a number of other reasons which in our view justify the use of seasonally adjusted data:

i. greater flexibility is warranted in the specification of the seasonal element which may have an additive character for some and a multiplicative character for other variables;
ii. shifts in the seasonal pattern can be taken into account, provided an appropriate seasonal adjustment procedure is used;
iii. there are less parameters to be estimated;

---

4. Apart from the number of unemployed persons which is published monthly.

iv. seasonal dummies represent the net effect of the seasonal influences of all variables and may therefore bias the results;
v. the output of a model built with seasonally adjusted data can be directly applied in analysing the current economic situation.

The summing up of arguments in favour of seasonally adjusted time series does not mean that there are no objections against their use. It is a well-known fact that moving averages of time series are serially correlated even if the original series are not. In addition, most seasonal adjustment methods use moving averages and imply, therefore, the loss of a number of degrees of freedom. Another drawback of this approach is that undoubtedly errors are introduced which can lead to a wrong interpretation of the results and their statistical properties.

Nevertheless we are in favour of seasonally adjusted series because to our mind the above mentioned advantages outweigh the disadvantages and because we can work with a very flexible and accurate method reducing errors inherent in the application of a seasonal adjustment procedure to negligible proportions. It may here suffice to give its main characteristics.

The procedure for estimating seasonal components of time series has been developed in the Central Planning Bureau by Mr. R. J. A. DEN HAAN and programmed for computer by Mr. D. BREKELMANS. Their seasonal adjustment method allows for gradual changes in the underlying basic seasonal pattern and at the same time for a changing multiplicative influence due to fluctuations in the trend-cycle component. This can be illustrated as follows.

Let an original time series Y_{ij} be defined as the sum of a trend cycle component D_{ij}, a seasonal component S_{ij} and a disturbance term U_{ij} in quarter i of year j. The seasonal component S_{ij} is then estimated by the following set of equations:

(2.1) $\quad S_{ij} = s_{ij} k_{ij}$

(2.2) $\quad s_{ij} = a_{0i} + a_{1i} t$

(2.3) $\quad k_{ij} = b_0 + (1 - b_0) \dfrac{D_{ij}}{\bar{D}}$

where $\quad S$ = seasonal component;
$\quad\quad\quad\; s$ = basic seasonal deviation, i.e. after adjustment for the trend-cycle component;
$\quad\quad\quad\; t$ = time trend;
$\quad\quad\quad\; k$ = multiplicator;
$\quad\quad\quad\; D$ = trend-cycle component;
$\quad\quad\quad\; \bar{D}$ = average trend-cycle component in a mid-year, when $t = 0$.

This model has three equations and also three unknown parameters. The way in which the trend-cycle component and the parameters a_0, a_1 and b_0 are estimated is described in appendix D.

2.4. USE OF LOGARITHMS

Variables in reaction equations have been mostly measured in natural logarithms. Equations describing final demand components, imports and employment have been expressed in log-linear form, whereas wage equations and equations explaining prices of final demand components have been estimated on the basis of first differences of logs between corresponding quarters. We have used these four-quarter differences rather than one quarter differences in order to avoid the time series to become too erratic. The use of logarithms implies that the regression coefficients may be considered as partial elasticity coefficients.

There are two main reasons for the use of the logarithmic transformation. The first one is the empirical fact that there have been considerable changes in the greater part of the time series which tends to invalidate the assumption of a constant relationship between the absolute values of variables. Although linear relationships in terms of absolute levels seem on *a priori* grounds equally valid as log-linear relationships there have been considerable changes in marginal coefficients, so that elasticities seem to be the more structural parameters. This conclusion could be drawn from a comparison of two versions of the model, one estimated with variables expressed in absolute values and one with variables expressed in logarithms. It is outside the scope of this book to discuss the findings of this comparison extensively. One remarkable result, however, was that when absolute values were used a relationship between prices or relative prices and the volume of a dependent variable, if any, could hardly be found.

The second reason is that, when using the logarithmic transformation the efficiency of the estimates is increased because heteroscedasticity is reduced. In this case residuals are prevented to have a variance varying with the level of the explanatory variables, which can be expected when they are not of similar order of magnitude for the different observations.[5]

It will be understood that the use of the logarithmic transformation is an important tool in finding appropriate causal relationships and in assessing

---

5. See MALINVAUD (1966), p. 256.

their dynamic aspects. It is remarkable that the equations of so many macro-economic models have been estimated with variables expressed in absolute levels, without paying attention to the above mentioned problems and without taking measures – either logarithmic transformation or premultiplication – to solve them.[6]

2.5. ESTIMATION OF THE MODEL EQUATIONS

In the model the relationships between the endogenous variables are of a recursive rather than of an interdependent nature. This means that, apart from a few variables,[7] the relationships are one-way-directed indicating unilateral relations between the variables. As has been shown by WOLD (1954) a complete recursive system can be estimated by the method of ordinary least squares providing asymptotically unbiased estimates of the parameters. However, our model is in fact a quasi-recursive one with a few coefficients outside the block-triangular form. Nevertheless the model can be estimated as if it was a completely recursive model when these coefficients outside the block-triangular form are forced to have *a priori* determined values.[8]

Up to now the reaction equations of the model have been estimated with the method of ordinary least squares, but this cannot be fully defended on the above mentioned grounds. The reason is that the use of certain hypotheses of dynamic adjustment, to be explained later, contradicts one of the basic assumptions of the ordinary least squares method, *viz.* serial independence of the disturbance terms. Under such circumstances unbiased estimates of the parameters are obtained, but they are inefficient.

For the time being ordinary least squares estimates have been used for simulation and prediction experiments. In the future other methods of estimation have to be applied in order to achieve more sophisticated statistical results. If residuals of estimated equations were significantly autocorrelated, an iterative procedure, to be explained later, has been used to obtain proper results in simulation and extrapolation tests.

---

6. The premultiplication procedure must be applied when the value of a variable can become negative which invalidates the use of logarithms. Compare chapter XI on monetary phenomena.
7. It will be shown in Appendix G that the values of four endogenous variables have to be known before the remaining part of the model can be solved recursively.
8. For this procedure see SENGUPTA'S (1965) article on specification and estimation of structural relations.

2.6. CAUSES AND TYPES OF LAG STRUCTURES

An important and perhaps the most difficult problem in constructing a quarterly model is the estimation of the lag structure of the variables. Before going into the details of the estimating procedure used we have to look at the causes of lags in general and try to understand their appearance on the basis of the behaviour of economic subjects. In his study of the timeshape of economic reactions Koyck distinguishes *objective* from *subjective* causes, the objective causes being divided into technological and institutional ones.[9]

Technological causes are mainly related to the fact that physical production of investment and consumers' goods requires time. Once an entrepreneur has decided to react to a change in the price level and, for instance, to adjust his production capacity it takes time for him to buy new equipment, have it installed, etc., and once machines are installed it takes time to produce goods. So adjustments needed to bring about a new equilibrium are often time consuming for technical reasons. Other reasons leading to a lagged reaction are those resulting from institutional circumstances arising from laws or customs. These circumstances are different from country to country and they can vary over time. Examples are: the fact that salaries are usually paid at the end of the month, dividends once or two times a year, taxes in a certain quarter, etc.

Next we come to subjective reasons for lagged responses, mostly the result of imperfect knowledge of the market and psychological circumstances. For instance, a change in price is not immediately known to every potential buyer. This will be more important in the behaviour of consumers than in that of producers. Psychological inertia may prevent instantaneous readjustment of the behaviour of economic subjects to a changed situation, where habits lead to lagged reactions. An important psychological phenomenon is the existence of expectations. The behaviour of economic subjects is situated in a world full of uncertainty. Producers are uncertain about the level of their future sales and future prices of inputs and outputs.[10] Consumers on the other hand are not quite certain about their disposable incomes in the future, the prices that will prevail for consumer goods and the rate of interest at which they can borrow or lend. Consequently people will base their decisions on expectations about future developments and the problem is how these expectations are made and how they can be adequately converted into observable values.

9. KOYCK (1954), pp. 6–9.
10. It can be argued that firms are not uncertain about their product prices when they are fixed by them. Nevertheless price setting requires knowledge of the elasticity of demand, which may change over time.

The analysis of reasons why economic reactions may be spread over time has been especially developed for the behaviour of the individual economic subject. It will be clear that, whatever the reasons of the lag, it may consist of one, or more, definite periods of time. In general we may say that the lag in the reaction of an individual economic subject will have a determinate length: either the length of a *single* lag or the length of a *distributed* lag, *viz.* when the reaction is not instantaneous but is distributed over a period of time. It seems reasonable that when dealing with the reactions of a collection of individual subjects the total reaction will be spread over a longer period of time. This may be due to the fact that for different individuals single lags are not identical and because there are differences in the starting points of reactions. So, the distributed lags one expects when analyzing reactions on the macro economic level, may be caused by aggregation of diverse single lags or by combination of different single and distributed lags.

An other classification of lags that can be made is the distinction between *finite* and *infinite* lags. Single lags are by definition finite, but distributed lags may be of a finite or an infinite character. By a finite lag we mean a scheme in which past signals are translated within a fixed period of time, whereas with infinite lag structures the adjustment proceeds during an infinite number of periods.

2.7. FORMALIZATION OF DISTRIBUTED LAGS

In this section we will concentrate on the formalization and estimation of distributed lags. The reasoning is according to Jorgenson's analysis of rational distributed lag functions.[11]

A distributed lag function is defined by:

(2.4) $\quad y_t = p_0 x_t + p_1 x_{t-1} + p_2 x_{t-2} + \ldots$

where y_t and x_t are values of dependent and independent variables at time t and the coefficients $\{p_k\}$ are unknown parameters. We impose the restriction that the sequence $\{p_k\}$ corresponds to the probability distribution of a non negative, integer valued, random variable, so that:

$$p_k \geq 0 (k = 0, 1, 2, \ldots), \text{ and } \sum_{k=0}^{\infty} p_k = 1.$$

This restriction implies that a finite change in the value of the independent variable which persists indefinitely will result in a finite change in the depen-

---

11. See JORGENSON (1966).

dent variable. According to Jorgenson's line of thought distributed lag functions may be called rational when the sequence $\{p_k\}$ of coefficients has a rational generating function.

Let the generating function of the sequence $\{p_k\}$ be represented by $P(s)$ where

(2.5) $\quad P(s) = p_0 + p_1 s + p_2 s^2 + \ldots$

If this function is rational, we may write $P(s) = \dfrac{G(s)}{H(s)}$ where $G(s)$ and $H(s)$ are polynomials in s:

(2.6) $\quad G(s) = g_0 + g_1 s + g_2 s^2 + \ldots + g_m s^m$

(2.7) $\quad H(s) = h_0 + h_1 s + h_2 s^2 + \ldots + h_n s^n$

Under the restriction that these polynomials have no characteristic root in common, a rational distributed lag function may be represented by the ratio of two polynomials.

Distributed lag function (2.4) can be written as:

(2.8) $\quad y_t = P(L) x_t = [p_0 + p_1 L + p_2 L^2 + \ldots] x_t$

where L is the lag operator, defined as $L^n x = x_{t-n}$. Alternatively this relationship may also be formulated as:

(2.9) $\quad y_t = P(L) x_t = \dfrac{G(L)}{H(L)} x_t$

where $G(L)$ and $H(L)$ are polynomials in the lag operator (L). This general formulation of a distributed lag of the variable x_t on y_t includes a number of different distributed lag models. If we take, for instance, $G(L) = \gamma_0 + \gamma_1 L + \ldots + \gamma_m L^m$ and $H(L) = 1$ a finite distributed lag is obtained of the form:

(2.10) $\quad y_t = \gamma_0 x_t + \gamma_1 x_{t-1} + \ldots + \gamma_m x_{t-m} = \sum_0^m \gamma_i x_{t-i}$

The γ's, or reaction coefficients, give the response of the variable y to a shock in the variable x over m periods earlier. The immediate, or short run, response is described by γ_0 and the total, or long run, response is $\sum_0^m \gamma_i$. If the γ's are all positive γ_i may be regarded as the weight given to the lag of length i. The average lag may then be calculated as $\sum i \gamma_i / \sum \gamma_i$.

An example of an infinite distributed lag arising from the general equation (2.9) is the geometrically distributed lag function used by KOYCK (1954).

In this case we may take $G(L) = 1 - \lambda$ and $H(L) = 1 - \lambda L$ so that

(2.11) $\quad y_t - \lambda y_{t-1} = (1 - \lambda) x_t$

This is the so-called Koyck transformation of the form[12]

(2.12) $\quad y_t = (1 - \lambda) \sum_{i=0}^{\infty} \lambda^i x_{t-i} \qquad\qquad 0 \leqslant \lambda < 1$

A more general infinite distributed lag function is the Pascal distribution,[13] in the case of which $G(L) = (1 - \lambda)^r$ and $H(L) = (1 - \lambda L)^r$. The final form of this distributed lag function, for $r = 2$, is

(2.13) $\quad y_t = (1 - \lambda)^2 x_t + 2\lambda y_{t-1} - \lambda^2 y_{t-2}$

An attractive property of this lag function is that the influence of x on y_t can first rise and then decline. This and other properties of rational distributed lag functions are formulated by JORGENSON (1966) and discussed in some detail by GRILICHES (1967). We need not repeat their argument here, but it is useful to pay attention to some problems in relation to estimating infinite distributed lag functions and regard the frequently used method developed by ALMON (1965) as well.

2.8. ESTIMATION OF DISTRIBUTED LAGS

In this section we consider the estimation of distributed lags in the model. This means that we will consider two groups of problems connected herewith. The first group of problems is related with the making of hypotheses of dynamic economic behaviour and their formalization. Up to this section formalization of distributed lags has been handled without paying attention to any underlying behavioural hypothesis. The existence of distributed lags was only postulated. The second group of problems are those related with the estimation of the distributed lags. The foregoing section was only concerned with deterministic specifications rather than with stochastic ones. It will be clear, that the discussion of statistical problems of estimating

---

12. In fact Koyck used the form $y_t = x_t + \lambda x_{t-1} + \lambda^2 x_{t-2} + \ldots = \sum_{i=0}^{\infty} \lambda^i x_{t-i}$, which is then transformed to $y_t = \lambda y_{t-1} + x_t$. Throughout this book we will use specification (2.12). The difference is that the sum of weights in equation (2.12) adds up to unity, whereas in Koyck's original specification this is not necessarily so.
13. See SOLOW (1960).

distributed lags must be rather limited here.[14] Therefore it will not go further than what is necessary for the understanding of the model equations.

We mentioned already the geometrically distributed lag postulated by Koyck in his analysis of the investment behaviour. Such a lag function was derived by CAGAN (1956) and NERLOVE (1958) by formulating hypotheses on economic behaviour.

According to Cagan's hypothesis – the adaptive expectations hypothesis – expectations of a variable (x^*) are revised in proportion to the error associated with the previous level of expectations, thus

(2.14) $\quad x_t^* - x_{t-1}^* = (1 - \lambda)(x_t - x_{t-1}^*) \qquad 0 \leqslant \lambda < 1$

Substitution of this hypothesis in a relationship of the type

(2.15) $\quad y_t = \alpha + \beta x_t^* + u_t$

where u_t is an error term with usual statistical properties,[15] yields after the Koyck transformation,

(2.16) $\quad y_t = \alpha(1-\lambda) + \beta(1-\lambda)x_t + \lambda y_{t-1} + (u_t - \lambda u_{t-1})$

Nerlove formulated a model, the partial adjustment model, in which a 'desired' level of y, say y^*, depends on the current value of an exogenous variable x

(2.17) $\quad y_t^* = \alpha + \beta x_t + u_t$

but only some fixed fraction of the desired adjustment is accomplished within a particular period of time, i.e.

(2.18) $\quad y_t - y_{t-1} = (1 - \lambda)(y_t^* - y_{t-1}) \qquad 0 \leqslant \lambda < 1$

hence

(2.19) $\quad y_t = \alpha(1-\lambda) + \beta(1-\lambda)x_t + \lambda y_{t-1} + (1-\lambda)u_t$

Although the adaptive expectations model and the partial adjustment model have essentially an identical final specification, their consequences for statistical estimation may differ. In Nerlove's model the error term in the final equation is free of autocorrelation, whereas in Cagan's model serial correlation in the disturbances is introduced. The consequences of applying ordinary least squares in the latter case are that inefficient coefficient estimates and

---

14. The reader may consult GRILICHES (1967) and WALLIS (1969) for further details and references to the literature.
15. See for example CRAMER (1969), Chapter 5.

biased estimates of the standard errors result. In addition, when the lagged dependent variable appears among the explanatory variables and autocorrelation in disturbances is present, inconsistent least squares estimates are obtained. Furthermore the Von Neumann ratio, as a measure of serial correlation, is badly biased in this situation.[16]

Although specification (2.16) is statistically inferior to specification (2.19) it is clear that empirically any discrimination between the two hypotheses mentioned is hardly possible. Similarly, when both models of lagged adjustment are assumed to be present in the same equation one is not able to distinguish between them.[17] We have therefore simplified the discussion of dynamic equations in the following chapters by omitting the error terms. When a specification of the type of equations (2.16) or (2.19) was chosen error terms were tested for the presence of serial correlation. In only one case, the equation for labour supply, we could determine residual autocorrelation.

A problem we have neglected up to now is whether, if more than one independent variable is included in the estimating equation, all these variables have identical lag distributions or not. There are no *a priori* reasons for the time shape of different independent variables to be of similar form and length. Neither through theoretical reasoning nor empirically we have been able to reach conclusions which could support such a phenomenon. Some variables have only technological lags, others have lags mainly arising from psychological inertia and still others a mixture of adaptative and expectation lags. It is for these reasons that we have some doubts with respect to the simulation performance of equations involving uniform lags for all explanatory variables. In the models mentioned in section 2.3 of this chapter this type of relationship is frequently found. Apart from the reasons just given and apart from a number of problems, mentioned in the beginning of this section, arising from statistical reasoning we have found that, in general, the procedure using the lagged dependent variable among the explanatory variables does often not yield acceptable *economic* results.

When a uniform time pattern of reaction for each of the explanatory variables is postulated or is derived from one of the behavioural hypotheses mentioned an equation usually takes on the form

(2.20) $\quad y_t = \lambda y_{t-1} + \alpha_1 (1-\lambda) x_t + \alpha_2 (1-\lambda) w_t + \alpha_3 (1-\lambda) z_t + (1-\lambda) \alpha_4$

where y_t is the dependent variable and x_t, w_t and z_t are three independent

---

16. See GRILICHES (1961).
17. See WALLIS (1969), pp. 774–775.

variables with an identical lag distribution, its form being dependent on the value of λ. Especially when the series y_t has a strong trend, as is usual in most of the quarterly models we mentioned, y_t and y_{t-1} are highly correlated. The result is that usually high values for λ are found (.7, .8 or .9), suggesting that *all* explanatory variables have a slow adjustment process. This seems by no means realistic. It may be true that certain variables need a relatively long time of adjustment, such as price or relative price variables, but on the other hand there are a number of variables reacting in a relatively short period. Another drawback of the described estimation procedure, particularly if one is working with trending data, is that the impact of the independent variables is considerably reduced and therefore does not provide an adequate explanation for these trends.

It will be clear that similar difficulties may arise when for each independent variable an adjustment pattern of the Pascal type is chosen. It is true that in that case the reaction first rises and then declines, which may be sometimes more realistic than the geometrically declining curves of the Koyck type, but it seems just as unrealistic to postulate identical humped curves of adjustment for *each* explanatory variable. In addition, as GRILICHES (1967) has pointed out, the use of the Pascal distributed lags requires the fulfilment of a number of rather stringent conditions, otherwise one will arrive at unacceptable results.[18]

A flexible method for estimating different distributed lags for different explanatory variables is the method developed by ALMON (1965). This method assumes the weights of the lag distribution to be coefficients of Lagrange polynomials. The degree and length of the polynomial determines the lag scheme. After varying both these parameters the distribution yielding the highest coefficient of determination is accepted, provided the right sign and sufficient significance of the regression coefficients. Applied to one independent variable and provided a limited number of variations with the degree of the polynomial are made, one can obtain acceptable results within a reasonable time. Things become more difficult when the Almon procedure is applied to more than one independent variable because a considerable amount of combinations is then possible and a considerable number of iterations with both the degree and length of several polynomials has to be made. An advantage of Almon's method is that no specific statistical problems arise, although the empirical literature suggests positive autocorrelation of the residuals to be a frequently occurring phenomenon related with its application.

When estimating the equations of the present model we did not have at

---

18. Compare for instance the findings of STREIT (1970).

our disposal a computer program for the application of the Almon procedure. So, since we had set our mind to obtain flexible lag structures we had to use an equally uncomfortable estimating and selection procedure. To avoid research into the estimating of lags becoming too extensive we have imposed, in principle, infinite distributed lag structures on price or relative price variables. Although this assumption is mainly used on practical grounds and its choice is subjective and not fully defensible by objective theory, there are arguments in favour of its introduction. For that matter one has to acknowledge that prices play an important part in the economic process and that economic subjects cannot permanently withdraw from the working of the price mechanism. Signals of prices present themselves regularly and the above mentioned hypothesis that these signals are translated into decisions during an infinite number of periods is based on the assumptions that, in general, the subject cannot foresee price changes exactly and that they are outside his control. A gradual adjustment to price changes according to an infinite lag scheme seems therefore not unrealistic. However, it should be kept in mind that the use of an infinite lag structure may imply an average adjustment time of reaction which is relatively short.[19]

Two examples may illustrate this proposition. Changes in the price level abroad are outside the control of importers and are known to them when they are actually involved in a transaction of a specific commodity or service. Transactions of commodities or services are distributed over time and this may cause that the reactions to a changed price situation are gradually spread over a rather long period of time. In this example the lag is caused by partial adjustment but a similar conclusion will hold good in the case of expectations.[20] For instance, a producer has to decide on the labour capital ratio to be installed and takes his decision by assessing the future price level of labour relative to the expected price level of capital goods. It may be postulated that expected factor prices are based on the permanent part of factor prices in the past and that transitory components are not taken into consideration in the expectations. Given the importance of the decision for the future utilization rate of the production factors and the installation time involved, it seems adequate to approximate the process of formation of

---

19. The average adjustment time is defined as the time period involved to bring about 50 per cent of the total reaction. See FERBER and VERDOORN (1962), p. 317.

20. In his *Value and Capital* HICKS (1946) classifies three sorts of influences to which price expectations may be subject. In agreement with his line of thought we treat the influence consisting of actual experience of prices, *viz.* experience in the past and experience in the present, as endogenous changes. Influences arising from the weather, from political news and from news bearing on movements of demand and supply are considered as autonomous changes.

expectations by an infinite lag structure. Additional examples might be given in order to support our choice of imposing, in general, infinite lag structures on price or relative price variables. Rather than doing this here we will discuss the general form of our estimating equations. In each of the coming chapters, however, we will show what kind of lag structure has been chosen for each independent variable.

The estimating procedure of the model equations to which we will often refer in the next chapters can be described as follows. Let us assume a relationship between a dependent variable y_t and two independent variables, viz. a price variable z_t and a non price variable x_t. In addition, let the relationship between y_t and (z_t, x_t) be represented by rational distributed lag functions. Then we have

$$(2.21) \quad y_t = \alpha_1 \frac{G(L)_1}{H(L)_1} z_t + \alpha_2 \frac{G(L)_2}{H(L)_2} x_t + c$$

Omitting an error term and supposing that the price variable has an infinite and the non-price variable a finite lag distribution, more specifically supposing that $G(L)_1 = 1 - \lambda, H(L)_1 = 1 - \lambda L, G(L)_2 = \sum_{i=0}^{m} \gamma_i x_{t-i}$ and $H(L)_2 = 1$, then the final form of this equation, implying a Koyck lag [21] of z_t on y_t, is

$$(2.22) \quad y_t - \lambda y_{t-1} = \alpha_1 (1 - \lambda) z_t + \alpha_2 \left[\sum_{i=0}^{m} \gamma_i x_{t-i} - \lambda \sum_{i=1}^{m+1} \gamma_{i-1} x_{t-i} \right] + \\ + (1 - \lambda) c$$

It should be borne in mind that in this example the lag distribution starts in period t, but this is, of course, not necessary and in a quarterly model even most unlikely.[22]

Rather than estimating this equation with the one period lagged dependent variable among the independent variables, as is usual, we have always estimated the model equations in the form of specification (2.22). Intercorrelation between y_t and y_{t-1} is then avoided and for high values of λ one is not far from regressions in first differences, so that the effect of multicollinearity is reduced. The parameters of the equations have been estimated by applying an estimating procedure in which a reasonable number of trial values for λ was chosen in the interval (0,1). We used the values 0, .1, .2, ..., .9 of λ, applied ordinary least squares and then selected the equation for which the

---

21. This Koyck lag may represent the partial adjustment hypothesis discussed in the beginning of this section.
22. When in the following chapters a specification of the type of equation (2.22) occurs, the reader should be aware of this remark.

sum of squared residuals was the lowest. Variables with a wrong sign were dropped and the procedure was applied again until all variables had acceptable signs. Variables with relatively high standard errors have been maintained when theory required their appearance. It will be clear that the applied estimation procedure is not fully satisfactory because

i. *general* lag distributions are postulated in the basic specifications, but we were only able to estimate rather simple lag distributions; the lag distributions found are therefore presumably not optimal;
ii. autocorrelation of residuals may be introduced since the same reduced form can arise from different adjustment hypotheses (compare the partial adjustment and the adaptive expectation models discussed earlier).

As concerns the latter problem we have always tested whether the residuals of the estimating equation showed significant autocorrelation. If so, an iterative procedure, approximately equal to the application of the method of generalized least squares, was put into practice.[23]

Finally one additional remark must be made with respect to the shape of the lag distributions. It sometimes follows from *a priori* reasoning that a lag distribution in the form of a humped curve is required. For instance, assume that people react with a lag on the expected price level and that price expectations are in their turn based on past experience. Instead of equation (2.21) we then have the following general specification:

$$(2.23) \quad y_t = \beta_1 \frac{G(L)_1 G(L)_3}{H(L)_1 H(L)_3} z_t + \beta_2 \frac{G(L)_2}{H(L)_2} x_t + c$$

Suppose furthermore, in addition to specification (2.21), that $G(L)_3 = \frac{1}{n} \sum_{i=1}^{n} z_{t-i}$ and $H(L)_3 = 1$. In its final form we have now

$$(2.24) \quad y_t - \lambda y_{t-1} = \beta_1 (1-\lambda) \frac{1}{n} \sum_{i=1}^{n} z_{t-i} + \beta_2 \left[\sum_{i=0}^{m} \gamma_i x_{t-i} - \lambda \sum_{i=1}^{m+1} \gamma_{i-1} x_{t-i} \right]$$
$$+ (1-\lambda) c$$

The difference in the lag structure of z_t in equation (2.22) and (2.24) can now be easily seen. The weighting scheme underlying equation (2.22) is $(1-\lambda)$, $(1-\lambda)\lambda$, $(1-\lambda)\lambda^2$, $(1-\lambda)\lambda^3$, ... whereas in equation (2.24) – assuming for

---

23. See JOHNSTON (1963), pp. 193–194.

Figure 2.1. Different distributed lags of the Koyck type for $\lambda = .3$, $\lambda = .7$, $n = 2$ *and* $n = 4$

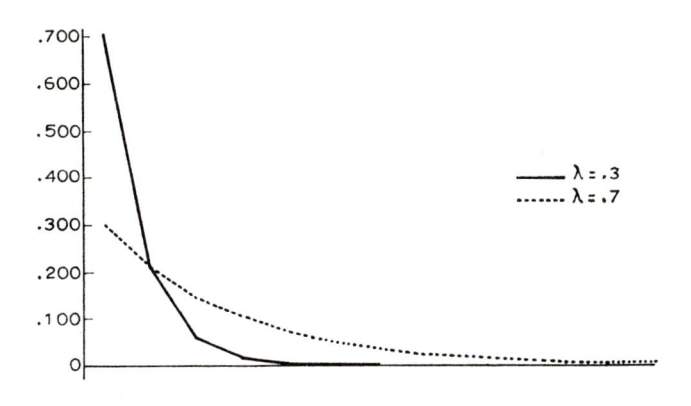

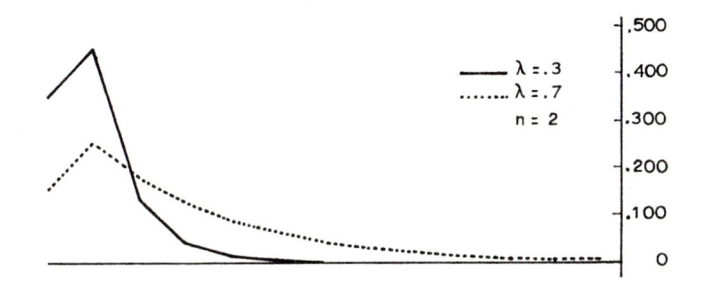

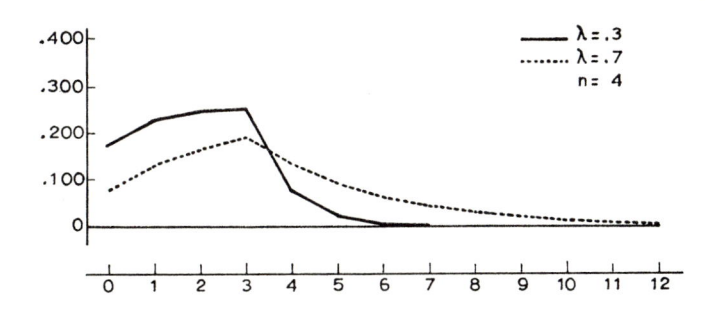

instance $n = 3$ – we have $\frac{1}{n}(1-\lambda)$, $\frac{1}{n}(1-\lambda)(\lambda+1)$, $\frac{1}{n}(1-\lambda)(\lambda^2+\lambda+1)$, $\frac{1}{n}(1-\lambda)(\lambda^2+\lambda+1)\lambda$, ... The conclusion is that application of the Koyck distributed lag to an arbitrary weighted average of a variable yields humped curves of reaction as well. In figure 2.1 the simple Koyck distribution and more complicated versions are compared for $\lambda = .3$, $\lambda = .7$, $n = 2$ and $n = 4$.

2.9. NOTATION

With a few exceptions we refer in the following chapters to the value of a variable in current prices by an upper case symbol, whereas lower case symbols indicate the value of a variable in constant prices of 1963 and price indexes (1963 = 100). Amounts in guilders are on an annual basis. Symbols with a hat (^) represent variables in a situation of full utilization, while an asterisk (*) indicates an expected or a desired value of a variable.

Standard errors, expressed in per cent of the regression coefficient, are given in brackets below this coefficient. Furthermore the Von Neumann ratio is mentioned expressing the degree of autocorrelation of residuals. The rate of explanation is expressed by $\bar{R}^2$ *viz.* the coefficient of determination corrected for bias defined as

$$(2.25) \quad \bar{R}^2 = R^2 - \frac{1-R^2}{n}[(k+1)-(1-R^2)(1+2R^2)]$$

where n is number of observations and k is number of explanatory variables (except constant term).[24] The sample period covers sixty quarters from 1951:1–1965:4, so $n = 60$.

It should be noted that $\bar{R}^2$ does not measure goodness of fit of specifications like equation (2.22), but is computed as if y_{t-1} was written on the right side of the equation. $\bar{R}^2$ as calculated from equation (2.22) may, obviously, differ considerably from the reported $\bar{R}^2$.

---

24. See BARTEN (1962).

III. The labour market

3.1. INTRODUCTION

The equations describing the labour market have, together with the equations explaining investment behaviour and wage determination, a predominant position in the model. This model, it is repeated, is built to generate both cyclical fluctuations and medium term growth in a near full employment economy. It will be clear from the outset that a successful treatment of these and related problems heavily depends on the quality of the single relationships describing labour demand and supply.

The philosophy underlying the analysis of the labour market is neoclassical in that we have adopted a labour demand function which determines the amount of labour for a given production, relative factor prices, labour time, and state of technology. In addition, and unlike the Keynesian theory, the labour supply function relates the labour offered to the real instead of the nominal wage rate.

This very rough description of both sides of the labour market is especially related to the long run situation. In order to represent cyclical influences on labour demand and supply we have used the utilization rate of labour as additional variable. This utilization rate is approximately equal to one minus the unemployment ratio (see section 3.7 of this chapter). In summary we have the following system of labour market equations in mind:

(3.1) $\quad L = L(y, \dfrac{p_k}{w}, q_L, h, t)$

(3.2) $\quad P_S = P_S(P_{ST}, \dfrac{w}{p_c}, q_L)$

25

(3.3) $U = P_S - L$

(3.4) $q_L = q_L(U, L, U_0)$

Labour demand (employment) (L) is determined by the level of production (y), the price of capital (p_k) relative to the wage rate (w), the state of technology (t), the utilization rate of labour (q_L) and labour time (h). Labour supply (P_S) is dependent on the trend of the working population (P_{ST}), as determined by demographic factors, the real wage rate $\left(\dfrac{w}{p_c}\right)$ and the utilization rate of labour (q_L). The unemployed labour force (U) is defined as labour supply minus employment. The utilization rate of labour (q_L) is derived from the number of unemployed workers (U), employed workers (L) and the minimum number of workers which is usually unemployed (U_0) (frictional and structural unemployment).

The following six sections present estimations of these relationships and explain the underlying theoretical concepts. In the last section it is shown, that under certain hypotheses, the utilization rate of labour may act as an overall measure of capacity utilization in a near full employment economy.

3.2. DEMAND FOR LABOUR THEORY

The central assumption in the analysis of the demand for labour is that firms determine their demand of factors of production by finding the combination of factor inputs that will maximize profits subject to a technical constraint, the production function. Because the production function is the constraint for decisions to all factor inputs, individual factor demands must be interrelated. Each factor demand equation must therefore contain parameters from this production function. It will be clear that common parameters in different factor demand relationships should be consistent, i.e. not significantly different. To accept this theme for the analysis of factor demand relations is not new and has been advocated by several authors, as NADIRI and ROSEN (1969) and COEN and HICKMAN (1970). However, when adequate statistical data of the capital stock are lacking the requirements for estimating consistent factor demand equations are not easily fulfilled. Especially when one factor demand equation is in fact a relationship explaining gross investment rather than investment for expansion, problems of identification arise. In chapter IV on investment behaviour we will return to this problem.

Under dynamic conditions the production function is a constraint for firms relating desired or expected production to desired factor inputs. In other words, the production function relates the long run equilibrium values of production to long run equilibrium values of inputs. We assume that a Cobb Douglas production function is valid with unconstrained returns to scale and disembodied technological progress. This function connects expected (desired) long run production (y^*) with desired capital input (K^*) and desired labour input (L^*). The rate of technological progress, for the time being represented by an exponential function, is δ, while A is a scale factor. For the sake of simplicity we abstract temporarily from the influence of hours worked, both for workers and for capital.[1]

(3.5) $\quad y^* = A\, e^{\delta t}\, (L^*)^\alpha\, (K^*)^\beta$

The next assumption is that the economic process proceeds in a world with imperfect competition in both markets of products and production factors; so market subjects cannot supply or demand unconstrained quantities at the current price level. Firms are confronted in their selling market with a decreasing price demand curve and in the market of production factors they are faced with curves representing rising marginal costs of labour and capital.

Suppose for instance that demand for a certain product is represented by the following equation[2]:

(3.6) $\quad y^* = B_1\, p_y^{*\,e_y} \qquad\qquad -\infty < e_y < 0$

where B_1 is a constant, e_y the price elasticity of demand and p_y the price of the product. Let us assume furthermore that the supply curves of labour and capital have the following simple form, viz.:

(3.7) $\quad L^* = B_2\, p_l^{*\,e_L} \qquad\qquad 0 < e_L < \infty$

(3.8) $\quad K^* = B_3\, p_k^{*\,e_K} \qquad\qquad 0 < e_K < \infty$

where B_2 and B_3 are constants, e_L and e_K price elasticities of supply, while p_l represents the price of labour and p_k the user cost of capital to be defined later.[3] For the time being the elasticities e_y, e_L and e_K are assumed to be con-

---

1. It should be noted that in production function (3.5) the flow of production is related to the stock of labour and the stock of capital. In fact capital and labour *services* are an input to the productive process. It is assumed that both stocks are multiplied by a factor representing the rate of service per period of time. In the representation of the production function this factor is normalized at unity. See also JORGENSON (1965), p. 54.
2. The line of thought is adopted from BROWN (1966), chapter VI and can also be found in a more general form in FERGUSON (1969), chapter 8.
3. The supply of labour function is much simpler than the one which is empirically estimated and actually used in the model. The formulation of the relationships (3.14) and (3.15), however, would not be altered when, for instance the real wage rate was included and/or the utilization rate of labour was added in equation (3.7).

stant. Finally, it is hypothesized that firms maximize their desired profits subject to the constraint of production function (3.5) by minimizing the expected costs of producing a given expected output.

This constraint is written in the form:

(3.9) $\quad F = y^* - A e^{\delta t} (L^*)^\alpha (K^*)^\beta = 0$

The desired amount of profits Z^* is defined as:

(3.10) $\quad Z^* = p_y^* y^* - p_l^* L^* - p_k^* K^*$

To attain the maximum profit goal there are three necessary conditions, *viz.*

(3.11) $\quad \dfrac{\partial Z^*}{\partial y^*} - \lambda \dfrac{\partial F}{\partial y^*} = (1 + 1/e_y) B_1^{-1/e_y} y^{*1/e_y} - \lambda = 0$

(3.12) $\quad \dfrac{\partial Z^*}{\partial L^*} - \lambda \dfrac{\partial F}{\partial L^*} = -(1 + 1/e_L) B_2^{-1/e_L} L^{*1/e_L} + \lambda \dfrac{\alpha y^*}{L^*} = 0$

(3.13) $\quad \dfrac{\partial Z^*}{\partial K^*} - \lambda \dfrac{\partial F}{\partial K^*} = -(1 + 1/e_K) B_3^{-1/e_K} K^{*1/e_K} + \lambda \dfrac{\beta y^*}{K^*} = 0$

where λ is the multiplicator of Lagrange. From equations (3.6) and (3.11) we find $\lambda = (1 + 1/e_y) p_y^*$. After appropriate algebraic manipulation and using this value of λ we arrive at

(3.14) $\quad \dfrac{\alpha y^*}{L^*} = \dfrac{p_l^*(1 + 1/e_L)}{p_y^*(1 + 1/e_y)}$

(3.15) $\quad \dfrac{\beta y^*}{K^*} = \dfrac{p_k^*(1 + 1/e_K)}{p_y^*(1 + 1/e_y)}$

It is a well-known fact that partial differentiation of production function (3.5) leads to the formulation of a constant relationship between the average and marginal products of labour and capital respectively:

(3.16) $\quad \dfrac{\partial y^*}{\partial L^*} = \alpha \dfrac{y^*}{L^*}$

(3.17) $\quad \dfrac{\partial y^*}{\partial K^*} = \beta \dfrac{y^*}{K^*}$

Substitution of these relationships in equations (3.14) en (3.15) shows that the ratio of these equations establishes that to minimize cost subject to a given output, production factor inputs should be purchased in quantities such that their marginal rate of technical substitution $\frac{\partial y^*}{\partial L^*} / \frac{\partial y^*}{\partial K^*}$ equals the incremental input-cost ratio.

From equations (3.14) and (3.15) the so-called expansion path function may be derived in which the desired labour-capital ratio is related to expected relative factor prices 'corrected' for elasticities of supply because firms are not confronted with a perfectly elastic supply of production factors.[4]

(3.18) $\quad \dfrac{L^*}{K^*} = \dfrac{\alpha}{\beta} \dfrac{p_k^*}{p_l^*} \dfrac{(1 + 1/e_K)}{(1 + 1/e_L)}$

It is important to note that this expansion path function is a long run equilibrium relation. It should be borne in mind that, by definition, in the long run the firm is able to substitute capital for labour completely because the absolute value of the elasticity of substitution $d \ln \dfrac{L^*}{K^*} / d \ln \dfrac{p_k^*}{p_l^*}$ is unity. However, the substitution elasticity at any given moment can be less than that what is technologically specified because, once the capital goods are installed it may be difficult to replace them by labour in the short run. In addition, although it is generally taken for granted that labour is a variable input factor in the short run,[5] there are a number of considerations which suggest that labour is a rather rigid factor of production especially in a downward direction.[6] One could think of the following arguments:

i. a minimum number of workers is necessary to operate the plant and equipment and produce output at all;
ii. a minimum amount of labour is required to perform the routine clerical and secretarial functions;
iii. large amounts of training and re-orientation may be required to adjust a worker to a new organization and new equipment;
iv. contractual agreements relating to the duration of employment may limit the reduction of labour;
v. laying off workers and later hiring additional workers is a costly procedure.

The fact that labour is a quasi fixed production factor in the short run is one of the reasons why employment functions without a relative factor price

---

4. The term corrected is used by SCHNEIDER (1963), p. 208.
5. We disregard the aspect of labour time at the moment.
6. The role of labour rigidities in production functions has been extensively investigated by HUBBARD (1968).

variable have been estimated by BRECHLING (1965), BALL and ST. CYR (1966), BRECHLING and O'BRIEN (1967) and IRELAND and SMYTH (1967).[7] In their equations production and a time trend are the sole explanatory variables and actual employment (incl.-hours) adjusts gradually to equilibrium employment with a distributed lag. We agree with the above mentioned authors that in the short run the input of labour and capital services is more or less fixed, although, as far as capital is concerned, this seems only approximately true since the utilization rate of the capital stock is more flexible than the capital stock itself. However, since we wish to generate both the cycle and the trend we should consider the consequences of substitution between labour and capital, especially when labour is relatively scarce as in a near full employment economy.[8]

When equations (3.5) and (3.18) are combined and it is assumed that they may be applied on the macro-economic level as well, the following function for desired labour input is obtained

(3.19)
$$L^* = y^{*1/(\alpha+\beta)} \left(\frac{p_k^*}{p_l^*}\right)^{\beta/(\alpha+\beta)} \left(\frac{1 + 1/e_K}{1 + 1/e_L}\right)^{\beta/(\alpha+\beta)} e^{-\delta t/(\alpha+\beta)} \left(\frac{\alpha}{\beta}\right)^{\beta/(\alpha+\beta)} A^{-1/(\alpha+\beta)}$$

Up to now we have abstracted from the dimension of the number of working hours per worker and per unit of capital in the production function. This aspect can be introduced in (3.5) in more than one way. First, the production flow may be assumed to result from the number of workers employed, the number of working hours per worker, the number of utilized units of capital and the number of working hours per unit of capital. The production function then reads

(3.20) $\quad y = A e^{\delta t} (Lh)^{\alpha} (Kh)^{\beta}$

where h is the number of working hours.[9] In this specification the elasticity coefficient of the working hours variable is equal to the sum of the production elasticities of both factor inputs, *viz.* $\alpha + \beta$. FELDSTEIN'S (1967) findings in a cross section analysis of production functions for the United Kingdom show indeed an elasticity coefficient of hours greater than that of labour input.

---

7. A survey of neoclassical models of labour is given by KILLINGWORTH (1970).
8. In his survey article of neoclassical models of labour demand KILLINGWORTH (1970) distinguishes between the 'crude profit maximizing' theory, the 'instantaneous hours-cost-minimizing' theory and the 'employment-cost-minimizing-over-time' theory. Our approach belongs to the first category like the studies of NADIRI (1968) and DHRYMES (1969).
9. This approach is slightly different from what is usual in the literature. See for example KILLINGWORTH (1970) BRISCOE, O'BRIEN and SMYTH (1970) and HILTON and DOLPHIN (1970).

On the contrary DENNISON's (1962) research suggests a relatively low elasticity for the hours variable. It can be argued that by increasing the average hours of work, production per worker will decrease reflecting fatigue in the short run and ill health in the long run. But there is the argument that an increase in hours increases the flow of capital services as well. In addition, Feldstein has argued that increases in the official working time entail a more than proportionate increase in the actual number of hours worked because a number of hours may be regarded as fixed, *viz.* setting up time, refreshment breaks etc. Anyway, there are reasons not to fix the coefficient of the hours variable in advance. We have therefore chosen a second approach, *viz.* a production function in which the variable working hours has an unknown coefficient and is not directly related to specific inputs. The revised equation for desired labour input now reads:

(3.21)
$$L^* = y^{*1/(\alpha+\beta)} \left(\frac{p_k^*}{p_l^*}\right)^{\beta/(\alpha+\beta)} \left(\frac{1 + 1/e_K}{1 + 1/e_L}\right)^{\beta/(\alpha+\beta)} h^{*1/(\alpha+\beta)} e^{-\delta t/(\alpha+\beta)} \left(\frac{\alpha}{\beta}\right)^{\beta/(\alpha+\beta)} A^{-1/(\alpha+\beta)}$$

We are now faced with two problems, *viz.* what is the relationship between actual labour employment and desired labour input and how are expected values of variables transformed into observable values.[10] To solve the first problem we postulate that actual employment is related to desired labour input by means of a, for the time being, unknown adjustment process. In addition to this general assumption we want to allow this adjustment to be influenced by a number of factors, *viz.* the cyclical situation on the labour market, the rate of return on invested capital and the liquidity ratio.

It seems plausible that a near full employment economy would have short term elasticities different from a substantially underutilized economy. When relatively large amounts of underutilized factors of production are available only a small quantity of additional labour will be required for production expansion. On the other hand when the economy is operating near full employment larger additional labour inputs will be required to expand production because bottlenecks are likely to occur more frequently and production is less efficiently organized. The foregoing considerations suggest that the way in which the labour market situation influences the adjustment mechanism will probably be of a non-linear nature, but this has to be tested.

Cyclical influences in the employment function may as well arise from fluctuations in the rate of return on invested capital. For example, a low

---

10. See also NADIRI (1968).

profitability will induce firms to rationalize the use of labour which will also effect the adjustment of actual to desired labour input. In addition, the rate of return is an expression of the availability of internal funds. It seems reasonable to suppose that the adjustment referred to is positively influenced by the internal liquidity position of firms.

A similar argument holds good for the availability of external funds. The adjustment of actual to desired labour input is therefore postulated to be affected by the liquidity ratio, the total amount of liquidities relative to turnover, as well.

The foregoing considerations lead to the following employment function in which unknown adjustment processes are represented by unknown rational distributed lag functions:

$$(3.22) \quad \ln L = \xi_1 \frac{G(L)_1}{H(L)_1} \ln q_L + \xi_2 \frac{G(L)_2}{H(L)_2} \ln \frac{L_q}{V} + \xi_3 \frac{G(L)_3}{H(L)_3} \left[\ln \frac{Z - T_Z}{p_i} - \ln \hat{K} \right] + \frac{G(L)_4}{H(L)_4} \ln L^* + c_1$$

where q_L is the rate of utilization of the labour force, $\frac{L_q}{V}$ is the liquidity ratio, Z is non-wage income (incl. corporate profits), T_Z is direct taxes on non-wage income and p_i is price level of gross fixed investment. This function describes how actual employment is adjusted to desired employment modified by the demand/supply situation in the labour market, the liquidity position and the rate of return on invested capital. Note that the constant term c_1 represents the long run or normal value of the liquidity ratio and the rate of return in such a way that when labour is fully utilized ($q_L = 1$) actual employment equals desired employment in the long run.

With respect to the transformation of long run equilibrium employment into an observable value, it is assumed that each variable determining the desired labour input has its own adjustment process. We have therefore no uniform adjustment of actual values towards expected values with respect to production, relative factor prices, hours of work, labour utilization, liquidity ratio and rate of return.

Let us first rewrite equation (3.21) in log-linear form:

$$(3.23) \quad \ln L^* = \frac{1}{\alpha + \beta} \ln y^* + \frac{\beta}{\alpha + \beta} \ln \frac{p_k^*}{p_i^*} + \frac{\beta}{\alpha + \beta} \ln \frac{(1 + 1/e_K)}{(1 + 1/e_L)} + \frac{\iota}{\alpha + \beta} \ln h^* - \frac{1}{\alpha + \beta} \delta t + \frac{\beta}{\alpha + \beta} \ln \frac{\alpha}{\beta} - \frac{1}{\alpha + \beta} \ln A$$

It is furthermore assumed that expected values of variables are functions of their values in the past, these relationships being described by unknown rational distributed lag functions.

(3.24) $\quad \ln y^* = \dfrac{G(L)_5}{H(L)_5} \ln y$

(3.25) $\quad \ln \dfrac{p_k^*}{p_l^*} = \dfrac{G(L)_6}{H(L)_6} \ln \dfrac{p_k}{p_l}$

(3.26) $\quad \ln h^* = \dfrac{G(L)_7}{H(L)_7} \ln h$

Hence we obtain a relationship for desired labour input in terms of observable values which, substituted in equation (3.22), gives an equation for employment:

$$\begin{aligned}
(3.27) \quad \ln L =\ & \frac{1}{\alpha+\beta} \frac{G(L)_4}{H(L)_4} \frac{G(L)_5}{H(L)_5} \ln y + \frac{\beta}{\alpha+\beta} \frac{G(L)_4}{H(L)_4} \frac{G(L)_6}{H(L)_6} \ln \frac{p_k}{p_l} + \\
& + \frac{\beta}{\alpha+\beta} \frac{G(L)_4}{H(L)_4} \ln \frac{(1+1/e_K)}{(1+1/e_L)} + \xi_1 \frac{G(L)_1}{H(L)_1} \ln q_L + \\
& + \xi_2 \frac{G(L)_2}{H(L)_2} \ln \frac{L_a}{V} + \xi_3 \frac{G(L)_3}{H(L)_3} \left[\ln \frac{Z-T_Z}{p_i} - \ln \hat{K} \right] + \\
& + \frac{1}{\alpha+\beta} \frac{G(L)_4}{H(L)_4} \frac{G(L)_7}{H(L)_7} \ln h - \frac{1}{\alpha+\beta} \frac{G(L)_4}{H(L)_4} \delta t + \\
& + \frac{\beta}{\alpha+\beta} \ln \frac{\alpha}{\beta} - \frac{1}{\alpha+\beta} \ln A + c_1
\end{aligned}$$

This relationship can be estimated, provided there is a decision on the treatment of the supply elasticities e_L and e_K and the nature of the lag distributions. We analyse first the aspect of imperfectness of competition in the factor markets.

3.3. IMPERFECT COMPETITION ON MARKETS FOR PRODUCTION FACTORS

It is a wellknown fact that in a situation of perfect competition both elasticity coefficients e_L and e_K are infinite. The assumption of imperfect competition implies on the one hand that prices of final products will be higher than in the case of perfect competition. On the other hand the reward of production factors will be lower than the money value of their marginal product.[11]

In the empirical macro-economic literature the phenomenon of the imperfectness of the market is treated in a rather stepmotherly fashion. One often restricts oneself to assuming that even in the short run the elasticities e_L and e_K are constant.[12] It is very easy to say that this hypothesis is not realistic, but this does not solve the problem how to take into consideration the consequences of the market structure in empirical macro-economics. A possible solution, based on rather strong assumptions, which heavily leans on thoughts developed by EVANS and KLEIN (1967) is the following. Let us first define two variables representing the rate of utilization of production factors $q_L = \dfrac{L}{\hat{L}}$ and $q_K = \dfrac{K}{\hat{K}}$, where q_L and q_K are the rate of utilization of labour and capital respectively, L is employment, $\hat{L}$ is full employment supply of men, K is utilized capital stock and $\hat{K}$ is the capital stock installed.[13] In addition, let us assume that both supply elasticities are not constants but vary with the respective utilization rates. Then we have for example[14]

(3.28) $\quad (1 + 1/e_L) = q_L^{-\xi_4} c_2$

and

(3.29) $\quad (1 + 1/e_K) = q_K^{-\xi_5} c_3$

So it is assumed that the wage elasticity of labour supply will increase with tensions in the labour market, given the level of wages. A similar reasoning goes for capital.

---

11. See CHAMBERLAIN (1933), chapter VIII.
12. See for instance NADIRI (1968). Another possibility is to assume that e_L and e_K are equal but this is not acceptable at all.
13. Throughout this study fully utilized labour and capital means: after deduction of frictional underutilization.
14. Alternatively we could have written $(1 + 1/e_L) = e^{-\xi_4 q_L} \cdot c_2$ and $(1 + 1/e_K) = e^{-\xi_5 q_K} \cdot c_3$. In the following we have used either these formulations or equations (3.28) and (3.29) dependent on the form in which other relevant explanatory variables, especially the labour utilization rate, occur in the reaction equation under consideration.

In section 3.7 of this chapter we will explain that in a near full employment economy fluctuations in the utilization rate of capital can be approximated by the utilization rate of labour. In anticipation of a more complete analysis of this result ln q_K is written as a function of ln q_L

(3.30) $\ln q_K = \xi_6 \ln q_L + c_4$

Combination of equations (3.28), (3.29) and (3.30) now enables us to write

(3.31) $\ln \dfrac{(1+1/e_K)}{(1+1/e_L)} = (\xi_4 - \xi_5 \xi_6) \ln q_L + c_5$

where $c_5 = -\ln c_2 + \ln c_3 - \xi_5 c_4$. Substituting this relationship in the labour demand equation (3.27) yields:

(3.32) $\ln L = \dfrac{1}{\alpha+\beta} \dfrac{G(L)_4}{H(L)_4} \dfrac{G(L)_5}{H(L)_5} \ln y + \dfrac{\beta}{\alpha+\beta} \dfrac{G(L)_4}{H(L)_4} \dfrac{G(L)_6}{H(L)_6} \ln \dfrac{p_k}{p_l} +$

$+ \left\{ \dfrac{\beta}{\alpha+\beta} (\xi_4 - \xi_5 \xi_6) \dfrac{G(L)_4}{H(L)_4} + \xi_1 \dfrac{G(L)_1}{H(L)_1} \right\} \ln q_L +$

$+ \xi_2 \dfrac{G(L)_2}{H(L)_2} \ln \dfrac{L_q}{V} + \xi_3 \dfrac{G(L)_3}{H(L)_3} \left[\ln \dfrac{Z - T_Z}{p_i} - \ln \hat{K} \right] +$

$+ \dfrac{\iota}{\alpha+\beta} \dfrac{G(L)_4}{H(L)_4} \dfrac{G(L)_7}{H(L)_7} \ln h - \dfrac{1}{\alpha+\beta} \dfrac{G(L)_4}{H(L)_4} \delta t +$

$+ \dfrac{\beta}{\alpha+\beta} \ln \dfrac{\alpha}{\beta} - \dfrac{1}{\alpha+\beta} \ln A + c_1 + \dfrac{\beta}{\alpha+\beta} c_5$

Thus we have obtained a labour demand function of a dynamic form based on the Cobb Douglas production function.
This means that:
i. the sum of the partial production elasticities α and β indicate the degree of returns to scale;
ii. the long run elasticity of substitution between factors of production is unity;
iii. technological change is autonomous and neutral.

As far as technological change is concerned we have not actually used the time trend t. It is generally adopted that the greater part of technological change is incorporated in new capital goods. Therefore we follow the procedure of Dhrymes in making employment dependent on the capital stock. In the words of Dhrymes this '... allows, rather elegantly, the entire history of capital stock accumulation to extend an influence on the marginal productivity of labour'.[15] This influence has been formalized by including a distributed lag on investment expenditures in the basic specification (3.32). The use of the distributed lag formulation implies that the impact of recent vintages of the capital stock on labour productivity is larger than the influence of older vintages.

After introduction of this new formulation for the impact of technological change on the labour demand function (3.32), the equation can be estimated provided the capital stock variable ($\hat{K}$) is further specified because capital stock data are lacking in the Netherlands.[16] If we postulate in this case for $\hat{K}$ a specification identical to that for technological change, i.e. a distributed lag on investment outlays, the final labour demand equation reads

$$(3.33) \quad \ln L = \frac{1}{\alpha+\beta} \frac{G(L)_4}{H(L)_4} \frac{G(L)_5}{H(L)_5} \ln y + \frac{\beta}{\alpha+\beta} \frac{G(L)_4}{H(L)_4} \frac{G(L)_6}{H(L)_6} \ln \frac{p_k}{p_i} +$$

$$+ \left\{ \frac{\beta}{\alpha+\beta} \frac{G(L)_4}{H(L)_4} (\xi_4 - \xi_5\xi_6) + \xi_1 \frac{G(L)_1}{H(L)_1} \right\} \ln q_L +$$

$$+ \xi_2 \frac{G(L)_2}{H(L)_2} \ln \frac{L_q}{V} + \xi_3 \frac{G(L)_3}{H(L)_3} \ln \frac{Z-T_z}{p_i} +$$

$$+ \frac{\iota}{\alpha+\beta} \frac{G(L)_4}{H(L)_4} \frac{G(L)_7}{H(L)_7} \ln h - \rho \frac{G(L)_8}{H(L)_8} \ln i +$$

$$+ \frac{\beta}{\alpha+\beta} \ln \frac{\alpha}{\beta} - \frac{1}{\alpha+\beta} \ln A + c_1 + \frac{\beta}{\alpha+\beta} c_5$$

where ρ and $\frac{G(L)_8}{H(L)_8}$ are an additional coefficient and an additional distributed lag function expressing the total impact of gross fixed investment (i) on labour demand.

15. DHRYMES (1969), p. 144.
16. We have made an effort to compute the rate of return on the basis of replacement value of the capital stock of enterprises assessed by the Netherlands CBS in 1952. See DRIEHUIS (1968). The results can be found in *The Dutch Economy in 1973* (in Dutch) and the Central Economic Plans 1971 (p. 96) and 1972 (p. 91). In the future we will experiment with quarterly data of the rate of return computed along the lines described in the mentioned references.

3.4. EMPIRICAL RESULTS OF DEMAND FOR LABOUR

The estimation of relationship (3.33) is difficult because it has many complex distributed lags. On *a priori* grounds two variables are to be considered for a relatively long lag. These variables are the factor prices ratio and the investment variable. Actually we have alternatively tried a Koyck distributed lag on both variables, thus allowing the influence of the successive vintages of the capital stock or the influence of relative factor prices to have declining weights over time. More specifically, in the case of an infinite lag on investment, it was assumed, in first instance, that $G(L)_8 = 1 - \lambda$ and $H(L)_8 = 1 - \lambda L$. Furthermore the remaining lag functions $G(L)_1$ up to $G(L)_7$ were assumed to be finite and $H(L)_1 = H(L)_2 = \ldots = H(L)_7 = 1$. It is repeated that this choice is probably not an optimal one. Other and perhaps more complicated lag distributions may yield better results, although the empirical results to be discussed below suggest that the lag distributions found are not so bad.

Using the rules of selection given in section 2.7 we have adopted the following equation regarding labour demand by enterprises

$$
\begin{aligned}
(3.34) \quad \ln L = &\ .8 \ln L_{-1} \underset{(-)}{} + \\
& + .800 \left[\sum_{-1}^{-7} \gamma_1 \ln y - .8 \sum_{-2}^{-8} \gamma_1 \ln y \right] + \\
& \underset{(-)}{} \\
& + .267 \left[\sum_{-1}^{-10} \gamma_2 (\ln p_k - \ln w) - .8 \sum_{-2}^{-11} \gamma_2 (\ln p_k - \ln w) \right] + \\
& \underset{(11.0\%)}{} \\
& + .712 \left[\sum_{-3}^{-7} \gamma_3 q_L - .8 \sum_{-4}^{-8} \gamma_3 q_L \right] + \\
& \underset{(39.7\%)}{} \\
& + .040 \left[\sum_{-3}^{-5} \gamma_4 \ln \frac{L_q}{V} - .8 \sum_{-4}^{-6} \gamma_4 \ln \frac{L_q}{V} \right] + \\
& \underset{(49.0\%)}{} \\
& + .061 \left[\sum_{-4}^{-7} \gamma_5 \ln \frac{Z - T_Z}{p_{i-sa}} - .8 \sum_{-5}^{-8} \gamma_5 \ln \frac{Z - T_Z}{p_{i-sa}} \right] - \\
& \underset{(28.5\%)}{} \\
& - .742 \left[\sum_{-2}^{-3} \gamma_6 \ln h_c - .8 \sum_{-3}^{-4} \gamma_6 \ln h_c \right] - .043 \sum_{-3}^{-6} \gamma_7 \ln i_{-sa} + \\
& \underset{(23.3\%)}{} \hspace{6cm} \underset{(10.1\%)}{} \\
& + .030 \left[L_{aut} - .8 L_{aut-1} \right] + .265 \hspace{1cm} \bar{R}^2 = .998 \\
& \underset{(20.8\%)}{} \hspace{3cm} \underset{(59.6\%)}{} \hspace{2cm} NR = 1.46
\end{aligned}
$$

37

where L = employment in enterprises;
y = production of enterprises, in 1963 prices;
p_k = user cost of capital, 1963 = 100;
w = wage sum per worker in enterprises excluding lump sum payments, 1963 = 100;
q_L = utilization rate of labour;
$\dfrac{L_q}{V}$ = liquidity ratio, after correction for its decreasing trend;
Z = non-wage income (incl. corporate profits);
T_Z = direct taxes on non-wage income (cash basis);
p_{i-sa} = price of gross fixed investment in enterprises excluding housing, ships and airplanes, 1963 = 100;
h_c = contractual working hours, 1963 = 100;
i_{-sa} = gross fixed investment in enterprises excluding housing, ships and airplanes, in 1963 prices;
L_{aut} = impact cold winters on employment in 1956:1 and 1963:1;
γ_1 = .400, .300, .154, .075, .036, .022, .013;
γ_2 = .21, .17, .15, .12, .10, .08, .06, .05, .04, .02;
γ_3 = .14, .23, .26, .23, .14;
γ_4 = .33, .34, .33;
γ_5 = .10, .20, .30, .40;
γ_6 = .50, .50;
γ_7 = .25, .25, .25, .25.

This labour demand equation is in agreement with the theoretical basic specification. In first instance this was not so because straightforward estimation did not yield an acceptable influence of relative factor prices. This fact did not come as a surprise as work on an earlier version of this model gave a similar result.[17] Actually we have estimated a labour demand relationship in which the variable to explain was formulated as

$$(\ln L - \frac{1}{\alpha+\beta} \sum_{i=j}^{m} \gamma_i \ln y_{t-i}) - \lambda(\ln L_{t-1} - \frac{1}{\alpha+\beta} \sum_{i=j+1}^{m+1} \gamma_{i-1} \ln y_{t-i})$$

The accepted value of the coefficient $\dfrac{1}{\alpha+\beta}$ in the model equation of .80 was chosen after successive estimation of the basic equation with different values of $\dfrac{1}{\alpha+\beta}$ in the range from .65 to 1.0.

17. See DRIEHUIS (1970), p. 32.

Figure 3.1. Actual and computed employment in enterprises (in logs) according to equation (3.34)

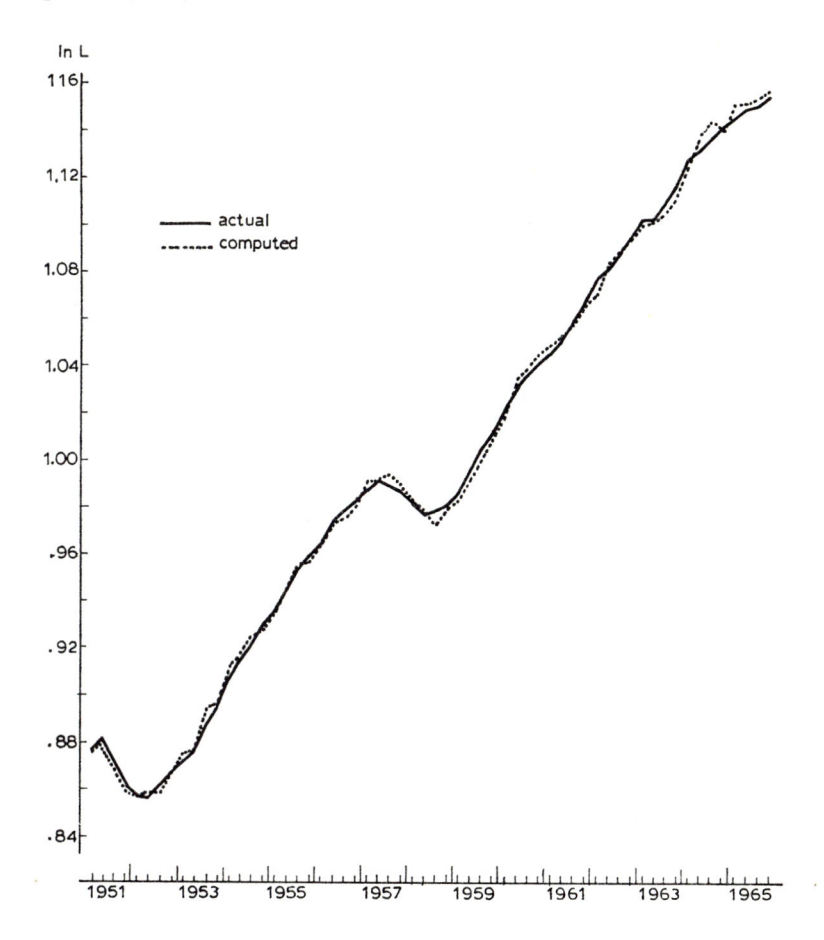

As concerns the measurement of the variables a few remarks must be made. The variable production of enterprises has for 1960 been corrected for the effect of an exceptional increase in agricultural production of about 30% due to an extremely good harvest. The price of labour input was measured by the wage rate in enterprises, the wage sum per worker in enterprises, corrected for lump sum payments in 1956 and 1965, because these incidental payments are not relevant for the demand for labour. The price of capital input, the user cost of capital, is compiled from the price of gross fixed business investment, the present value of a twenty year annuity for a given, changing, interest rate and corporation tax allowances, in the form of accelerated depreciation or investment deduction (see equation 25 in appendix A).[18] Furthermore, we had to use a dummy variable in order to account for disturbing effects of very cold weather, especially in the years 1956 and 1963. Under these conditions labour demand reduces at once, especially in the building industry, whereas the weather effect in the production of enterprises manifests itself in labour demand in subsequent quarters given the employment function used. Finally, we have tried both actual working time and contractual working time in the regressions. The latter variable yielded the most acceptable and significant results. The influence of actual working time is difficult to determine because the fluctuations of this variable are not independent of the fluctuations of the utilization rate of labour.

In line with the theory given in previous sections most variables have a lag distribution with weights rising first and then declining. A considerable average lag has been found for investment expenditures as could be expected. The average lag of the utilization rate of labour, which has a non-linear reaction, the liquidity ratio and real non-wage income was about four or five quarters. The application of the Koyck distributed lag on a weighted average of the investment variable gave results superior to the use of a simple geometric declining lag distribution. The average lags for all expla-

Table 3.1. Average lags of variables explaining employment in enterprises (equation 3.34)[a]

Variable	0	1	2	3	4	5	6	7	8	9	10
1. Production			x	x							
2. Relative factor prices			x	x							
3. Utilization rate of labour						x					
4. Liquidity ratio					x						
5. Real non-wage income							x				
6. Contractual working hours			x	x							
7. Gross fixed investment									x	x	

a. A mark in two columns indicates an average lag between the respective quarters.

18. Our definition of user cost of capital is different from the definitions used by other researchers. See HALL and JORGENSON (1967) and HALEY (1971).

natory variables are given in table 3.1[19]. Similar to findings by others, among whom COEN and HICKMAN (1970), BISCHOFF (1969) and VAN DEN BELD (1968), the average lag for relative factor prices is greater than for production.

Finally we have to consider which long term values for the parameters of the Cobb Douglas production function used in the previous sections are implicitly found in the estimated labour demand equation.

As concerns the production elasticities of production factors labour and capital we see that $\frac{1}{\alpha+\beta} = .800$ and the coefficient of the relative factor prices $\frac{\beta}{\alpha+\beta} = .267$, which yields $\alpha = .916$ and $\beta = .334$. The coefficient of hours of work in the production function can computed to be .928 which is a relatively high figure more in line with the findings of Feldstein than with Dennison's results, discussed earlier. The influence of technological progress can only be approximated since the investment term in the labour demand equation represents two effects (see page 36). When we start from an average annual growth rate of gross fixed investment in enterprises of 6.5 per cent the influence of technological progress on the production of enterprises during the sample period can assessed to be 1.3 per cent per year.[20] The mentioned values of the production function parameters enable us, finally, to estimate the average growth rate of the capital stock. For that purpose the production function is written in terms of average growth rates, which are denoted by a bar over a variable

(3.35) $\overline{\Delta \ln y} = .916 \overline{\Delta \ln L} + .334 \overline{\Delta \ln(\hat{K}.q_K)} + .928 \overline{\Delta \ln h_c} + .013$

---

19. The average lag can be computed in different ways. In general it may be computed as a weighted average in which each quarter is weighted with its respective coefficient: $\Sigma_j \beta_j / \Sigma \beta_j$, where j is the quarter and β_j is the reaction coefficient for that quarter. When a variable has a geometric declining distributed lag the average lag can be easily found by computing the formula $\frac{\lambda}{1-\lambda}$.

20. The computation is as follows. The long run coefficient of the investment variable in equation (3.34) is .215, which is equal to $\left(\xi_3 + \frac{\delta'}{\alpha+\beta}\right)$, where $\xi_3 = .061$, viz. the coefficient of $\ln\left(\frac{Z-T_z}{p_{i-sa}}\right)$ in equation (3.34), and $\alpha+\beta = 1.25$. After substitution of the average growth rate of investment of .065 per year δ' can be computed given ξ_3. This value of δ' may act as an approximation for the technical progress coefficient in the original production function (equation 3.5).

Substitution of the average growth rates during the period 1951–1965 of production, employment and hours of respectively 5%, 2% and − .4%, the average growth rate of the utilized capital stock can be computed as a residual, *viz.* 7 per cent per year. Assuming that $\Delta \ln q_K$ averages zero during these years this is approximately the average annual growth rate of the capital stock. One obtains a higher growth rate, *viz.* about 9 per cent, when the self-employed are included in the definition of employment.

3.5. SUPPLY OF LABOUR THEORY

In this section we do not consider the long run determinants of labour supply but we restrict ourselves to medium term labour supply as it depends on demographic factors, participation rates, the real wage level and external migration.

Given the demographic factors and participation rates we consider first of all domestic labour supply in the medium term, for instance a period of five years. Within that period we can assume the age distribution, the distribution of educational levels and the institutional factors in relation to the participation to the labour market to be exogenous. In addition, if we assume that people do not suffer from money illusion and react to real instead of nominal wages we can postulate the following labour supply function in log-linear form[21]

$$(3.36) \quad \ln P_{ST} = \ln P + \mu_1 \ln \overline{\frac{w}{p_c}}$$

where P_{ST} represents domestic labour supply in the medium term, P represents all demographic factors and the factors determining labour participation and $\overline{\frac{w}{p_c}}$ is the trend of the real wage level in enterprises. The last variable appears as a constant rate of growth in a first difference formulation of equation (3.36)

$$(3.37) \quad \Delta \ln P_{ST} = \Delta \ln P + \mu_1 c_1$$

c_1 being the average percentage change in the real wage sum per worker. The relative change in medium term domestic labour supply is then mainly

---

21. For the impact of money illusion on labour supply see FAIR (1970) and LUCAS and RAPPING (1969).

determined by exogenous factors and the medium term trend in real wage rates.

However, actual changes in labour supply differ from their medium term trend and show cyclical variations. Deviations from this trend are mainly due to the actual supply and demand situation in the labour market. With a tight labour market more people are prepared to join the labour force. One may think e.g. of married women, old age pensioners, etc., whereas in a situation of rising unemployment the reverse will take place. In addition, when the actual change in real wages deviates from its normal or average change labour supply will be influenced, other things being equal. If the change in current real wages is abnormally high, more labour is supplied than would be implied by the medium term supply function. If the change in current real wages is below their 'normal' change relatively less labour is offered.[22] If the average change in real wages is expressed by an unknown rational distributed function in the lag operator (L) and the expected values of other variables are represented by such distributed lag functions as well we have the following dynamic first difference equation for domestic labour supply, in which the real wage elasticity of labour supply varies, as was assumed in section 3.2, with the utilization rate of labour:

$$(3.38) \quad \frac{\Delta P_{SD}}{P_S} = \Delta \ln P_{ST} + \mu_2 \frac{G(L)_1}{H(L)_1} \left(\Delta \ln \frac{w}{p_c} - \frac{G(L)_2}{H(L)_2} \Delta \ln \frac{w}{p_c} \right) +$$

$$+ \mu_3 \frac{G(L)_3}{H(L)_3} \Delta \ln q_L + c_2$$

This equation describes only one part of total labour supply, *viz.* domestic labour supply (P_{SD}). Foreign migration and commuting play their part in the determination of total labour supply as well. It is desirable to have separate relationships for each of these components but, lack of quarterly data over the whole sample period makes it impossible to introduce such a set of relationships. Nevertheless for each component theoretical specifications have been developed in the following and these have finally been aggregated into one labour supply function.

First of all we are concerned with the balance of foreign migration including foreign labourers from Italy, Morocco, Spain, Jugoslavia, etc. Using annual data it has been found that this balance shows, *ceteris paribus*,

---

22. The deviation between the actual and the average change in real wages is used in a labour supply relationship constructed by LUCAS and RAPPING (1969), pp. 726–733 on the basis of a utility analysis of the goods-leisure choice.

a negative relationship with the growth of medium term labour supply. Also there appears to be a positive relation between the number of foreign labourers and the utilization rate of labour. The wage level as such is less relevant here because people coming from the above mentioned countries are first of all looking for work with a higher payment than they can get in their own country and seem rather indifferent to a specific country. The residence choice seems to depend on the labour market situation in the new country, its institutional regulations, its housing accommodation, etc., but these factors are difficult to consider in a macro-economic analysis.

We specify the following relationship for the change in labour supply arising from foreign migration (ΔP_{SF})[23]

$$(3.39) \quad \frac{\Delta P_{SF}}{P_S} = -\mu_4 \frac{G(L)_4}{H(L)_4} \Delta \ln P_{ST} + \mu_5 \frac{G(L)_3}{H(L)_3} \Delta \ln q_L + c_3$$

Finally, we need a specification for border commuting, mainly from Belgium to the Netherlands and from the Netherlands to Western Germany. First of all there is a positive relationship with labour utilization in the Netherlands. In addition, relative wages play a part. It will be clear that nominal wages are relevant here because the price level abroad is of less importance. It is furthermore not impossible that the labour utilization rate abroad is a relevant variable. In equation form we then have:

(3.40)

$$\frac{\Delta P_{SC}}{P_S} = \mu_6 \frac{G(L)_5}{H(L)_5} \Delta \ln \frac{w}{w_F} + \mu_7 \frac{G(L)_3}{H(L)_3} \Delta \ln q_L - \mu_8 \frac{G(L)_6}{H(L)_6} \Delta \ln q_{LF} + c_4$$

where ΔP_{SC} is the change in the balance of border commuting, w_F is a weighted average of the wage levels in Western Germany and Belgium and q_{LF} is the utilization rate of labour abroad.[24]

Combination of equations (3.38), (3.39) and (3.40) yields the basic specification for total labour supply (P_S)[25]:

---

23. Investigations with annual data have shown that it is allowed to take the same lag distribution for the labour utilization rate variable as in equation (3.38).
24. Assuming regional differences in wage levels, the wage rate in Belgian and German border districts would be a more appropriate variable.
25. By definition we have $\Delta P_S = \Delta P_{SD} + \Delta P_{SF} + \Delta P_{SC}$. Dividing by P_S yields equation (3.41) assuming $\Delta P_S/P_S \cong \Delta \ln P_S$.

$$(3.41) \quad \Delta \ln P_S = \Delta \ln P_{ST} + \mu_2 \frac{G(L)_1}{H(L)_1}\left(\Delta \ln \frac{w}{p_c} - \frac{G(L)_2}{H(L)_2} \Delta \ln \frac{w}{p_c}\right) +$$

$$+ \mu_9 \frac{G(L)_3}{H(L)_3} \Delta \ln q_L - \mu_8 \frac{G(L)_6}{H(L)_6} \Delta \ln q_{LF} -$$

$$- \mu_4 \frac{G(L)_4}{H(L)_4} \Delta \ln P_{ST} + \mu_6 \frac{G(L)_5}{H(L)_5} \Delta \ln \frac{w}{w_F} + c_5$$

where $c_5 = c_2 + c_3 + c_4$ and $\mu_9 = \mu_3 + \mu_5 + \mu_7$.

3.6. EMPIRICAL RESULTS OF LABOUR SUPPLY

We have assumed that the adjustment of changes in labour supply to the difference between the actual and the average change in real wages takes place rather gradually. Therefore it has been postulated that $G(L)_1 = 1 - \lambda$ and $H(L)_1 = 1 - \lambda L$. Furthermore we have assumed that $H(L)_2 = H(L)_3 = H(L)_4 = H(L)_5 = H(L)_6 = 1$ and that $G(L)_2 - G(L)_6$ are finite distributed lag structures.

In first instance the estimating results were rather disappointing because

i. an influence of the Dutch wage level relative to those of Germany and Belgium could not be determined, probably due to inappropriate statistical time series (national instead of regional data);
ii. an influence of the labour utilization rate abroad could not be determined, and
iii. the residuals showed a considerable degree of auto-correlation, the Von Neumann ratio being only .80.

We therefore dropped the relative wage rate variable as well as the variable representing the utilization rate of labour abroad. The equation involving the remaining variables of the basic specification was then estimated but showed still considerable positive auto-correlation, despite the fact that real wages had a relatively long distributed lag, the optimal value of λ being .8. After applying the weighting scheme representing this lag distribution to the real wage rate variable, the labour supply equation was estimated again in a form in which each variable was transformed according to a first order Markov auto-regressive scheme.[26] Ultimately labour supply equation (3.42) was

---

26. See JOHNSTON (1963), pp. 193-194.

obtained, where the coefficient of medium term labour supply was pinpointed at unity.

(3.42) $\ln P_S - \ln P_{S-4} = \underset{(-)}{.4}(\ln P_{S-1} - \ln P_{S-5}) +$

$+ \underset{(-)}{1.000} \left[(\ln P_{ST} - \ln P_{ST-4}) - .4(\ln P_{ST-1} - \ln P_{ST-5})\right] -$

$- \underset{(75.3\%)}{.083} \left[\sum_{-2}^{-3} \gamma_6 (\ln P_{ST} - \ln P_{ST-4}) - .4 \sum_{-3}^{-4} \gamma_6 (\ln P_{ST} - \ln P_{ST-4})\right] +$

$+ \underset{(17.0\%)}{.071} \left[\sum_{-1}^{-9} \gamma_8 \left\{\left(\ln \frac{w}{p_c} - \ln \frac{w_{-4}}{p_{c-4}}\right) - \sum_{-1}^{-4} \gamma_7 \left(\ln \frac{w}{p_c} - \ln \frac{w_{-4}}{p_{c-4}}\right)\right\} -\right.$

$\left. - .4 \sum_{-2}^{-10} \gamma_8 \left\{\left(\ln \frac{w}{p_c} - \ln \frac{w_{-4}}{p_{c-4}}\right) - \sum_{-1}^{-4} \gamma_7 \left(\ln \frac{w}{p_c} - \ln \frac{w_{-4}}{p_{c-4}}\right)\right\}\right] +$

$+ \underset{(9.4\%)}{.208} \left[\sum_{-1}^{-3} \gamma_4 (q_L - q_{L-4}) - .4 \sum_{-2}^{-4} \gamma_4 (q_L - q_{L-4})\right] +$

$+ \underset{(25.2\%)}{.162} \left[\sum_{-4}^{-6} \gamma_4 \Delta (q_L - q_{L-4}) - .4 \sum_{-5}^{-7} \gamma_4 \Delta (q_L - q_{L-4})\right] +$

$+ \underset{(5.3\%)}{.012} [P_{Saut} - .4 P_{Saut-1}] - \underset{(70.6\%)}{.001}$

$\bar{R}^2 = .963$
$NR = 1.89$

where P_S = labour supply;
P_{ST} = trend of working population;
w = wage sum per worker in enterprises excluding lump sum payments, 1963 = 100;
p_c = price of private consumption, 1963 = 100;
q_L = utilization rate of labour;
P_{Saut} = cyclical variation in the labour participation of married women (four-quarter changes);
γ_4 = .33, .34, .33;

$$\gamma_6 = .50, .50;$$
$$\gamma_7 = .25, .25, .25, .25;$$
$$\gamma_8 = .30, .21, .15, .11, .08, .06, .04, .03, .02.$$

Figure 3.2. Actual and computed four – quarter changes in supply of labour according to equation (3.42)

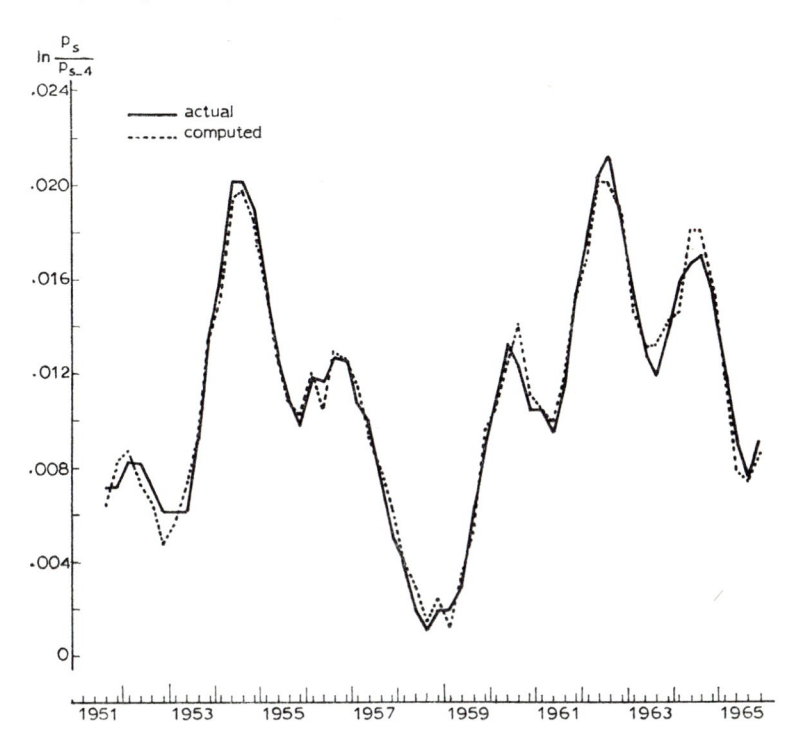

It can be seen that the change in labour supply is mainly determined by the change in the trend of working population, the first and the second difference of the labour utilization rate and the difference between the average four quarter change of the real wage and the average change in the real wage during the preceding four quarters. The latter variable appeared with the positive sign but it should be kept in mind that when a longer period is considered the relationship between labour supply and real wages may be negative when more leisure time is preferred above more real wage. The reaction of the change of the utilization rate on labour supply is curvilinear.

An additional influence of the labour market situation could be determined in the form of a quasi accelerator of the labour utilization rate. Both variables, however, were not able to give a complete explanation of the cyclical fluctuations of labour supply. Therefore a dummy variable was used to represent the fact that married women were prepared to join the labour market in the upswing of the cycle and to leave it in the downswing. This variable was constructed on the basis of experiences with annual data.

Finally we mention the average lags of the most important explanatory variables. It appears that the ratio of the change in real wages to the average changes in real wages and the second difference of the labour utilization rate have the longest lags, *viz.* about 4–5 quarters. Similar to findings by VAN DEN BELD (1968) for the Netherlands the change in the labour utilization rate influences the change in labour supply after about two quarters. This phenomenon seems responsible for the fact that when in a recession unemployment starts to rise, usually in the beginning of the second quarter, the rate of increase of unemployment weakens in the beginning of the next year.

Table 3.2. Average lags of variables explaining changes in labour supply (equation 3.42)[a]

Variable	\multicolumn{7}{c}{Number of quarters}
	0	1	2	3	4	5	6
1. Change in working population (+sign)	×						
2. Change in working population (−sign)			×	×			
3. Change in ratio of real wage rate to average real wage rate					×	×	
4. Change in utilization rate of labour			×				
5. Second difference in utilization rate of labour						×	

a. A mark in two columns indicates an average lag between the respective quarters.

3.7. THE UTILIZATION RATE OF LABOUR

It has already become clear from the foregoing sections and it will be clear from the coming ones that capacity (labour) utilization is an important variable for the explanation of many events in a near full employment economy. The ratio of potential to actual production reflects as does no other variable the business cycle and is therefore very important in our analysis.

The concept of a capacity ceiling on production has played an important part in post war empirical econometrics as well as in aggregate economic theory, especially in the cyclical growth models developed by SMITHIES (1957), PHILLIPS (1961), BERGSTRÖM (1962) and others. The practical measurement of capacity utilization, or the complementary concept of excess capacity, has also received widespread attention. It is, however, beyond the scope of this study to examine several alternative ways of estimating full capacity production.[27] In this section we concentrate on the rate of capacity utilization rather than on the full capacity level of production itself.[28] We will use the concept of the production function again.

Let actual production be described by the already used Cobb Douglas production function:

(3.43) $\quad y = A\, e^{\delta t}\, L^\alpha\, K^\beta\, h^\iota$

For full capacity production the same relation is assumed to be valid:

(3.44) $\quad \hat{y} = A\, e^{\delta t}\, \hat{L}^\alpha\, \hat{K}^\beta\, \hat{h}^\iota$

where $\hat{y}$ is the full capacity production flow, $\hat{L}$ is the input flow of the fully utilized labour force, $\hat{K}$ is the flow of services from the fully utilized capital stock and $\hat{h}$ is contractual labour time. If the following definitions are used, viz. $q_y = \dfrac{y}{\hat{y}}$, $q_L = \dfrac{L}{\hat{L}}$, $q_K = \dfrac{K}{\hat{K}}$ and $q_h = \dfrac{h}{\hat{h}}$, the next relationship between the respective utilization rates can be obtained from equations (3.43) and (3.44)

(3.45) $\quad \ln q_y = \alpha \ln q_L + \beta \ln q_K + \iota \ln q_h$

This equation cannot be directly applied for the construction of a utilization variable in terms of production because we have no data on the capital stock and an aggregate capital utilization rate is lacking for the Netherlands. This has forced us to postulate a relationship between the utilization rate of capital and the utilization rate of labour. Such a relation has been suggested by SOLOW (1957) and is furthermore used by KLEIN and PRESTON (1967) and many others.

---

27. For such a discussion see, for instance, KLEIN and PRESTON (1967), HILTON and DOLPHIN (1970) and BRISCOE, O'BRIEN and SMYTH (1970).
28. Compare PHILLIPS' (1961) cyclical growth model which is finally written as a differential equation in the utilization rate. See also ALLEN (1967), chapter 20.

It is clear from relationship (3.45) that the relative impact of the respective utilization rates on the utilization rate in terms of production depends on the parameters α, β and ι. Our findings concerning the parameters of the production function described in section 3.4 suggest the influence of the labour utilization rate to be about three times that of capital because $\alpha = .916$ and $\beta = .334$. Even when fluctuations in the capital utilization rate are relatively large as compared to the labour utilization rate, the fluctuations in total capacity utilization may be moderate when the utilization rate of labour is fluctuating moderately.

As has already been mentioned no official data of capital utilization are available in the Netherlands. Nevertheless we had at our disposal a few data on capital utilization rates obtained from annual interviews held by the Central Planning Bureau in cooperation with the Netherlands' Employers Association.[29] In these interviews a number of important firms in the Netherlands are asked, among other things: 'Can you indicate approximately the percentage rate of utilization of your installed productive capacity.' When these replies are aggregated and reweighted according to the relative size of the firms the following aggregate capital utilization rates are obtained for the years 1963–1970.

Table 3.3. Estimated capital utilization rate in enterprises, 1963–1970 (as per cent)

1963	0.863	1967	0.844
1964	0.892	1968	0.855
1965	0.864	1969	0.874
1966	0.863	1970	0.860

Source: CPB questionnaires on short term economic developments, 1963–1970.

These data, showing a cyclical pattern, should be compared with the utilization rate of labour during the same period. Before we do so we will discuss the measurement of the latter variable.

The utilization rate of labour is defined as the ratio of actual to potential employment. We have used as available labour force the employment in enterprises, as explained by equation (3.34). As full capacity labour force we have taken labour supply less 10 000 persons, the minimum number of people included in the registered labour reserve who find it difficult to join

29. We are indebted to this association for their consent in publishing the data of table 3.3, although it is not responsible for the aggregation of the individual utilization rates.

the labour market for reasons of age, profession, etc., and after deduction of the number of government employees and the self employed working population.[30] In addition, the ratio of employment to the thus corrected labour force was reduced by the minimum percentage of unemployed labour force during the sample period reflecting the percentage of normal frictional unemployment (.6%). In summary, the utilization rate of labour (q_L) was defined as

(3.46) $$q_L = \frac{L}{P_S - L_g - L_s - .01} + .006$$

where: q_L = utilization rate of labour;
L = employment in enterprises;
P_S = labour supply;
L_g = employment by the government;
L_s = self employed working population.

In this way we arrived at the following annual data.

Table 3.4. Utilization rate of labour, 1963–1970. (as per cent)

1963	0.998	1967	0.983
1964	0.999	1968	0.987
1965	0.998	1969	0.992
1966	0.996	1970	0.995

Confrontation of the data in tables 3.3 and 3.4 gives the following relationship between the utilization rates of capital and labour. It should be noted that the utilization rates of table 3.3 have been recalculated on the basis of a maximum utilization rate of 90 per cent. The resulting equation is:

(3.47) $\ln q_K = 1.920 \ln q_L - 4.265$
(40.8%) (86.5%) $\bar{R}^2 = .488$

We consider this equation as a confirmation of the hypothesis that the utilization rate of capital can be approximated by the utilization rate of labour. An important result of the estimation is that the elasticity coefficient describing the relationship between the two utilization rates is greater than

---

30. For a similar reasoning see KRISHNAMURTY (1961), p. 316.

one.[31] On the one hand this phenomenon may be explained by the existence of invisible unemployment, which is not reflected by the utilization rate of labour which is based on registered unemployment. The real utilization of the labour force is therefore probably underestimated which may explain an elasticity above unity in equation (3.47). The other and more important explanation for the greater fluctuations in the use of capital than of labour is that in a near full employment economy the entrance or leaving of marginal workers has a more than proportional effect on capital utilization and therefore causes greater fluctuations.

It should be borne in mind that the estimated relationship is clearly valid for a specific period of time. It is possible that a sample period covering a greater number of years would yield different estimates of the parameters, although we expect the elasticity coefficient then to be greater than unity as well.

We have not discussed the 'utilization rate' of hours so far. If it is assumed that the ratio of actual to contractual working time, the 'utilization rate' of hours, also shows a positive relationship with the utilization rate of labour, we conclude that equation (3.45) can be transformed into a relationship where the utilization rate in terms of production is written as a function of the utilization rate of labour alone.[32] We then arrive at:

(3.48) $\quad \ln q_y = (\alpha + \beta \, \xi_6 + \iota \xi_7) \ln q_L + \beta c_4 + \iota c_5$

using equation (3.30)

(3.49) $\quad \ln q_K = \xi_6 \ln q_L + c_4$

and using

(3.50) $\quad \ln q_h = \xi_7 \ln q_L + c_5$

where q_h is the 'utilization rate' of contractual working time.

---

31. Findings of this sort are not new. See for instance PAISH (1962) for Great Britain. He considers, however, the relationship between fluctuations in total capacity and fluctuations in unemployment and finds that fluctuations in the former are about five times the changes in the latter.
32. See also the study of VERDOORN and POST (1964) on the use of the unemployment rate as a proxy for capacity utilization in the Netherlands.

IV. Investment behaviour of enterprises

4.1. INTRODUCTION

One of the greatest difficulties in the construction of an econometric model is the empirical explanation of gross fixed investment in enterprises and all the more so because a great number of variables is potentially acceptable each with its own merits and its own grade of realism. An equation explaining both fluctuations and growth of investment outlays requires consequently many relevant variables. Therefore the theoretical starting points must be sufficiently flexible allowing for a relatively great number of explanatory variables.

Properly speaking our approach of investment analysis contains some criticism on the widely admired but also criticized studies of investment behaviour in the United States by JORGENSON and his collaborators.[1] These authors choose their assumptions in such a fixed manner that the role of financial variables is partly neglected to name but one instance. This holds as well for a number of other variables which have been found to be relevant for US-investment behaviour of firms, by among others, MEYER and KUH (1957), KUH (1963), DHRYMES and KURZ (1967), EISNER (1967) and ANDERSON (1967).

Another feature of the here presented analysis of investment behaviour is that it is based on assumptions already used in explaining demand for labour. We especially have in mind the Cobb-Douglas production function constraint. The investment equation to be accepted must therefore include values of the parameters of this function which are consistent with their values in the demand for labour relationship. As in the case of employ-

---

[1] See, among others, JORGENSON (1963), JORGENSON (1965), HALL and JORGENSON (1967), JORGENSON and STEPHENSON (1968), and JORGENSON and SIEBERT (1968).

ment starting point is again the behaviour of the individual firm, maximizing expected profits in an imperfect competition world full of uncertainties. In line with other recent work on investment behaviour of the Netherlands the analysis is split up into two parts, one relating to investment for expansion and the other related to investment for replacement.[2]

4.2. THE THEORY OF INVESTMENT FOR EXPANSION

Point of departure is the flexible accelerator model of investment behaviour originated by CHENERY (1952) and KOYCK (1954). In this model the firm is supposed to have a desired level of capital determined by considerations for the long run. In a given time period investment is a function of the discrepancy between the desired and the actual capital stock. Denoting the actual level of the capital stock by $\hat{K}$ and the desired level by $\hat{K}^*$ we have the following general specification

(4.1) $\quad i_e = i_e(\hat{K}^* - \hat{K}_{-1})$

where i_e is investment for expansion.

It has been shown by Jorgenson that under certain assumptions regarding the distribution of completion of initiated investment projects over time, investment for expansion is a distributed lag function of period to period changes in desired capital stock.[3] Then we have

(4.2) $\quad i_e = \dfrac{G(L)_1}{H(L)_1} (\hat{K}^* - \hat{K}^*_{-1})$

where $G(L)$, and $H(L)$, are unknown rational distributed lag functions in the lag operator (L).

This relationship can be replaced by one in which the causality is written in log-linear form. Therefore we have to assume that the long run growth of the capital stock over time can be approximated by the following exponential function[4]

(4.3) $\quad \hat{K} = \hat{K}_0 \, e^{\varepsilon_1 t}$,

---

2. See DEN HARTOG and FALKE (1970).
3. See JORGENSON (1965), pp. 47–48.
4. This assumption is different from the one used in chapter III. The reason is that when we should have used the hypothesis that the capital stock is approximated by a weighted average of past investment we would arrive at a rather naive explanation of investment.

where $\hat{K}_0$ is the capital stock in a base year and t a time trend. The log-linear approximation of equation (4.2) can now be written as

$$(4.4) \quad \ln i_e = \frac{G(L)_1}{H(L)_1}(\ln \hat{K}^* - \ln \hat{K}^*_{-1}) + \varepsilon_1 t + c_1,$$

where $c_1 = \ln \hat{K}_0 + \ln(1 - \hat{K}_0^{-\varepsilon_1})$.[5] This reformulation of the simple stock adjustment equation from the beginning of this chapter shows the logarithm of investment for expansion to be a function of the long term growth rate of capital modified by short term changes in the desired level of the capital stock.

The desired capital stock can easily be determined with the help of the Cobb Douglas production function already used. Following the same set of assumptions mentioned in the previous chapter it can be derived that, analogous to equation (3.21)

$$(4.5) \quad \hat{K}^* = y^{*1/(\alpha+\beta)} \left(\frac{p_k^*}{p_l^*}\right)^{-\alpha/(\alpha+\beta)} \left(\frac{1+1/e_K}{1+1/e_L}\right)^{-\alpha/(\alpha+\beta)} h^{*-1/(\alpha+\beta)} e^{-\delta t/(\alpha+\beta)}$$

$$\left(\frac{\alpha}{\beta}\right)^{-\alpha/(\alpha+\beta)} A^{-1/(\alpha+\beta)}.$$

This relationship relates desired capital input to expected relative factor prices, expected (desired) production, expected working hours and technological development, in a situation of imperfect competition. If we approximate the variables representing the latter phenomenon, viz. the ratio of supply elasticities of labour and capital, by equation (3.31) of the previous chapter[6] we obtain in logarithmic form:

$$(4.6) \quad \ln \hat{K}^* = \frac{1}{\alpha+\beta}\ln y^* - \frac{\alpha}{\alpha+\beta}\ln \frac{p_k^*}{p_l^*} - \frac{\alpha}{\alpha+\beta}(\xi_4 - \xi_5\xi_6)\ln q_L^* -$$

$$- \frac{1}{\alpha+\beta}\ln h^* - \frac{1}{\alpha+\beta}\delta t - \frac{\alpha}{\alpha+\beta}\ln \frac{\beta}{\alpha} - \frac{1}{\alpha+\beta}\ln A - \frac{\alpha}{\alpha+\beta}c_5.$$

Furthermore we write expected values of variables as a function of their

---

5. We have omitted the distributed lag formulation for constants and instead of $\varepsilon_1 t_{-1}$, which is the real outcome of the transformation, we have simply written $\varepsilon_1 t$.
6. Equation (3.31) was:

$$\ln \frac{(1+1/e_K)}{(1+1/e_L)} = (\xi_4 - \xi_5\xi_6)\ln q_L + c_5.$$

values in the past, these relationships being described by rational distributed lag functions:

$$(4.7) \quad \ln y^* = \frac{G(L)_2}{H(L)_2} \ln y$$

$$(4.8) \quad \ln \frac{p_k^*}{p_l^*} = \frac{G(L)_3}{H(L)_3} \ln \frac{p_k}{p_l}$$

$$(4.9) \quad \ln q_L^* = \frac{G(L)_4}{H(L)_4} \ln q_L$$

$$(4.10) \quad \ln h^* = \frac{G(L)_5}{H(L)_5} \ln h$$

Hence we obtain a first difference relationship for desired capital input in terms of observable values.

$$(4.11) \quad \Delta \ln \hat{K}^* = \frac{1}{\alpha+\beta} \frac{G(L)_2}{H(L)_2} \Delta \ln y - \frac{\alpha}{\alpha+\beta} \frac{G(L)_3}{H(L)_3} \Delta \ln \frac{p_k}{p_l} +$$

$$+ \varepsilon_2 \frac{G(L)_4}{H(L)_4} \Delta \ln q_L - \frac{\iota}{\alpha+\beta} \frac{G(L)_5}{G(L)_5} \Delta \ln h - \frac{1}{\alpha+\beta} \delta$$

where $\varepsilon_2 = -\frac{\alpha}{\alpha+\beta}(\xi_4 - \xi_5\xi_6)$. Assuming $\frac{1}{2}\xi_4 < \xi_5$ because $\xi_6 \approx 2$ and taking into account the estimated values of the parameters α and β we draw the conclusion that ε_2 is positive.

Before this relationship is substituted in the modified stock adjustment specification of investment for expansion (equation 4.4) we consider some factors influencing the adjustment process postulated in that equation. We look for the same sort of factors as used in the analysis of labour demand, *viz.* the utilization rate of capital, the rate of return on invested capital and the liquidity ratio.

The impact of capital utilization is discussed by many authors, among whom CHENERY (1952), KOYCK (1954), HICKMANN (1957), GREENBERG (1964) and JANUNKAR (1970). They all draw the conclusion that the adjustment between investment and one or another form of the change in the capital stock will vary according to the degree of capital utilization. With capital not fully utilized firms consider the need to expand capacity less urgent and restrict investment outlays. It is not unreasonable to expect the influence of capital utilization to be of a non-linear nature but this has to be tested.

Similar to the explanation of labour demand the rate of return on invested capital plays a part in the adjustment of investment plans to their realisation. On the one hand the rate of return is an indicator of the availability of profits for the financing of investment expenditures; on the other hand it may influence the profit expectations of entrepreneurs.[7] On the mentioned grounds there seems to exist a positive relationship between the realization of investment plans and the rate of return.[8]

Finally we think the liquidity ratio to be a relevant variable, expressing the availability of external funds for the financing of investment outlays. The role of financial factors in investment behaviour is emphasized, among others, by MEYER and KUH (1957) and BISCHOFF (1968).

When the three factors are taken into consideration as determinants of the speed of adjustment of actual to long run equilibrium capital stock a more elaborate version of aggregation (4.4) is obtained:

$$(4.12) \quad \ln i_e = \varepsilon_3 \frac{G(L)_6}{H(L)_6} \ln \frac{L_q}{V} + \varepsilon_4 \frac{G(L)_7}{H(L)_7} \left[\ln\left(\frac{Z-T_Z}{p_i}\right) - \ln \hat{K}_{-1} \right] +$$

$$+ \varepsilon_5 \frac{G(L)_8}{H(L)_8} \ln q_K + \frac{G(L)_1}{H(L)_1} \Delta \ln \hat{K}^* + \varepsilon_1 t + c_1.$$

Substitution of the determinants of the change in desired capital stock as obtained in equation (4.11) in this specification and rearranging terms yields a dynamic equation for investment for expansion:

$$(4.13) \quad \ln i_e = \frac{1}{\alpha+\beta} \frac{G(L)_1}{H(L)_1} \frac{G(L)_2}{H(L)_2} \Delta \ln y - \frac{\alpha}{\alpha+\beta} \frac{G(L)_1}{H(L)_1} \frac{G(L)_3}{H(L)_3} \Delta \ln \frac{p_k}{p_i} +$$

$$+ \varepsilon_2 \frac{G(L)_1}{H(L)_1} \frac{G(L)_4}{H(L)_4} \Delta \ln q_L - \frac{1}{\alpha+\beta} \frac{G(L)_1}{H(L)_1} \frac{G(L)_5}{H(L)_5} \Delta \ln h +$$

$$+ \varepsilon_3 \frac{G(L)_6}{H(L)_6} \ln \frac{L_q}{V} + \varepsilon_4 \frac{G(L)_7}{H(L)_7} \left[\ln\left(\frac{Z-T_Z}{p_i}\right) - \ln \hat{K} \right] +$$

$$+ \varepsilon_5 \frac{G(L)_8}{H(L)_8} \ln q_K - \frac{1}{\alpha+\beta} \delta + \varepsilon_1 t + c_1.$$

---

7. See also EISNER (1967).
8. For investment equations with both a sales or production variable and a profit variable see, for instance, KUH (1963), EISNER (1964) and DUESENBERRY (1958).

4.3. THE THEORY OF INVESTMENT FOR REPLACEMENT AND MODERNIZATION

Most recent econometric studies of investment behaviour rely on the assumption that investment for replacement and modernization is proportional to the capital stock. When gross investment is chosen as the dependent variable the one period lagged capital stock is added to the basic specification of investment for expansion and its coefficient is assumed to represent the rate of depreciation. The assumption that the ratio of replacement investment to the capital stock is constant is based on the statement that in the long run, if the capital stock is growing at a constant rate, replacement investments approach a constant proportion of the capital stock, whatever the initial age distribution and replacement rates for individual capital goods.[9]

FELDSTEIN and FOOT (1971) recently proposed an alternative hypothesis for investment of replacement which was independently and at about the same time used by DEN HARTOG and FALKE (1970). The alternative theory says that, although their may be a long run constantness of replacement investment to the capital stock these investment expenditures may very well show cyclical variations in the short run caused by factors similar to those relevant for investment for expansion. As possible variables responsible for cyclical variation around a fixed non zero level of replacement investment we mention the expected change in production, the change in relative factor prices, the rate of return on invested capital, the liquidity ratio and the utilization rate of the capital stock.

Short run activation of replacement investment can be caused by changes in the expected or desired level of production. This positive relationship between production and replacement investment is, among others, supported by findings of EISNER (1970) and DEN HARTOG and FALKE (1970). Moreover we think that relative factor prices play a part in explaining replacement investment. When the price of labour is high in comparison with the price of capital goods it may be desirable to have existing equipment replaced by new equipment using less labour than continuing with the old equipment. Furthermore a large proportion of fixed business investment is financed internally and these funds are likely to affect the timing of replacement investment as they do expansion investment. The same may be true for the liquidity position of the firm. Finally, when capital utilization is high equipment with higher variable cost is coming into use. Therefore the pressure to replace existing relatively expensive equipment for equipment with lower costs will increase the higher the utilization rate of capital.

9. See JORGENSON (1965), p. 51.

In summary we postulate the following dynamic log linear specification for investment for replacement (i_r):

(4.14) $\ln i_r = \ln \vartheta + \ln \hat{K} + \varepsilon_6 \Delta \ln y^* - \varepsilon_7 \Delta \ln \left(\dfrac{p_k}{p_i}\right)^* +$

$+ \varepsilon_8 \ln \left(\dfrac{L_q}{V}\right)^* + \varepsilon_9 \left[\ln \left(\dfrac{Z-T_z}{p_i}\right)^* - \ln \hat{K}^*\right] +$

$+ \varepsilon_{10} \ln q_K^* + c_2,$

where the constant term c_2 is assumed to have such a value as necessary to make investment for replacement a constant fraction ϑ of the capital stock in the long run. To keep the final basic specification for gross investment within manageable proportions the dynamization of expected variables in equation (4.14) must be based upon assumptions already used in the equation for investment for expansion (4.13) viz.

(4.15) $\Delta \ln y^* = \dfrac{G(L)_1}{H(L)_1} \dfrac{G(L)_2}{H(L)_2} \Delta \ln y$

(4.16) $\Delta \ln \dfrac{p_k^*}{p_i^*} = \dfrac{G(L)_1}{H(L)_1} \dfrac{G(L)_3}{H(L)_3} \Delta \ln \dfrac{p_k}{p_i}$

(4.17) $\ln \left(\dfrac{L_q}{V}\right)^* = \dfrac{G(L)_6}{H(L)_6} \ln \left(\dfrac{L_q}{V}\right)$

(4.18) $\ln \left(\dfrac{Z-T_z}{p_i}\right)^* - \ln \hat{K}^* = \dfrac{G(L)_7}{H(L)_7} \left[\ln \dfrac{Z-T_z}{p_i} - \ln \hat{K}\right]$

(4.19) $\ln q_K^* = \dfrac{G(L)_8}{H(L)_8} \ln q_K$

After substitution of these five relationships into equation (4.14) and combining this dynamic relationship for investment for replacement with the dynamic relationship for investment for expansion, according to:

(4.20) $\ln i = \varepsilon_{11} \ln i_e + \varepsilon_{12} \ln i_r$ $\qquad \varepsilon_{11} + \varepsilon_{12} = 1$

where i is gross investment in enterprises less investment in housing and where ε_{11} is a weighting factor representing the share of investment for expansion in gross investment in the previous period $\left(\frac{i_{e-1}}{i_{-1}}\right)$, we ultimately arrive at:

$$(4.21) \quad \ln i = \left(\frac{1}{\alpha+\beta}\varepsilon_{11} + \varepsilon_6\varepsilon_{12}\right)\frac{G(L)_1}{H(L)_1}\frac{G(L)_2}{H(L)_2}\Delta \ln y - \left(\frac{\alpha}{\alpha+\beta}\varepsilon_{11} + \varepsilon_7\varepsilon_{12}\right)$$

$$\frac{G(L)_1}{H(L)_1}\frac{G(L)_3}{H(L)_3}\Delta(\ln p_k - \ln p_l) + \varepsilon_2\varepsilon_{11}\frac{G(L)_1}{H(L)_1}\frac{G(L)_4}{H(L)_4}\Delta \ln q_L$$

$$-\frac{1}{\alpha+\beta}\varepsilon_{11}\frac{G(L)_1}{H(L)_1}\frac{G(L)_5}{H(L)_1}\Delta \ln h +$$

$$+ (\varepsilon_3\varepsilon_{11} + \varepsilon_8\varepsilon_{12})\frac{G(L)_6}{H(L)_6}\ln\left(\frac{L_q}{V}\right) +$$

$$+ (\varepsilon_4\varepsilon_{11} + \varepsilon_9\varepsilon_{12})\frac{G(L)_7}{H(L)_7}\ln\left(\frac{Z - T_Z}{p_i}\right) + (\varepsilon_5\varepsilon_{11}\xi_6 + \varepsilon_{10}\varepsilon_{12}\xi_6)$$

$$\frac{G(L)_8}{H(L)_8}\ln q_L + \varepsilon_{13}t + c_3$$

where[10] $\varepsilon_{13} = (1 - \varepsilon_4)\varepsilon_1\varepsilon_{11} + (1 - \varepsilon_9)\varepsilon_1\varepsilon_{12}$ and

$$c_3 = [(1 - \varepsilon_9)\varepsilon_{12} - \varepsilon_4\varepsilon_{11}]\ln \hat{K}_0 + (\varepsilon_{12})\ln \vartheta + \varepsilon_{11}c_1 + \varepsilon_{12}c_2 -$$

$$-\frac{1}{\alpha+\beta}\delta\varepsilon_{11} + (\varepsilon_5\varepsilon_{11} + \varepsilon_{10}\varepsilon_{12})c_4$$

This estimation equation has been derived by substitution of equation (4.3) for each term $\hat{K}$ and by replacing $\ln q_K$ for its equivalent in terms of q_L (see chapter III, equation 3.30).

This relationship is much more flexible than Jorgenson's estimation equation developed for the Brookings model.[11] It will be worth while to consider the most striking differences. Compared with Jorgenson's analysis of investment behaviour and in contrast to his specification our analysis has been resulting in:

i. separate lag structures for each explanatory variable;

10. The term c_4 is the constant of equation (3.30).
11. See JORGENSON (1965).

60

ii. explicit acknowledgement of the role of financial variables, such as the rate of return and the liquidity ratio, and the capital utilization rate in the adjustment of a disequilibrium situation[12];
iii. the inclusion of a variable representing imperfect competition;
iv. a separate relative factor prices variable rather than pinpointing the coefficient of this variable on its theoretical value;
v. the possibility of having variations in the replacement ratio;
vi. estimating in logarithms rather than in absolute levels of variables.

Before presenting and discussing the relationship which was actually included in the model we draw attention to the fact that the weighting factors ε_{11} and ε_{12} from equation (4.20) are not constant but vary over time around some average level.[13] We have to assume that the deviations are represented by the utilization rate variable or otherwise have resulted in residuals of the estimating equation.

4.4. EMPIRICAL RESULTS

Similar to our earlier work on the explanation of investment behaviour of firms in the Netherlands we have imposed an infinite distributed lag on relative factor prices.[14] All other variables have been considered as having finite lag distributions.

The most satisfactory result, ultimately included in the model, was:

$$(4.22) \quad \ln i_{-sa} = .8 \ln i_{-sa-1}$$
$$(-)$$
$$+ .704 \left[\sum_{-1}^{-5} \gamma_9 \Delta \ln y - .8 \sum_{-2}^{-6} \gamma_9 \Delta \ln y \right] -$$
$$(48.7\%)$$
$$- .146 \sum_{-5}^{-6} \gamma_{10} (\Delta \ln p_k - \Delta \ln w) +$$
$$(63.1\%)$$
$$+ 6.384 \left[\sum_{0}^{-2} \gamma_4 q_L - .8 \sum_{-1}^{-3} \gamma_4 q_L \right] +$$
$$(25.0\%)$$

12. Jorgenson includes the rate of return in the user cost of capital.
13. In their paper on the analysis of investment in equipment in the Netherlands DEN HARTOG and FALKE (1970) mention values of .87 for ε_{11} and .13 for ε_{12}. When investment in industrial building and in means of transport are included in the definition of investment a lower value of ε_{11} seems reasonable.
14. See DRIEHUIS (1970), p. 24.

$$+ 2.103 \underset{(79.6\%)}{\left[\sum_{-2}^{-3} \gamma_6 \Delta q_L - .8 \sum_{-3}^{-4} \gamma_6 \Delta q_L\right]} +$$

$$+ .613 \underset{(70.9\%)}{\left[\sum_{-3}^{-5} \gamma_4 \frac{L_q}{V} - .8 \sum_{-4}^{-6} \gamma_4 \frac{L_q}{V}\right]} +$$

$$+ .245 \underset{(43.9\%)}{\left[\sum_{-1}^{-5} \gamma_{11} \ln \frac{Z-T_Z}{p_{i-sa}} - .8 \sum_{-2}^{-6} \gamma_{11} \ln \frac{Z-T_Z}{p_{i-sa}}\right]} +$$

$$+ .012 \underset{(13.3\%)}{[t - .8\, t_{-1}]} -$$

$$- .722 \underset{(407.5\%)}{\left[\sum_{-3}^{-4} \gamma_6 \Delta \ln h_c - .8 \sum_{-4}^{-5} \gamma_6 \Delta \ln h_c\right]} +$$

$$+ .026 \underset{(9.6\%)}{[T_c - .8\, T_{c-1}]} + .079 \underset{(31.4\%)}{[i_{aut} - .8\, i_{aut-1}]} - .993 \underset{(35.4\%)}{}$$

$$NR = 1.72 \qquad \bar{R}^2 = .996$$

where i_{-sa} = gross fixed investment in enterprises excluding housing, ships and airplanes, in 1963 prices;
Z = non-wage income (incl. corporate profits);
T_Z = direct taxes on non-wage income, cash basis;
p_{i-sa} = price of gross fixed investment in enterprises excl. housing and excl. ships and airplanes, 1963 = 100;
y = production of enterprises, in 1963 prices;
$\frac{L_q}{V}$ = liquidity ratio, after correction for its decreasing trend;
p_k = user cost of capital, 1963 = 100;
w = wage sum per worker in enterprises excluding lump sum payments, 1963 = 100;
q_L = utilization rate of labour;
t = time trend;
h_c = contractual working hours, 1963 = 100;
i_{aut} = effect of anticipatory purchases of investment goods in in 1965:4;
T_c = minimum temperature below 0° centigrade;
γ_4 = .33, .34, .33;
γ_6 = .50, .50;
γ_9 = .60, .24, .10, .04, .02;
γ_{10} = .20, .80.
γ_{11} = .10, .20, .25, .30, .15;

Figure 4.1. Actual and computed gross fixed investment in enterprises, excluding housing, ships and airplaines (in logs) according to equation (4.22)

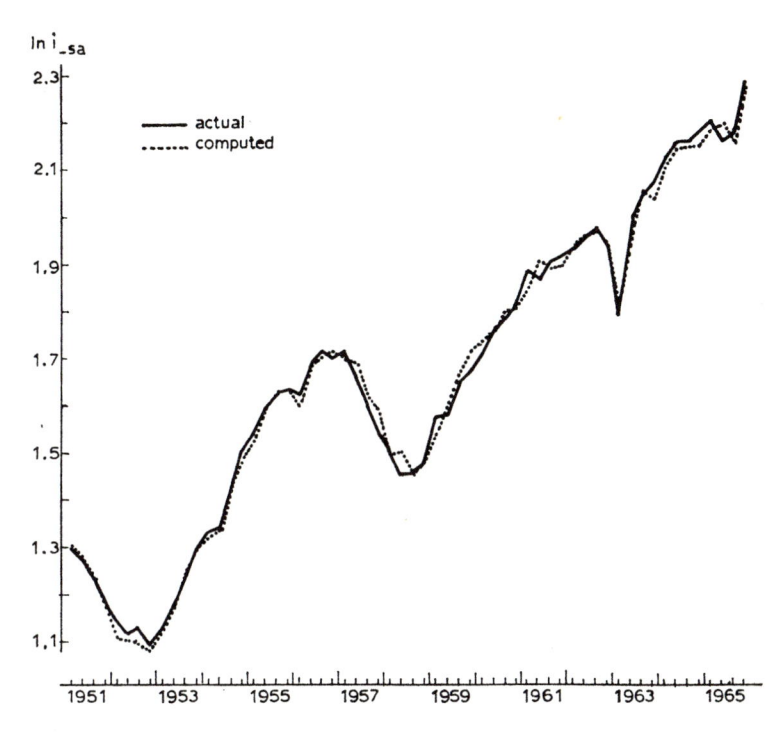

This equation contains all the variables of the postulated theory and it has a good fit during the sample period. Consistency with the estimates of the parameters α and β in the employment function requires a long run elasticity of the relative change in production of .800, a long run elasticity of relative factor prices of .733, and a long run elasticity of .928 of the relative change in contractual labour time. However, when gross investment is considered the elasticities will probably differ from these values. Actually we have found an elasticity of .704 for the production variable, an elasticity of .722 for labour time and an elasticity of .730 for relative factor prices. These estimates suggest that these variables have lower coefficients for replacement investment compared to investment for expansion. The conclusion is that investment for replacement and modernisation and investment for expansion are influenced by a number of identical variables. The estimation result supports the conclusion reached in the analysis of labour demand *viz.* that relative factor prices have a longer lag than the production variable.

Such a result has also been found by BISCHOFF (1969) for the United States. Our findings are in contrast with the results of COEN (1968) who finds that, when a profit variable is added to an accelerator model, the influence of relative factor prices will be lower. The high coefficient of the labour utilization rate confirms the important role of capital utilization in investment behaviour and it corroborates furthermore that the elasticity above unity between the utilization rates of labour and capital, as found in chapter III, was a realistic estimate. Moreover, the positive sign of the change in the labour utilization rate is in agreement with the postulated influence of market imperfections and may be seen as a confirmation of the hypotheses used in this context. The coefficient of real non-wage income after taxes is lower than usually found in investment equations in which the acceleration principle is lacking and profits after taxes play a predominant role.[15]

As might be expected the liquidity ratio has a much greater influence on investment compared with labour demand and consumption. Similar to the findings by VAN DEN BELD (1968) the average lag is about one year. The average lags for the remaining variables are given in table (4.1). Finally, if we assume that the values $\varepsilon_{11} = .7$ and $\varepsilon_{12} = .3$ are valid the elasticity of the time trend variable seems somewhat on the low side when the findings on the growth rate of the capital stock in chapter III are taken into consideration.

Table 4.1. *Average lags of variables explaining gross fixed investment in enterprises (equation 4.22)*[a]

Variable	Number of quarters
	0　1　2　3　4　5　6　7　8　9　10
1. Change in production	x　x
2. Change in relative factor prices	x　x
3. Utilization rate of labour	x
4. Change in utilization rate of labour	x　x
5. Liquidity ratio	x
6. Real non-wage income	x　x
7. Contractual working hours	x　x

a. A mark in two columns indicates an average lag between the respective quarters.

15. See for example the investment equation of the annual model of the CPB. See VERDOORN (1967) and VERDOORN, POST and GOSLINGA (1970).

V. Private consumption expenditures

5.1. INTRODUCTION

Micro economic theory of consumer behaviour explains that each subject distributes his available income over present and future consumption according to the rule that the marginal utility of the last money unit is equalized over time. The decisions connected herewith depend on total income available for the distribution over present and future consumption, the desired equilibrium between consumption and savings over lifetime and the rate of discount between present and future goods.

The total amount available for consumption depends on disposable income and wealth. The desired equilibrium position both depends on the present possibilities to consume and the present needs as well as on income, wealth etc., and needs in the future. The ratio of exchange of present and future goods depends on the real rate of interest i.e. the nominal interest rate corrected for the expected change in the price level.

In the context of an explanation of private consumption on the macro level we mention as important factors determining the present possibilities to consume: the level of disposable income, the level of wealth including liquid assets, the price of consumer goods and the distribution of income and wealth, while expectations on disposable income, wealth, business cycle, price level, etc. govern the expected buying power.

The following analysis of the macro economic private consumption expenditures starts in first instance from a static consumption function in which the level of private consumption expenditures in constant prices (c) is dependent on real disposable wage and transfer income (w_D), real disposable non-wage income (z_D), consumer prices (p_c), real wealth (s), the real rate of interest (r^r) and cyclical influences measured by the utilization rate of labour (q_L):

(5.1) $\quad c = c(w_D, z_D, p_c, s, r', q_L)$.

The sequence of the analysis is as follows. Firstly, we deal with the role of incomes and prices. Secondly, other relevant variables are considered and finally we are concerned with the estimating of the resulting basic consumption function.

5.2. THE ROLE OF INCOMES AND PRICES

In most consumption functions appearing in econometric models total disposable income is the main determinant of private consumption. We don't think this to be correct because the impact of changes in income distribution is neglected in such a specification. In the Netherlands the share of disposable wage and transfer income was 61.8% in 1951, whereas in 1965 this share was 71.0%, mainly due to a considerable rise of disposable transfer income at the cost of non-wage income. Given also the fact that non-wage income has a relatively low marginal propensity to consume, the use of a total disposable income variable may seriously disturb the finding of economic meaningful results.

For the time being we neglect the discussion of what the most appropriate formulation of income variables should be and distinguish between two types of real disposable income, *viz.* real disposable wage income (w_D) and real disposable non-wage income (z_D) First of all the following very simple functions are defined under quite static conditions:

(5.2) $\quad c = c_w + c_z$

(5.3) $\quad c_w = w_D^{x_1}$

(5.4) $\quad c_z = z_D^{x_2}$

where c, private consumption in real terms, is equal to the sum of real consumption by wage earners and persons with transfer incomes (c_w) and real consumption out of non-wage income (c_z). After taking differences of equation (5.2) and dividing by c we have

(5.5) $\quad \dfrac{dc}{c} = \dfrac{dc_w}{c} + \dfrac{dc_z}{c}$

If we then write $\dfrac{dc}{c} = d \ln c$, $\dfrac{dc_w}{c_w} = d \ln c_w$, $\dfrac{dc_z}{c_z} = d \ln c_z$ and, in addition, rewrite the terms in equation (5.5) the result is

(5.6) $\quad d \ln c = \dfrac{c_w}{c} d \ln c_w + \dfrac{c_z}{c} d \ln c_z$

Similar to most of the other equations in the model we prefer a consumption function in log-linear form. Integration of equation (5.6) and substitution of the logarithmic equivalent of equation (5.3) and (5.4) in this relationship yields:

(5.7) $\quad \ln c = \varkappa_1 \left[\dfrac{c_w}{c} \ln w_D \right] + \varkappa_2 \left[\dfrac{c_z}{c} \ln z_D \right] + c_1$

where c_1 is a constant term.

This equation contains two unobservable ratios, viz. $\dfrac{c_w}{c}$ and $\dfrac{c_z}{c}$. Their values have been approximated by using a method developed by VERDOORN (1968) which is already applied in the annual model of the Central Planning Bureau. He derived that, using $y_D = w_D + z_D$

(5.8) $\quad \dfrac{c_w}{c} = \varphi \approx \dfrac{\dfrac{\Delta c_w}{\Delta w_D} \dfrac{w_D}{y_D}}{\dfrac{\Delta c_w}{\Delta w_D} \dfrac{w_D}{y_D} + \dfrac{\Delta c_z}{\Delta z_D}\left(1 - \dfrac{w_D}{y_D}\right)}$

and

(5.9) $\quad \dfrac{c_z}{c} = 1 - \varphi.$

Verdoorn has estimated $\dfrac{\Delta c_w}{\Delta w_D}$ and $\dfrac{\Delta c_z}{\Delta z_D}$ to be .86 and .41 respectively in 1957. However, our earlier experiments with a quarterly consumption function have shown that when these consumption quota's are used for the computation of φ the estimated marginal propensities differ considerably from their mentioned values.[1] The marginal consumption quota of disposable wage and transfer income of .86 seems on the low side and that of disposable non-wage income of .41 much too high. So we must experiment with different ratio's of the two marginal propensities. This will be done in section 5.4.

1. See DRIEHUIS (1970), p. 16.

For the time being equation (5.7) is written as follows:

(5.10) $\ln c = \varkappa_1 [\varphi \ln w_D] + \varkappa_2 [(1-\varphi) \ln z_D] + c_1$

This specification takes into consideration the shifts in income distribution by pre-multiplying the different types of income with their estimated share in total consumption.

The consumer demand function as it now stands is homogenous of degree zero in money incomes and the price level. Real consumption is a function of real incomes but not of the price level. While we may expect this to be a rational hypothesis in the long run it is not so certain that consumers are free of money illusion in the short run.[2] To leave this possibility open we extend equation (5.10) with an independent price variable. We discuss two possibilities which are open here.

One possibility is to add the level of consumer prices to the consumption function obtained so far. In logarithmic form the function can then be written as

(5.11) $\ln c = \varkappa_1 [\varphi \ln w_D] + \varkappa_2 [(1-\varphi) \ln z_D] + \varkappa_3 \ln p_c + c_2$

With the consumption function formulated in this form we have absence of money illusion for $\varkappa_3 = 0$. On the contrary if there is money illusion in the sense that a proportionate increase in money income leads to an increase in real consumption we may expect $0 < \varkappa_3 \leqslant 1$. This formulation of money illusion in the consumption function which recently has been found to be valid for the United States by BRANSON and KLEVORICK (1969), has unpleasant implications because it presupposes that even in the long run consumers suffer from money illusion and never fully adjust their real expenditures of consumption goods.

This objection against the level-based approach of money illusion in the consumption function can be met by introducing a change-based formulation of consumer prices. Hence we would have:

(5.12) $\ln c = \varkappa_1 [\varphi \ln w_D] + \varkappa_2 [(1-\varphi) \ln z_D] + \varkappa_4 \Delta \ln p_c + c_3$.

In this case as well we must apply restrictions on the parameter $\varkappa_4$, i.e. absence of money illusion when $\varkappa_4 = 0$ and existence of money illusion when $0 < \varkappa_4 \leqslant 1$.

---

2. Remember that in chapter III the supply of labour was not influenced by money illusion in the long run. The supply of labour data are too bad to test such an influence.

It has been argued[3] that when consumers do not suffer from money illusion and there is a price expectations mechanism at work represented by the change (or expected change) in the price level of consumption, one would have found a specification similar to equation (5.12).[4] Such a mechanism can arise from the behaviour lying behind substitution between consumption and savings when prices are expected to rise and savings will have a lower real yield. Current consumption is then stimulated in particular when the expected rate of inflation is relatively high. Furthermore there is the so-called real wealth effect introduced by PIGOU (1941): a rise in the price level decreases the value of assets as a consequence of which consumption is reduced to compensate for the loss in the real value of cash balances, bonds etc.[5] However, it should be borne in mind that people having debts take advantage of rising prices and may, on the contrary, increase their consumption expenditures.

In what follows we consider equation (5.12) as the most appropriate formulation of the consumption function. The hypothesized behaviour lying behind is that if consumers are confronted with a change in the price level their consumption is initially not fully adjusted to the changed situation because they do not realize the price change to its full extent or do not want to change their original buying plans. Afterwards there is an adjustment of consumption expenditures in the opposite direction and consumption is moved from the present towards the future or vice versa. If money illusion and/or price expectations, two phenomena we can not distinguish in the chosen specification, are present to some degree we should find $\varkappa_4$ to be positive and significantly different from zero. This supposes, however, that the Pigou effect which suggests a negative effect on real consumption when prices are rising, is more than counterbalanced by positive price expectations and the effect of money illusion.

Before we turn to the dynamization of the consumption function we should consider an old problem with respect to the *estimating* of consumption functions, *viz.* whether they must be formulated in volume or in value terms.[6] A real income variable is not directly observable because nominal income is deflated by a consumer price index. This deflation procedure may yield biased estimates of the marginal propensities to consume because the consumption pattern of wage earners may be different from that of people

---

3. See BRANSON and KLEVORICK (1969) and POWER (1959).
4. In fact we anticipate now on the discussion of other than income and price variables which has been reserved for the following section.
5. See also TYRNI (1964).
6. See FERBER (1953).

spending non-wage income.[7] To avoid this drawback we have chosen for a nominal consumption function. Equation (5.12) must then be transformed into

(5.13) $\quad \ln C = \varkappa_1 [\varphi \ln W_D] + \varkappa_2 [(1-\varphi) \ln Z_D] +$
$\quad\quad\quad + \varkappa_4 \Delta \ln p_c + (1-\varkappa_5) \ln p_c + c_4$

where $\varkappa_5 = \varphi \varkappa_1 + (1-\varphi)\varkappa_2$. It seemed likely that a significant influence of the level of consumer prices could not be determined because $\varkappa_5$ was found to be slightly below unity in a consumption function appearing in an earlier version of the present model.[8] Therefore the term $(1-\varkappa_5) \ln p_c$ was dropped in the following specifications.

There is no reason to expect consumers to react instanteneously to changes in income or prices. It is much more plausible to suppose that there will be a lag before the reactions to these independent variables set in. Moreover, it seems plausible that in making consumption decisions in a particular quarter, consumers consider the more permanent part of their recent experience with regard to consumption determining variables. In fact distributed lag adjustments of these variables will be a mixture of institutional lags and lags induced by expectations.

As concerns income variables there is evidence for institutional lags but these are different for the two types of income under consideration. Most people receive their salary or transfer income once a week or once a month. So on the one hand there exists a rather continuous flow of wage and transfer income which is spent for a considerable part in a relatively short period of time. On the other hand there is a rather irregular flow of non-wage income, with a heterogenous composition which is not instanteneously known (dividends and profits become known with a lag, etc.).

So, if we introduce the permanent income concept which is developed by BROWN (1952) and FRIEDMAN (1957) as valid for consumer behaviour it seems appropriate to assume that the degree of permanentness is different for wage and transfer income on the one side and non-wage income on the

---

7. This hypothesis is confirmed by empirical facts. Estimating a quarterly real consumption function yielded a very high marginal propensity to consume for non-wage income. This result is probably due to the fact that the composition of non-wage income consumption is different from wage income consumption in the sense that the first mentioned variable contains relatively more spending on durables Prices of durables. have been rising less than other consumption categories during the sample period, so the total price index overestimates consumer prices relevant for non-wage income consumption. Real non-wage income is then underestimated and this probably leads to an overestimation of the marginal propensity to consume of non wage earners.

8. DRIEHUIS (1970), pp. 13–16.

other.[9] Hence we split both consumption of disposable wage and transfer income and disposable non-wage income into a permanent and a transitory part and do the same thing for the respective income variables.

If permanent disposable income variables are written as rational distributed lag functions of their past values we arrive at:

$$(5.14) \quad W_D^p = \frac{G(L)_1}{H(L)_1} W_D$$

$$(5.15) \quad Z_D^p = \frac{G(L)_2}{H(L)_2} Z_D$$

where p denotes the permanent income component.

Here we see another aspect of the distinction between the two types of income. Not only can one take into account the effects of a shifting income distribution and different marginal propensities to consume but one is forced to realize that the permanent component of non-wage income may be quite different from permanent wage and transfer income. In addition, when transitory components of consumption and disposable income are considered to be independent from permanent parts and when transitory components are assumed, as is usual in the literature, to have a zero expectation it can be shown that total aggregate consumption is a function of permanent income.[10]

This procedure now gives the following consumption function in which an unknown rational distributed lag function for the rate of change in the consumer price level is introduced as well:

$$(5.16) \quad \ln C = \varkappa_6 \left[\frac{G(L)_1}{H(L)_1} \varphi \ln W_D \right] + \varkappa_7 \left[\frac{G(L)_2}{H(L)_2} (1 - \varphi) \ln Z_D \right]$$

$$+ \varkappa_8 \frac{G(L)_3}{H(L)_3} \Delta \ln p_c + c_5 .$$

According to Friedman's theory a constant term should lack in the consumption function. It should be noted that this requirement need not to be fulfilled when variables other than income variables are also included in the equation.

---

9. We do not consider here DUESENBERRY's (1949) theory of consumer behaviour, because we think that his idea that the highest previous income is determining consumption expenditures is not relevant when real consumption shows a continuous rise.
10. See for example CRAMER (1969), p. 181–190.

5.3. THE ROLE OF OTHER VARIABLES

In the introduction of this chapter real wealth, the real rate of interest and the business cycle were mentioned as possible variables for explaining consumer behaviour.

As concerns wealth, i.e. accumulated savings, we will be very short. Personal wealth data are not available for the Netherlands and the impact of wealth on private consumption expenditure cannot adequately be tested. However, it is not unrealistic to suppose that wealth effects are at least partly reflected by other variables such as non-wage income, liquid assets and the real interest rate.

One portion of consumer wealth is held in the form of liquid assets and this variable is sometimes even used as an indication of total consumer wealth supposing that changes herein are closely related to changes in total wealth holding.[11] However, we should be careful in our interpretation of this idea because changes in liquid asset holdings may be the consequence of a change in the composition of wealth, leaving total assets unchanged. Nevertheless we want to open the possibility to find an influence of liquid assets on consumer behaviour because it may be a sensitive indicator of short run factors affecting consumer expenditures. We quote ZELLNER, HUANG and CHAU[12]: '..., if a consumer receives an unexpected temporary increment of income receipts, it will initially probably be incorporated in liquid asset holdings giving rise to a liquid asset imbalance which will be corrected with the passage of time, perhaps in part by an adjustment of expenditures. Or, suppose that a consumer plans to buy a major durable. He may very well build up his liquid assets above their 'normal' level prior to making the outlay on the durable. Again a liquid asset imbalance appears as an indicator of future expenditure behaviour.' So, these authors advocate the imbalance between actual and desired real liquid assets as a variable affecting personal consumption expenditures. Rather than following their line of thought in every respect we have adopted as an explanatory variable the total amount of liquidities relative to total expenditures.[13] The underlying hypothesis is that an increase of liquidities faster than an increase of expenditures would raise consumer expenditures and vice versa. In order to express that very short-run changes in the liquidity ratio do not effect the behaviour of consumers

---

11. See ACKLEY (1967), p. 275.
12. See ZELLNER, HUANG and CHAU (1965), p. 574.
13. A more appropriate variable would be liquid assets held by consumers, but such a time series is not available. In addition, the variable chosen has the advantage of being an endogenous variable in the model.

we only take into account the 'permanent' component of the liquidities expenditures ratio.

The impact of the interest rate on consumer expenditures is subject to controversy not in the least because the real rate of interest, which theoretical considerations indicate to be the relevant variable, is not directly observable. Along the lines suggested by FISHER (1930) we can define the real interest rate as the difference between the nominal interest rate and the anticipated rate of inflation:

$$(5.17) \quad r^r = r^n - \varkappa_9 \varDelta \ln p_c^*$$

where r^r is the real rate of interest, r^n the nominal rate of interest and $\varDelta \ln p_c^*$ the expected rate of change in the consumer price level. The formulation and the estimation of the real rate of interest is widely discussed in Chapter XI and it may suffice here to say that we don't want to restrain *a priori* $\varkappa_9$ to be unity[14] and that the expected rate of inflation can be more conveniently written as a rational distributed lag function

$$(5.18) \quad \varDelta \ln p_c^* = \frac{G(L)_4}{H(L)_4} \varDelta \ln p_c$$

This relation combined with equation (5.17) yields a measerable formulation for the real rate of interest:

$$(5.19) \quad r^r = r^n - \varkappa_9 \frac{G(L)_4}{H(L)_4} \varDelta \ln p_c$$

Another potential explanatory variable for private consumption expenditures is a variable representing cyclical fluctuations. This variable should be especially suited to express the cyclical changes in the propensity to save. When bad times are expected and people fear to become unemployed, they restrict their purchases, particularly of durable goods and increase their savings. It seems therefore not unreasonable to represent these consumer precautions by the rate of unemployment or, in our terminology, by the utilization rate of labour. As in many other situations people react to circumstances or changes in circumstances which they consider to be continuous for a certain period of time; very short run fluctuations are assumed to be out of consideration.

---

14. For a discussion see chapter XI, pp. 156-157.

In summary, we have now obtained the following aggregate consumption function:

$$(5.20) \quad \ln C = \varkappa_6 \frac{G(L)_1}{H(L)_1} \varphi \ln W_D + \varkappa_7 \frac{G(L)_2}{H(L)_2} (1 - \varphi) \ln Z_D$$

$$+ \varkappa_8 \frac{G(L)_3}{H(L)_3} \Delta \ln p_c + \varkappa_{10} \frac{G(L)_5}{H(L)_5} r^n + \varkappa_{10} \varkappa_9 \frac{G(L)_4}{H(L)_4}$$

$$\frac{G(L)_5}{H(L)_5} \Delta \ln p_c + \varkappa_{11} \frac{G(L)_6}{H(L)_6} \ln \frac{L_q}{V} + \varkappa_{12} \frac{G(L)_7}{H(L)_6} \ln q_L + c_6.$$

where $\varkappa_{10}$ and $\frac{G(L)_5}{H(L)_5}$ represent the influence of the real interest rate. It will be clear from the outset that estimation of this relationship will not give an acceptable result for the rate of change in prices. We have therefore assumed that the error introduced by postulating that the rational lag distributions $\frac{G(L)_3}{H(L)_3}$ and $\frac{G(L)_4}{H(L)_4} \frac{G(L)_5}{H(L)_5}$ are equal is not serious, in which case equation (5.20) can be simplified to:

$$(5.21) \quad \ln C = \varkappa_6 \frac{G(L)_1}{H(L)_1} \varphi \ln W_D + \varkappa_7 \frac{G(L)_2}{H(L)_2} (1 - \varphi) \ln Z_D$$

$$+ (\varkappa_8 + \varkappa_{10} \varkappa_9) \frac{G(L)_3}{H(L)_3} \Delta \ln p_c - \varkappa_{10} \frac{G(L)_5}{H(L)_5} r^n$$

$$+ \varkappa_{11} \frac{G(L)_6}{H(L)_6} \ln \frac{L_q}{V} + \varkappa_{12} \frac{G(L)_7}{H(L)_7} \ln q_L + c_6$$

5.4. EMPIRICAL RESULTS

The coefficients of basic specification (5.21) have been estimated under the assumption that $G(L)_3 = 1 - \lambda$, $H(L)_3 = 1 - \lambda L$ and that $G(L)_1$, $G(L)_2$, $G(L)_5$, $G(L)_6$ and $G(L)_7$ were finite distributed lags, while $H(L)_1 = H(L)_2$ $H(L)_5 = H(L)_6 = H(L)_7 = 1$. As will be seen below it is necessary to start the lag distribution of the price variable after one quarter. Its coefficient is not very significant and it represents both money illusion and price expectation effects. The long term coefficient amounts .668.

As expected the lag of disposable non-wage income is longer than the lag of disposable wage income, while their coefficients differ considerably. (See also table 5.1). The result suggests that there is hardly any reason to speak about 'permanent' wage income. Friedman's ideas seem more suited for other forms of income. The elasticities found for the income variables are obtained after iteration of the premultiplication factor φ.[15] For the application of this procedure one has to choose the ratio of the marginal propensities to consume of both wage and non-wage income in advance. The final result must then imply marginal consumption propensities equal to the propensities formerly assumed. In the middle of the sample period we have determined the following marginal propensities to consume:

disposable wage and transfer income: .92
disposable non-wage income: .22.

The ratio of these is 4.2 which is approximately identical to the ratio used in order to compute the premultiplicator.[16] It has furthermore been found that the rate of change of the labour utilization rate rather than its level contributed to the explanation of private consumption expenditures. This emphasizes the 'additional' character of this variable just as the overall influence of the business cycle seems to be expressed in the other explanatory variables, especially the income variables. Finally, the, non-linear, impact of

Table 5.1. *Average lags of variables explaining consumption expenditures (equation 5.22)*[a]

Variable	Number of quarters						
	0	1	2	3	4	5	6
1. Disposable wage income	×	×					
2. Disposable non-wage income			×				
3. Change in price level of consumption			×				
4. Interest rate					×	×	
5. Liquidity ratio			×	×			
6. Change in utilization rate of labour				×	×		

a. A mark in two columns indicates an average lag between the respective quarters.

15. For empirical reasons we have used one quarter lagged values of φ.
16. See equation 68 of the complete model in Appendix A.

the interest rate is very weak.[17] Relatively unimportant too is the influence of the liquidity ratio.

The equation included in the model is

$$
\begin{aligned}
(5.22) \quad \ln C = &\; .5 \ln C_{-1} \\
& \underset{(-)}{} \\
& + .837 \left[\sum_{0}^{-2} \gamma_{12}\, \varphi_{-1} \ln W_D - .5 \sum_{-1}^{-3} \gamma_{12}\, \varphi_{-1} \ln W_D \right] + \\
& \underset{(1.4\%)}{} \\
& + .308 \left[\sum_{0}^{-3} \gamma_{5}(1-\varphi_{-1}) \ln Z_D - .5 \sum_{-1}^{-4} \gamma_{5}(1-\varphi_{-1}) \ln Z_D \right] + \\
& \underset{(40.8\%)}{} \\
& + .334\, \Delta \ln p_{c-1} - \\
& \underset{(72.0\%)}{} \\
& - .003 \left[\sum_{-3}^{-4} \gamma_6\, r - .5 \sum_{-4}^{-5} \gamma_6\, r \right] + \\
& \underset{(63.7\%)}{} \\
& + .184 \left[\sum_{-1}^{-2} \gamma_6 \frac{L_q}{V} - .5 \sum_{-2}^{-3} \gamma_6 \frac{L_q}{V} \right] + \\
& \underset{(175.1\%)}{} \\
& + 1.238 \left[\sum_{-2}^{-3} \gamma_6\, \Delta q_L - .5 \sum_{-3}^{-4} \gamma_6\, \Delta q_L \right] + \\
& \underset{(78.5\%)}{} \\
& + .190\, [C_{aut} - .5\, C_{aut-1}] + \\
& \underset{(15.9\%)}{} \\
& + .466 \\
& \underset{(3.6\%)}{}
\end{aligned}
$$

$$\bar{R}^2 = .998$$
$$NR = 2.00$$

where C = private consumption, in current prices;
W_D = disposable wage and transfer income;
Z_D = disposable non-wage income;
p_c = price of private consumption, 1963 = 100;
r = long term interest rate (nominal);

17. For a more significant influence of the interest rate on private consumption, see HAMBURGER (1967). KEYNES (1936) thought that the short period influence of the rate of interest on individual spending out of a given income is secondary and relatively unimportant (see p. 110).

$\frac{L_q}{V}$ = liquidity ratio, after correction for its decreasing trend;
q_L = utilization rate of labour;
C_{aut} = effects of anticipatory purchases on private consumption in 1956:4, 1957:1 and 1965:4;
φ = share of wage-earners consumption in total consumption;
γ_5 = .10, .20, .30, .40;
γ_6 = .50, .50;
γ_{12} = .70, .20, .10.

Figure 5.1. Actual and computed private consumption expenditures (in logs) according to equation (5.22)

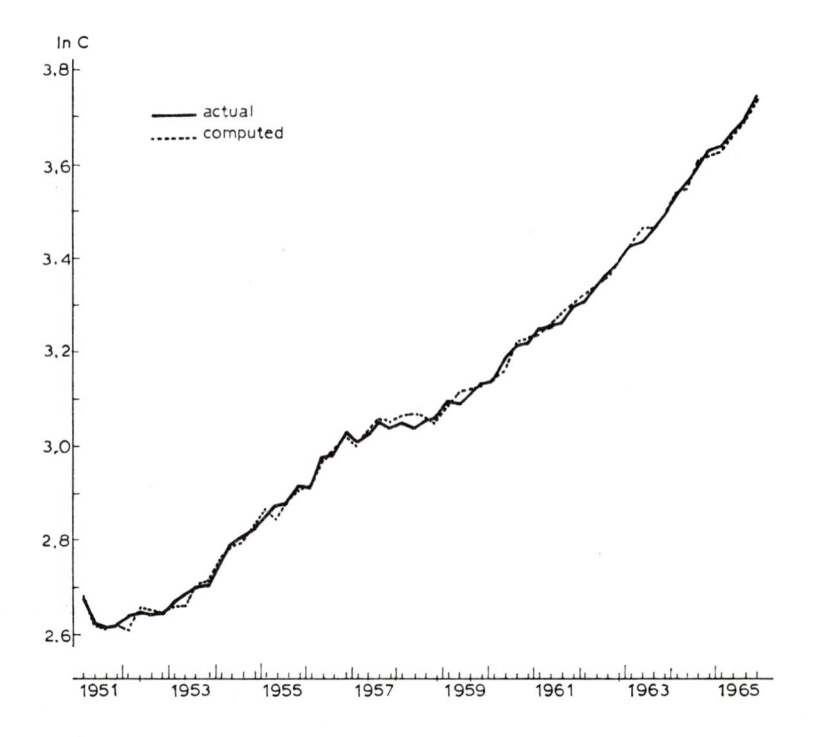

VI. Inventory formation

6.1. INTRODUCTION

Throughout the period of observation inventory investment has fluctuated more than any other component of aggregate demand. Thus a meaningful understanding of the determinants behind inventory investment behaviour and the lag structures involved are essential to an acceptable explanation of its cyclical fluctuations.[1] It should be noted that inventory formation fluctuates widely within the year and that the use of quarterly data may provide an additional insight into this type of investment that cannot be obtained appropriately from annual data. On the other hand quarterly inventory formation time series are often weak and this is certainly the case in this model. The present analysis of inventory investment starts, by considering three components of stockbuilding in combination with three well-known motives for inventory investment: the transactions motive, the precautionary motive and the speculative motive.

6.2. THEORY OF INVENTORY FORMATION

The explanation of inventory investment is based upon a small submodel in which three well-known components of stockbuilding are distinguished. These are the planned inventories, the unplanned inventories and speculative inventories. The planned inventories arise on the one hand from the transactions and the precautionary motive and on the other hand from the (partial) adjustment of a disequilibrium between the desired and the actual level of stocks.

---

1. This point has particulary been stressed by Colin CLARK (1949) when he constructed a quarterly model of the United States.

The transactions motive says that each firm considers the costs of holding or not holding inventories and, having decided upon these, determines some stock-sales ratio. The coefficient describing the equilibrium between planned inventory formation and the expected change in sales is called the 'marginal desired inventory coefficient'.[2] If we postulate that the expected change in sales is a function of changes in sales in the past and that this relationship can be described by an unknown rational distributed lag function in the lag operator (L) we have:

(6.1) $\quad \Delta n_{pt} = \eta_1 \Delta v^*$

and

(6.2) $\quad \Delta v^* = \dfrac{G(L)_1}{H(L)_1} \Delta v$

where Δn_{pt} is planned inventory investment arising from the transactions motive, v is sales, and v^* is expected sales, all in constant prices.

Apart from planned stocks related with the technical need to have a portion of the level of sales in stock either in the form of raw materials, semi-manufactured products or finished goods firms want to minimize the inconvenience of a lack of stocks at some future time. This demand for inventories arising from this precautionary motive is undoubtedly dependent on the expected level of transactions as well. But in addition the amount of precautionary inventories will show a relationship with the general conjunctural situation. When, to give an example, firms expect a recovery of the economy after recession they may feel the need for more stocks than on the basis of the transactions motive alone. When planned inventory investment arising from the precautionary motive (Δn_{pp}) is considered as a mark up over planned inventory investment arising from the transactions motive and an indicator of future cyclical developments is added we obtain the following specification:

(6.3) $\quad \Delta n_{pp} = \eta_2 \Delta n_{pt} + \eta_3 \dfrac{G(L)_2}{H(L)_2} \Delta q_L + c_1$

where the utilization rate of labour (q_L) is used as a general indicator of the conjunctural situation.

In addition to inventory formulation planned according to the transactions and the precautionary motive firms react on disequilibrium situations arisen in the past. When the expected change in sales is different from the actual one

---

2. See LOVELL (1961), p. 95.

an inventory position will result which is not foreseen and not desired, i.e. a divergence between desired stocks and actual stocks will appear. In the next periods firms will adjust their original inventory investment plans in a negative or positive direction dependent on the nature of the disequilibrium. This adjustment process will take time and we assume that this error adaptation will have a distributed lag, for the time being represented by an unknown rational distributed lag function. So we have the following specification for planned inventory investment arising from disequilibria (Δn_{pd}) between desired and actual stocks in the past:

$$(6.4) \quad \Delta n_{pd} = \eta_4 \frac{G(L)_3}{H(L)_3} (n_d - n)$$

where n_d is desired level of stocks and n is actual level of stocks. In an equilibrium situation $n = n_d$ and the part of planned inventory formation connected herewith is equal to zero.

In the foregoing analysis planned inventory investment was not simply geared to the actual change in the level of sales but to a normal or permanent change. It is clear that temporary or transitory changes in demand will result in temporary decumulation or accumulation of stocks. This part of inventory formation is not desired and therefore denoted as unplanned stockbuilding. The phenomenon of unplanned inventories can be written in the form of an equation, as follows:

$$(6.5) \quad \Delta n_u = -\eta_5 (\Delta v - \frac{G(L)_1}{H(L)_1} \Delta v)$$

where Δn_u represents unplanned inventory investment. One might ask whether it is necessary to have a reaction parameter written in this equation. The reason why we have adopted such a parameter is that the appearance of unplanned stockbuilding is especially valid for a part of the level of stocks (finished goods), so that a coefficient smaller than unity is needed to bring this to expression.

The speculative motive may be ultimately introduced by considering changes in the import price level because the import content of stockbuilding in the Netherlands is large. When import prices tend to rise inventory formation will take place in anticipation to a further rise in prices, and *vice versa*. So we arrive at the following simple specification for speculative inventory formation

$$(6.6) \quad \Delta n_s = \eta_6 \frac{G(L)_4}{H(L)_4} \Delta p_m$$

where Δn_s is speculative inventory investment and p_m is the price level of imported goods.

When equations (6.1) up to (6.6) are summarized according to the definition of total inventory investment (Δn)

(6.7) $\quad \Delta n = \Delta n_{pt} + \Delta n_{pp} + \Delta n_{pd} + \Delta n_u + \Delta n_s$

we arrive at

(6.8) $\quad \Delta n = (\eta_1 + \eta_1\eta_2 + \eta_5) \dfrac{G(L)_1}{H(L)_1} \Delta v + \eta_3 \dfrac{G(L)_2}{H(L)_2} \Delta q_L +$

$\qquad + \eta_4 \dfrac{G(L)_3}{H(L)_3} (n_d - n) - \eta_5 \Delta v + \eta_6 \dfrac{G(L)_4}{H(L)_4} \Delta p_m + c_1$

Before the estimation of this equation is discussed two remarks must be made. The first remark concerns the variable $(n_d - n)$. Usually the desired level of stocks is specified in terms of a normal level of sales[3] and this approximation is substituted in the inventory formation equation under consideration. Our basic specification (6.8) has been derived without applying this procedure. This was done to avoid the considerable multicollinearity between the level of stocks variable (n) and the level of sales (v). The implication is, however, the necessity of estimating a separate equation for the desired level of stocks. Such an equation can, for instance, be specified as follows:

(6.9) $\quad n_d = \eta_7 \dfrac{G(L)_5}{H(L)_5} v + c_2$

where the variable $\dfrac{G(L)_5}{H(L)_5} v$ represents the normal level of sales. It should be borne in mind that even when plans are fulfilled discrepancies may arise between planned and desired stocks due to technical limitations in, and factors affecting the speed of adjustment to be discussed later. So there is no *a priori* reason to restrict the variable v in equation (6.9) to have a lag distribution identical to that in equation (6.2).

The second remark is related to the fact that we have included the change in the rate of interest as a cost variable. A rising interest rate stimulates a more rational control of stocks and *vice versa*. So, the interest rate variable acts as a factor influencing the adjustment process between inventory formation and its determining factors. In this latter role a complicated lag between inventory investment and the interest rate seems not very plausible.

---

3. See, for instance, DARLIN and LOVELL (1965), BALL and DRAKE (1963), and VERDOORN, POST and GOSLINGA (1970).

6.3. EMPIRICAL RESULTS

Equation (6.8) can be estimated once the disequilibrium between the desired level of stocks and actual stocks can be quantified, more specifically once the desired level of stocks can be approximated in quantitative terms. As has been argued earlier the desired level of stocks is assumed to be a function of the expected normal level of sales (see equation 6.9). However, an additional variable was needed to quantify the decreasing trend in the stock-sales ratio that can be actually observed in the postwar years in the Netherlands.
This scale effect is probably due to a more efficient control of stocks. We have therefore estimated

$$(6.10) \qquad \frac{n}{\frac{G(L)_5}{H(L)_5} v} = -\eta_8 t + c_3$$

where t is a time trend. After rewriting the estimation result, the following equation for the desired level of stocks was obtained

$$(6.11) \qquad n_d = \left(.390 - .127 \, \frac{t}{100}\right)^{-4} \sum_{-1} \gamma_{13} v$$

where $\gamma_{13} = .40, .30, .20, .10$.

This equation is rather simple, probably too simple since we should include explanatory variables such as the rate of interest and labour costs as well. These variables seem, at least partly, responsible for the decreasing stock-sales ratio. Some time an alternative formulation for the desired level of stocks should be constructed and tested in the inventory investment equation.

The value of the desired level of stocks computed with the help of the parameters found in equation (6.11) can now be used in the estimating of an inventory formation equation.

The estimation of basic specification (6.8), enlarged by an interest rate variable, is based on the following assumptions with respect to the lags. $G(L)_1$, $G(L)_2$ and $G(L)_4$ are assumed to be unknown finite structures and $H(L)_1 = H(L)_2 = H(L)_4 = 1$. Furthermore, the discrepancy between desired and actual stocks was postulated to react with an infinite lag suggesting a relatively long adjustment time. Therefore $G(L)_3 = 1 - \lambda$ and $H(L)_3 = 1 - \lambda L$.

In this way the following model equation has been obtained:

$$(6.12) \qquad \Delta n = .5 \, \Delta n_{-1} + .506 \left[\sum_{-1}^{-3} \gamma_{14} \, \Delta v - .5 \sum_{-2}^{-4} \gamma_{14} \, \Delta v\right] +$$
$$ {\scriptstyle (-)} {\scriptstyle (19.5\%)}$$

$$+ .377(n_d - n_{-1})_{-1} - .134[\Delta v - .5 \, \Delta v_{-1}] +$$
$$ {\scriptstyle (27.8\%)} {\scriptstyle (34.0\%)}$$

$$+ .006 \left[\sum_{0}^{-1} \gamma_6 \Delta p_{mg-sa} - .5 \sum_{-1}^{-2} \gamma_6 \Delta p_{mg-sa} \right] -$$
(348.3%)

$$- .312 [\Delta r_{-1} - .5 \Delta r_{-2}] .705 \, Dum_1 + 1.021 \, Dum_2 + .142$$
(87.5%) (23.0%) (18.1%) (48.7%)

$$\bar{R}^2 = .792$$
$$NR = 2.20$$

where Δn = inventory formation, in 1963 prices;
v = total expenditures, less inventory formation, government wages, exports of services and factor incomes received from abroad, in 1963 prices;
n_d = desired level of stocks, in 1963 prices;
n = level of stocks, in 1963 prices;
p_{mg-sa} = price level of imports of goods excluding ships and airplanes, 1963 = 100;
r = long term interest rate;
Dum_1 = dummy variable for effects of Korean war and Suez crisis (1956);
Dum_2 = dummy variable for exceptional crops;
γ_6 = .50, .50;
γ_{14} = .17, .33, .50.

Figure 6.1. Actual and computed inventory formation (in billions of 1963 guilders) according to equation (6.12)

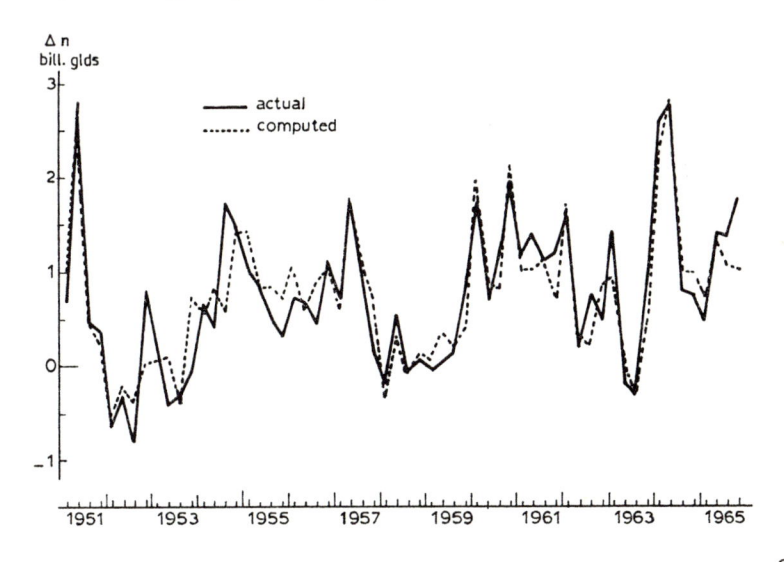

As usual in quarterly models the rate of explanation of inventory investment is not so very high. This confirms the rather erratic and weak character of the time-series of this part of aggregate demand. This is the more true when we see that the result has been obtained by using two dummy variables; one representing the effects of the Korean war and the Suez crisis in 1956 and one representing the effects of exceptional crops. The value of λ (.5) indicates that the adjustment of a disequilibrium between desired and actual stocks does not take place very fast. The long run coefficient of this variable is .754. This is a remarkable result since a long run coefficient of about unity, implying a complete elimination of the disequilibrium between desired and actual stocks, seems more reasonable. It was furthermore disappointing that no acceptable influence of a cyclical indicator could be found. According to the estimating result the impact of the change in import prices seems negligible. It may be that future research will improve the equation but in that respect we are rather pessimistic.

Table 6.1. *Average lags of variables explaining inventory formation (equation 6.12)*[a]

Variable	\multicolumn{7}{c}{Number of quarters}

Variable	0	1	2	3	4	5	6
1. Change in expenditures (+sign)			×	×			
2. Discrepancy between desired and actual stocks			×				
3. Change in expenditures (−sign)	×						
4. Change in price level of imports of goods	×	×					
5. Change in interest rate		×					

a. A mark in two columns indicates an average lag between the respective quarters.

VII. Exports and imports of goods and services

7.1. INTRODUCTION

The Netherlands' economy is of the type usually called 'open'. This can be illustrated by the fact that the share of exports and imports of goods and services averages 45 à 50 per cent of gross national product. An appropriate explanation of these trade flows is therefore extremely important. Another argument in favour of a careful study of the international trade relations is concerned with economic policy requirements. More than other countries open economies are confronted with the question whether their exchange rate still reflects the real fundamental position to the rest of the world and whether or not the exchange rate needs an alteration in order to return to a fundamental equilibrium.[1] Faced with policy decisions of this sort one needs the help of an econometric model involving appropriate international trade elements to show realistic effects on the economy of exchange rate adjustments either by the own country or by others.

The balance of payments reflects a country's position to the rest of the world, and consists, broadly speaking, of the following imports and exports items: goods, services, factor incomes, income transfers, capital and changes in the gold and exchange reserves as balance. In this model the international sector is represented by six behavioural equations, *viz.* equations for the volumes of exports and imports of goods and services and the prices of exports of goods and services. The price levels of imports of goods and services are treated as exogenous variables. This seems realistic for a small

---

1. During the sample period the Netherlands changed their exchange rate one time, *viz.* in March 1961.

85

country like the Netherlands because the supply of imports may be assumed to be infinitely elastic at the going (and exogenous) price level of foreign goods.

Except for the endogenously explained items, all the remaining imports and exports (factor incomes, transfer incomes and capital) are treated as exogenous variables. Indeed they are not really exogenous for the Netherlands but we treated them as such for the time being. Further research will probably enable us to include some of the items in the model in the future.

In this chapter we will discuss the analysis of the goods and services imports and exports volumes, whereas the export prices of goods and services are viewed in chapter IX on price formation.

7.2. EXPORTS OF GOODS AND SERVICES THEORY

Actual exports of goods and services are resulting from a demand and supply process. The equations to be described in this section therefore hold elements of both sides of the market: a demand variable and two variables representing supply factors all to be discussed later.

Visible and invisible trade are estimated separately in our model. This is obviously not self-evident. In none of the 25 models mentioned in NERLOVE'S (1966) survey of macro econometric models goods and services are treated in this way. We are of the opinion that a separate analysis of the two types of trade is to be preferred to equations for goods and services combined and we have two main reasons for this. One is that in international trade the roles of goods and services are different. The other is the need to evaluate as completely and realistically as possible the effects of international policy measures. Especially when exchange rates are altered one might expect different effects in visible and invisible trade respectively, quite apart from deviating effects arising from differences in the geographical composition of both trade flows.

We have shown elsewhere that the basic specification for exports of goods and services nevertheless has the same set of explanatory variables.[2] This specification is well-known and often successfully used in econometric models. In its most simple form this specification reads

$$(7.1) \quad \frac{b_A}{\Sigma b_j^{\vartheta_1}} = \left(\frac{p_{bA}}{\Sigma p_{bj}}\right)^{-\vartheta_2} c_1$$

---

2. See DRIEHUIS (1969).

hypothesizing that the volume of exports of country $A(b_A)$ relative to the export volumes of competitors (Σb_j) are a negative function of the price level of exports of that country relative to the price level of competitors.[3]

A more elaborate version of the hypothesis is that the capacity utilization rate in country A plays some role too:

$$(7.2) \qquad \frac{b_A}{\Sigma b_j^{\vartheta_1}} = \left(\frac{p_{bA}}{\Sigma p_{bj}}\right)^{-\vartheta_2} q_{yA}^{-\vartheta_3} c_2$$

where q_{yA} represents the capacity utilization rate in country A. The hypothesis is that, all other things being equal, country A is able to increase its market share when its utilization rate decreases, either by more favourable delivery times, or the availibility of servicing or trade credit facilities etc. Thus formulated the capacity variable acts as a proxy for non-price factors in competitiveness. Alternatively the level of capacity utilization exerts an influence on exports separate from the role of proxy for changes in competitiveness not detected by the relative price index. We have in mind the phenomenon that when the pressure on domestic capacity is relatively low suppliers will be able to fill more export orders. Conversely, when capacity is fully utilized an increase in domestic expenditures will probably lead to a pressure on exports.[4]

Although specification (7.2) is plausible it nevertheless seems not quite suitable for practical estimation. The reason is that exports of competitors are rather difficult to assess when the relationship must be used for practical forecasting purposes. We therefore replace the competitive exports variable by a variable representing import demand abroad (Σm_k). Such a variable has the advantage that it can be easier assessed on the basis of foreign production data.[5] We thus obtain.

$$(7.3) \qquad \frac{b_A}{\Sigma m_k^{\vartheta_4}} = \left(\frac{p_{bA}}{\Sigma p_{bj}}\right)^{-\vartheta_2} q_{yA}^{-\vartheta_3} c_3$$

---

3. For empirical applications see the annual model 63-d of the Central Planning Bureau in VERDOORN (1967) and our experiments in explaining exports of services of the Netherlands: DRIEHUIS (1969).
4. See for a more extensive treatment of the impact of domestic demand pressure on export fluctuations for example HENRY (1970), BALL, EATON and STEUER (1966).
5. Comparison of two export equations of goods in two versions of the annual model of the Central Planning Bureau of the Netherlands, one approximately according to specification (7.2) and one according to (7.3), shows that the price elasticity is not fundamentally different. Therefore we maintain the parameter ϑ_2 in equation (7.3).

Estimation of specification (7.3) requires the introduction of dynamic elements. In first instance we do not expect a lag in the demand variable: what has been exported has been, or will be, imported elsewhere and there may be some time between these two observations caused by clearing and outclearing and the like, but this will usually be not longer than one quarter. As concerns relative export prices we expect a distributed lag as the adjustment to a new situation will take place rather gradually. New prices are not instantaneously known to individual subjects and therefore their reactions will be spread over time. Apart from this reason, suppliers may react rather slowly to a new situation for technical reasons and reasons of market policy. Short term price elasticities may therefore differ considerably from long term elasticities. A distributed lag might be expected as well in the case of the capacity utilization variable. Suppose, for instance, that capacity utilization is decreasing because domestic demand slackens. Exporters will then try to increase their export performance by enlarging existing contacts and penetrating new markets either by using non-price instruments or by lowering their prices or by using both means simultaneously. This, however, requires time particularly when markets are imperfectly organized.

Representing unknown adjustment processes by rational distributed lag functions leads to the following general specification for the exports of goods or services[6]:

$$(7.4) \quad \ln b = \vartheta_4 \ln \Sigma m_k - \vartheta_2 \frac{G(L)_1}{H(L)_1} (\ln p_b - \ln \Sigma p_{bj}) - \vartheta_3 \frac{G(L)_2}{H(L)_2} \ln q_y + \ln c_3$$

7.3. EMPIRICAL RESULTS FOR EXPORTS

The actual regression based on this specification was run on the basis of $G(L)_1 = 1 - \lambda$, $H(L)_1 = 1 - \lambda L$, $H(L)_2 = 1$; $G(L)_2$ was un unknown finite distributed lag:

$$(7.5) \quad \ln b_t - \lambda \ln b_{t-1} = \vartheta_4 [\ln \Sigma m_k - \lambda \ln \Sigma m_{kt-1}] -$$
$$- \vartheta_2 (1 - \lambda)(\ln p_b - \ln \Sigma p_{bj}) -$$
$$- \vartheta_3 \left[\sum_{i=0}^{m} \gamma_i \ln q_{Lt-i} - \lambda \sum_{i=1}^{m+1} \gamma_{i-1} \ln q_{Lt-i} \right] +$$
$$+ (1 - \lambda) \ln c_3$$

6. The subscript A is dropped for sake of simplicity.

So relative prices are assumed to have an infinite lag structure of the Koyck type and the capacity utilization rate is approximated by the utilization rate of labour (see section 3.7). The infinite lag is also applied to a weighted average of the relative price variable allowing the adjustment to have a humped time shape of reaction. Furthermore, the demand variable has been alternatively specified as a weighted variable. In the equation for exports of goods imports of individual countries were reweighted according to the geographical distribution of Dutch commodity exports in the previous year.[7] As concerns the explanation of exports of services we do not have at our disposal quarterly time series of imports of services. The effect of world demand has in this case been approximated by a weighted OECD industrial production variable, i.e. industrial production of individual countries reweighted according to the geographical distribution of Dutch exports of services during the years 1962–1965.[7]

The weighting schemes for the export prices of competitors are obtained from trade flow matrices for goods and services. With the help of these matrices weights are computed for each competitor or group of competitors according to

$$(7.6) \quad \sum_{j=1}^{n} \frac{B_j}{B} \frac{B_{cj}}{M_j - B_j} \quad (j \neq c)$$

where, in current prices,

B = exports of goods (or services) of the Netherlands;
B_j = exports of goods (or services) of the Netherlands to country j;
B_{cj} = export of goods (or services) of competitor c to country j;
M_j = imports of goods (or services) of country j.

In this way the market share of each competitor in Dutch exports markets is weighted according to the relative importance of this export market for the exports of goods (or services) of the Netherlands (See appendix E.) A number of experiments has finally resulted in the following equation for the volume of exports of goods:

$$(7.7) \quad \ln b_{f-sa} = \underset{(-)}{.4 \ln b_{f-sa-1}} + \underset{(6.1\%)}{.930} \left[\sum_{0}^{-2} \gamma_{15} \ln m_w - .4 \sum_{-1}^{-3} \gamma_{15} \ln m_w \right] -$$

$$\underset{(15.4\%)}{- 1.227} (\ln p_{bf-sa} - \ln p_{bgw}) -$$

---

7. See appendix E.

$$-.554\left[\sum_{-3}^{-5}\gamma_4\ln q_L - .4\sum_{-4}^{-6}\gamma_4\ln q_L\right]+$$
(173.8%)

$$+.055\,[b_{feec}-.4\,b_{feec-1}]-.933$$
(39.6%) \hspace{3cm} (17.0%)

$$\bar{R}^2 = .992$$
$$NR = 2.09$$

where b_{f-sa} = exports of manufactured goods excluding ships and airplanes, in 1963 prices;

m_w = world imports of goods (reweighted according to the geographical distribution of Dutch exports of goods), 1963 = 100;

p_{bf-sa} = price of exports of manufactured goods excluding ships and airplanes, 1963 = 100;

p_{bgw} = price of exports of goods of competitors (reweighted) 1963 = 100;

q_L = utilization rate of labour;

b_{feec} = EEC effect on exports of goods (1959:1 – 1961:2 = 1, elsewhere 0);

γ_4 = .33, .34, .33;

γ_{15} = .50, .33, .17.

Exports of unprocessed agricultural products and ships and airplanes are excluded from the regression equation. Their volatile character made this desirable. The remaining part of commodity exports shows an elasticity with (reweighted) world demand slightly below unity. This is in agreement with the findings for the Netherlands by others.[8] It is remarkable that a, relatively short, distributed lag was required to obtain a satisfying result.

The long run price elasticity amounts −2.045 which is also similar to earlier findings. This estimate, however, is much higher than the price elasticity of −.66 we have found with the same specification from an eight quarter shorter sample period. When the years 1951 and 1952 were excluded, a period in which export prices were much more volatile compared with the rest of the sample period, we found the above mentioned long run price elasticity of −.66[9,10,11]. It seems to us that a value of −2.0 for the price

---

8. See VERDOORN, POST and GOSLINGA (1970).
9. See DRIEHUIS (1970), p. 29 .
10. A low value for the price elasticity of Dutch exports of goods, *viz.* −.82 has also been estimated by HOUTHAKKER and MAGEE (1969). Their estimate was based on annual data 1951–1966.
11. For similar problems with the export equations of the Brookings quarterly model, see RHOMBERG and BOISSONAULT (1965).

Figure 7.1. Actual and computed exports of manufactured goods excluding ships and airplanes (in logs) according to equation (7.7)

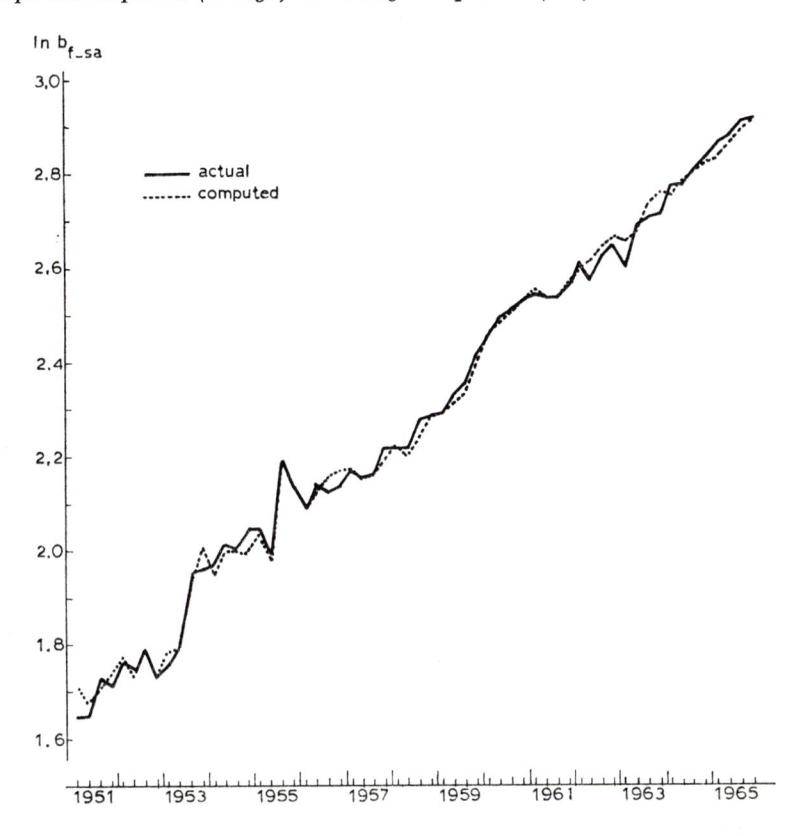

substitution effect is more a structural estimate than the low value which was found in the shorter sample period. Given the relative importance of finished products in total Dutch exports and given the high price elasticities found for these products in cross section analysis an average substitution elasticity below unity is not acceptable.[12] We therefore prefer the estimate of -2.0 which is moreover the result of a certain adjustment process which seems plausible in the light of the rigidity of international trade flows and market imperfections.

---

12. See for example BALASSA (1967) and DOSSER-HAN-HITIRIS (1969).

The average lag of the capacity variable is about a year (see table 7.1), which is twice as long as VERDOORN'S (1967) estimates and which corroborates the lag found by VAN DEN BELD (1968) in his annual cyclical growth model. It was remarkable that any substantial influence of the capacity utilization variable could only be determined when it was not formulated in a curvilinear form.

In addition to the theoretical basic specification we have attempted a dummy variable representing an 'autonomous' impact on exports of goods resulting from the EEC. Such a variable was meant to be an approximation of trade creation effects as suggested by VERDOORN and MEYER ZU SCHLOCHTERN (1964). Indeed we found such an influence and it was included in the model equation.

Table 7.1. Average lags of variables explaining exports of goods (equation 7.7)[a]

Variable	Number of quarters						
	0	*1*	*2*	*3*	*4*	*5*	*6*
1. World imports of goods	×	×					
2. Ratio of export prices to export prices of competitors	×	×					
3. Utilization rate of labour						×	

a. A mark in two columns indicates an average lag between the respective quarters.

The estimation of the exports of services equation was hampered by the lack of quarterly data on imports of services in demand countries. As mentioned, we have therefore used as a proxy variable the industrial production of these countries. However, a drawback connected with this procedure is that one needs the separate introduction of a variable representing (weighted) capacity utilization in demand countries. This difficulty has been solved more or less by including the unemployment rate in Western Germany in the regression equation. The assumption is that this rate is representative for the conjunctural situation in western european countries and anyway important in connection with the exports of travel services of the Netherlands to Western Germany.

We have ultimately included the following equation for exports of services in the model:

(7.8) $\ln b_{s-t} = .5 \ln b_{s-t-1} \underset{(-)}{} + 1.126[\ln y_w - .5 \ln y_{w-1}] \underset{(6.1\%)}{} -$

$$- .284 \underset{(39.3\%)}{} \left(\sum_{0}^{-1} \gamma_6 \ln p_{bs-t} - \sum_{-1}^{-2} \gamma_6 \ln p_{bsw} \right) -$$

$$- 1.628 \underset{(193.3\%)}{} \left[\sum_{0}^{-1} \gamma_6 \Delta \ln q_L - .5 \sum_{-1}^{-2} \gamma_6 \Delta \ln q_L \right] -$$

$$- .024 \underset{(83.4\%)}{} \left[\sum_{0}^{-1} \gamma_6 \ln U_G - .5 \sum_{-1}^{-2} \gamma_6 \ln U_G \right] +$$

$$+ .087 \underset{(26.6\%)}{} [b_{seec} - .5 \, b_{seec-1}] + .166 \underset{(14.5\%)}{} Dum_3 - 1.722 \underset{(9.2\%)}{}$$

$$\bar{R}^2 = .985$$
$$NR = 1.72$$

where b_{s-t} = exports of services excluding net receipts from transit trade, in 1963 prices;

y_w = industrial production in OECD countries, reweighted according to the geographical distribution of Dutch exports of services, 1963 = 100;

p_{bs-t} = price of exports of services, excluding transit trade, 1963 = 100;

p_{bsw} = price of exports of services of competitors (reweighted), 1963 = 100;

q_L = utilization rate of labour;
U_G = unemployment rate in Western Germany;
b_{seec} = EEC effect on exports of services (1959:1 – 1961:4 = 1, elsewhere 0);

Dum_3 = dummy for Korean war and Suez crisis;
γ_6 = .5, .5.

The erratic character of the net receipts from transit trade made it necessary to exclude this item from total exports of services. The remaining part of services exports shows an elasticity with respect to the weighted demand variable slightly above unity. Relative prices have been found to give a significant contribution to the explanation of exports of services, their long run coefficient being −.568. This value confirms our earlier findings that in the Netherlands the price elasticity in invisible trade is lower than in

Figure 7.2. Actual and computed exports of services excluding the receipts from transit trade (in logs) according to equation (7.8)

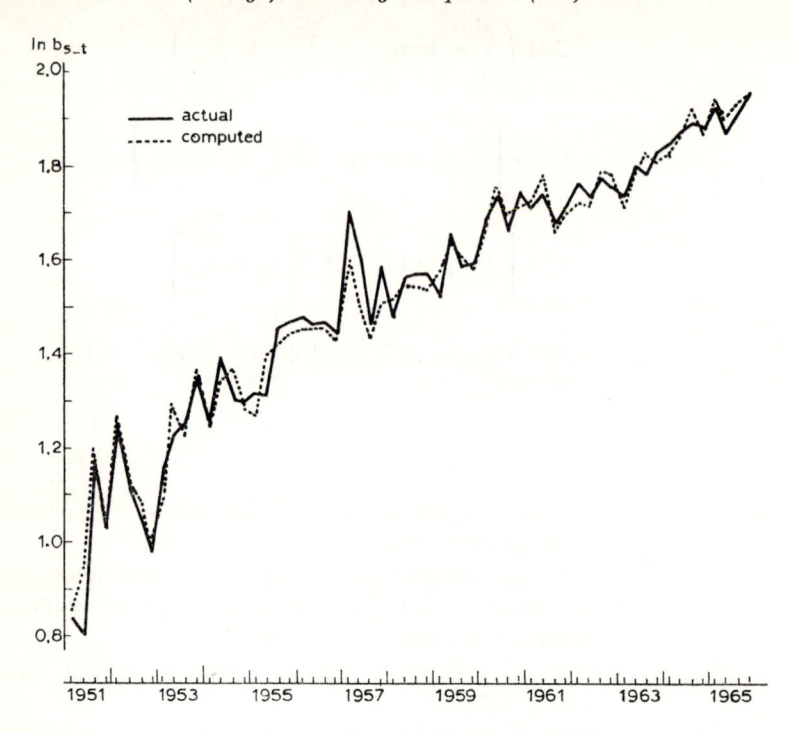

commodity trade.[13] Whether this conclusion will hold good for other countries as well will depend on the structure of their services exports. In general one might expect a relatively high price sensitivity in tourism and a relatively low price sensitivity in transportation services.[14] In contrast to the equation for commodity exports we could only determine the changes in the home pressure of demand to have an influence on exports of services. The average lag of this variable is also shorter than in the equation for exports of goods (see table 7.2). In addition, the German unemployment rate served as an approximation for cyclical circumstances abroad probably especially influencing expenditures for tourism in the Netherlands. Finally, an EEC effect could be found similar to this effect on exports of goods.

13. See DRIEHUIS (1969), p. 345.
14. See for some additional theory without measurement the reaction of GRAY (1971) on our study of invisible trade of the Netherlands.

Table 7.2. Average lags of variables explaining exports of services (equation 7.8)[a]

Variable	Number of quarters						
	0	1	2	3	4	5	6
1. OECD industrial production	×						
2. Ratio of export prices to export prices of competitors		×	×				
3. Change in utilization rate of labour		×	×				
4. Unemployment rate W-Germany		×	×				

a. A mark in two columns indicates an average lag between the respective quarters

7.4. IMPORTS OF GOODS AND SERVICES THEORY

The equations describing imports of goods and services are essentially demand relationships. They relate firstly imports to relevant demand components, more specifically they relate imports to aggregate demand reweighted according to the relative importance of individual demand categories for imports. The weighting procedure is required for considering the difference in import content in the expenditure components and the varying composition of demand over the cycle. It seems to us that the weighting of final demand categories, which has already been systematically applied by VERDOORN (1967) in his annual model, is particularly useful when alternative policy simulations have to be made.

Secondly, on the basis of the theory of international trade one would expect an influence of price differentials. When domestic prices are relatively high compared with import prices the propensity to import would rise and *vice versa*. Moreover, import prices should include import duties because these are relevant for the decision to import or not.

Thirdly, when the pressure of demand is high imports will speed up to ease the domestic supply situation. On *a priori* grounds one would expect a curvi-linear reaction of the utilization rate on imports.

After introduction of appropriate unknown dynamic elements we obtain the following specification:

$$(7.9) \quad \ln m = \vartheta_5 \frac{G(L)_3}{H(L)_3} \ln \Sigma v_j + \vartheta_6 \Delta n - \vartheta_7 \frac{G(L)_4}{H(L)_4} (\ln p_m - \ln \Sigma p_{vj}) +$$

$$+ \vartheta_8 \frac{G(L)_5}{H(L)_5} q_L + c_4$$

where Σv_j is a variable consisting of weighted final demand components v_j.[15]

Inventory formation has been specified separately since this variable cannot be transformed into logarithms because it can have negative values.

GREGORY (1971) has recently argued that not the relative price as such is relevant for the decision whether commodities are purchased from domestic or foreign supplies. He points out that price variables should be redefined as effective prices, i.e. the actual price plus elements as delivery time, trade credit terms, rebates and other aspects which are relevant for the decision to purchase or not. Most elements of this effective price are not easy to observe on a macro economic level, however, apart from the possibility to introduce such elements in foreign prices. We concentrate on the domestic effective price only and assume that non-price elements of this price have a positive functional relationship with the demand-supply situation in the home market. When excess supply exists waiting times, trade credit terms will be eased, rebates given, etc. In general this will result in a pressure on the domestic price level and will stimulate purchasing from domestic supplies. On the other hand when excess demand prevails the level of domestic prices will be influenced upwards and, *ceteris paribus*, imports will be stimulated.

When the mentioned disequilibria in the domestic market are simply represented by the rate of change of the domestic price level, and a simple lag is assumed to be valid, we arrive ultimately at the following basic specification for imports:

$$(7.10) \quad \ln m = \vartheta_5 \frac{G(L)_3}{H(L)_3} \ln \Sigma v_j + \vartheta_6 \Delta n - \vartheta_7 \frac{G(L)_4}{H(L)_4} (\ln p_m - \ln \Sigma p_{vj}) +$$

$$+ \vartheta_8 \frac{G(L)_5}{H(L)_5} q_L + \vartheta_9 \frac{G(L)_6}{H(L)_6} \Delta \ln p_v + c_5$$

Analogous to the equations for exports we have assumed the distributed lag on relative prices to be of the infinite type, therefore $G(L)_4 = 1 - \lambda$ and $H(L)_4 = 1 - \lambda L$. The remaining rational distributed lag functions describe finite lag structures, mainly representing adjustments arising from technical

---

15. The possibility to reweight final demand is an important reason to choose this variable and not production of enterprises.

reasons. In this way the import equations to be estimated are written in the following form

$$(7.11) \quad \ln m - \lambda \ln m_{-1} = \vartheta_5 \left[\sum_{i=0}^{m} \gamma_i \ln \Sigma v_{jt-i} - \lambda \sum_{i=1}^{m+1} \gamma_{i-1} \ln \Sigma v_{jt-i} \right] +$$

$$+ \vartheta_6 [\Delta n - \lambda \Delta n_{-1}] - \vartheta_7 (1-\lambda)(\ln p_m - \ln p_{vj}) +$$

$$+ \vartheta_8 \left[\sum_{i=0}^{n} \gamma_i q_{Lt-i} - \lambda \sum_{i=1}^{n+1} \gamma_{i-1} q_{Lt-i} \right] +$$

$$+ \vartheta_9 \left[\sum_{i=0}^{p} \gamma_i \Delta \ln p_{vt-i} - \lambda \sum_{i=1}^{p+1} \gamma_{i-1} \Delta \ln p_{vt-i} \right] + (1-\lambda) c_5$$

7.5. EMPIRICAL RESULTS FOR IMPORTS

As concerns the volume of imports of goods this specification was confirmed by the following empirical result:

$$(7.12) \quad \ln m_{g-sa} = \underset{(-)}{.3 \ln m_{g-sa-1}} + \underset{(9.3\%)}{1.009[\ln v_{mg} - .3 \ln v_{mg-1}]} +$$

$$+ \underset{(36.2\%)}{.365[\Delta \ln v_{mg-1} - .3 \Delta \ln v_{mg-2}]} + \underset{(17.2\%)}{.031}$$

$$[\Delta n - .3 \Delta n_{-1}] - \underset{(32.2\%)}{.491(\ln p_{mg-sa} - \ln p_{vmg})_{-1}} +$$

$$+ \underset{(39.2\%)}{1.684 \left[\sum_{-1}^{-3} \gamma_4 q_L - .3 \sum_{-2}^{-4} \gamma_4 q_L \right]} +$$

$$+ \underset{(39.5\%)}{.850 [\Delta \ln p_{v-1} - .3 \Delta \ln p_{v-2}]} - \underset{(37.7\%)}{1.091}$$

$$\bar{R}^2 = .996$$
$$NR = 2.26$$

where m_{g-sa} = imports of goods less ships and airplanes, in 1963 prices;
v_{mg} = expenditures reweighted according to the relative importance of expenditure categories for imports of goods, in 1963 prices;[16]
Δn = inventory formation, in 1963 prices;
p_{mg-sa} = price level of imports of goods excluding ships and airplanes, 1963 = 100;

16. The definition (see equation 51 of the complete model) is: $\ln v_{mg} = .42 \ln c + .17 \ln i_{-sa} + .08 \ln x + .30 \ln b_{f-sa} + .03 \ln b_{s-t}$. For the computation of the weighting scheme see appendix F).

p_{vmg} = price level of expenditures, reweighted according to the relative importance of expenditure categories for imports of goods, 1963 = 100[17];
q_L = utilization rate of labour;
p_v = price level of expenditures, excluding government wages, inventory formation, exports of services and factor incomes received from abroad 1963 = 100;
γ_4 = .33, .34, .33.

Figure 7.3. Actual and computed imports of goods excluding ships and airplanes (in logs) according to equation (7.12)

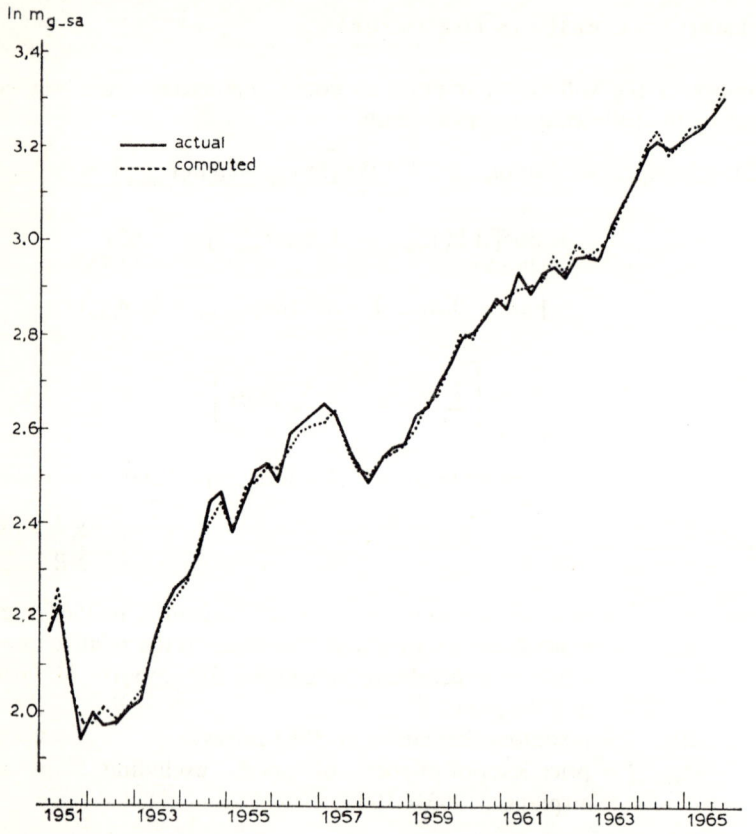

17. The weighting scheme is similar to that for the variable ln v_{mg}. Instead of the price deflator for private consumption we have used the endogenous consumer price index, *viz.* after correction for indirect taxes, rents etc.

This import equation gives a quite acceptable picture of past reality. It can be seen from equation (7.12) that the dynamics of demand have been estimated by adding the first difference of the demand variable (Δv_{mg}) rather than using lagged values of the import demand variable (v_{mg}). Relative prices contribute significantly to the explanation of imports of goods, their long run elasticity being about $-.7$, which is evidently lower than the substitution elasticity for exports of commodities because raw material and semi-manufactured products – goods with a relatively low price elasticity – take an important share in the imports of the Netherlands. It should be noted that rather than adding an indirect taxes term to the relative price variable to obtain the relevant price comparison, we have eliminated indirect taxes from consumer prices, just like other irrelevant items for import substitution, as rents.[18] In contrast to other import equations for the Netherlands the adjustment of imports to a new price ratio is not shorter than such an adjustment for exports of goods[19] (see table 7.3).

Relatively shorter, when compared with exports, is the reaction of imports on domestic capacity utilization. There is evidence for a curvilinear adjustment resulting in a sharp increase in imports when capacity limits are approached. Finally, the rate of change of domestic prices contributes significantly to the explanation of imports. This corroborates the findings of Verdoorn for the Netherlands and GREGORY'S (1971) results for the United States.

Table 7.3. Average lags of variables explaining imports of goods (equation 7.12)[a]

Variable	Number of quarters
	0 1 2 3 4 5 6
1. Expenditures	×
2. Change in expenditures	×
3. Inventory formation	×
4. Ratio of price level expenditures to price level of imports	× ×
5. Utilization rate of labour	×
6. Change in price level of expenditures	×

a. A mark in two columns indicates an average lag between the respective quarters.

18. The first mentioned procedure is applied in the annual model for the Netherlands. See VERDOORN (1967).
19. See VERDOORN (1967).

Almost similarly to the equation for goods we can arrive at an equation for imports of services. Imports of services in the Netherlands can be roughly divided into three main parts. Firstly, there are imports connected with exports of transportation services (port charges, ship's stores, expenditure on repairs, costs of bunkers etc.). So there is a more or less technical relationship between this import item and the rendering of transportation services abroad. Secondly, we distinguish consumption expenditures abroad for tourism and the third component consists of payments for other services, such as commission, brokerage, agency expenses etc.

Following the same line of thought as in the case of goods we have constructed a reweighted demand variable (see appendix F). According to the relative importance of the above mentioned items we may expect a much higher weight of exports of services in this demand variable. Furthermore, it seems correct that if we use the change in capacity utilization rate as explanatory variable for exports of services, the same variable must play its part in the imports of services equation. As can be seen below this expectation is confirmed but in contrast to the equation for exports of services relative prices appear in a rate of change form as well. This may be due to the way in which the Netherlands Bureau of Statistics deflates the value of imports of services, *viz.* by the import price of goods. This may be the reason that not the level of import prices but rather its rate of change appears as explanatory variable. Besides, it seems reasonable that in the long run the expenditures for tourism are more governed by weather conditions, both at home and abroad, the possibility of charter flights, changes in preferences, etc. and not by relative prices.

The equation included in the model is:

(7.13) $\ln m_s = .5 \ln m_{s-1} + .973 [\ln v_{ms} - .5 \ln v_{ms-1}] +$
${\scriptstyle(-)}\phantom{.5 \ln m_{s-1} + }{\scriptstyle(3.0\%)}$

$ + .421 [\Delta \ln v_{ms-1} - .5 \Delta \ln v_{ms-2}] -$
${\scriptstyle(26.9\%)}$

$ - .477 (\Delta \ln p_{ms-1} - \Delta \ln p_{vms-2}) +$
${\scriptstyle(54.7\%)}$

$ + 2.155 \left[\sum_{0}^{-2} \gamma_4 \Delta q_L - .5 \sum_{-1}^{-3} \gamma_4 \Delta q_L \right] +$
${\scriptstyle(155.9\%)}$

$ + .112\ Dum_4 - .791$
${\scriptstyle(24.0\%)}{\scriptstyle(4.5\%)}$

$\bar{R}^2 = .990$
$NR = 2.33$

where m_s = imports of services, in 1963 prices;
v_{ms} = expenditures, reweighted according to the relative importance of expenditure categories for imports of services, in 1963 prices[20];
p_{ms} = price level of imports of services, 1963 = 100;

Figure 7.4. Actual and computed imports of services (in logs) according to equation (7.13)

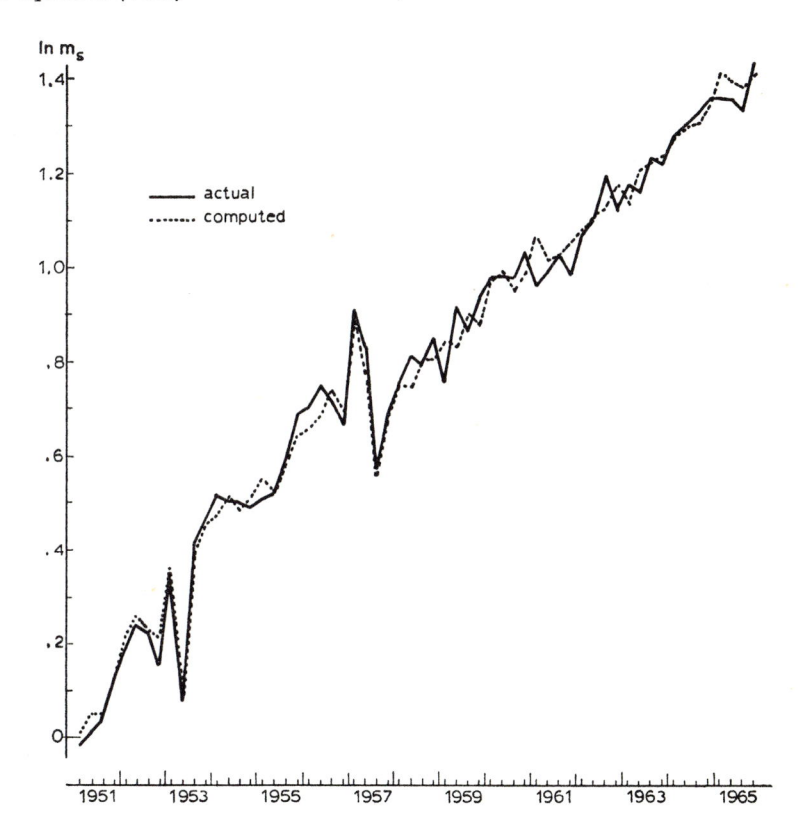

20. The definition (see equation 53 of the complete model) is: $\ln v_{ms} = .43 \ln c + .045 \ln i_{-sa} + .065 \ln x + .16 \ln b_{f-sa} + .30 \ln b_{s-t}$. In fact the weights are changing over time (see appendix F).

p_{vms} = price level of expenditures, reweighted according to the relative importance of expenditure categories for imports of services, 1963 = 100[21];
q_L = utilization rate of labour;
Dum_4 = Dummy for Korean war and Suez crises in 1956;
γ_4 = .33, .34, .33.

Table 7.4. *Average lags of variables explaining imports of services (equation 7.13)*

Variable	Number of quarters
	0 1 2 3 4 5 6
1. Expenditures	×
2. Change in expenditures	×
3. Change in ratio of price level of expenditures to price level of imports	×
3. Change in utilization rate of labour	×

21. The weighting scheme is similar to that of the variable ln v_{ms}. Instead of the price deflator for private consumption we have used the endogenous consumer price index, *viz.* after correction for indirect taxes, rents etc.

VIII. Wage determination and wage policy

8.1. INTRODUCTION

Post-war wage determination in the Netherlands has been influenced by specific institutional arrangements and a relatively long period of wage policy, the intensity of which was gradually decreasing in the course of time. One of the results was a more moderate rate of increase of the wage sum per worker during the fifties. In the years after 1960 wage increases were higher on the average and since 1968 there has been no wage policy based on narrow criteria. The question arises whether it is possible to arrive under these circumstances at a satisfactory analysis of wage determination for the Netherlands and if so whether one equation for wage determination would suffice for different periods of wage policy.

Up to 1962 the aggregate models of the Central Planning Bureau did not contain a wage equation. However, in recent versions of the annual model such an equation is included, covering both pre-war and post-war data. As concerns the impact of wage policy VERDOORN (1967) explains this somewhat astonishing fact by three reasons. We quote

i. Wage control has implicitly taken into account the same set of factors that in a free labour market is responsible for changes in wages, and that some components of wage increases such as black wages and, more generally, wage drift, partly escape from control.
ii. The effect of wage control has been on the whole gradual, and therefore represents a long-term rather than a short-term effect. Exactly this most important effect has been eliminated by the use of first differences.
iii. Even without its counterpart, price-control, wage-control tends to lower the level of prices. It follows that under a system of wage-control the 'normal' impact of the cost of living on wages is less than it otherwise would have been. For this reason and for those given under (i) and (ii) the probably sizeable, cumulative effects of wage-control cannot be inferred from the present reaction equation.

The following model of wage determination is based, in first instance, on rather narrow assumptions such as the marginal productivity theory and profit maximization of entrepreneurs. This already indicates that we will not arrive at a simple explanation of wages as suggested by Phillips: '... the rate of change of money wages can be explained by the level of unemployment and the rate of change of unemployment except in or immediately after those years in which is a sufficiently rapid rise in import prices to offset the tendency for increasing productivity to reduce the cost of living'.[1] Phillips' view on wage determination has been the subject of a number of investigations both for the United Kingdom and other countries.[2] The results of these studies suggest that a more complicated explanation is required.

8.2. A SIMPLE THEORY OF WAGE DETERMINATION

If we consider again the Cobb Douglas production function from chapter III, and we take into account the relationship between the marginal and average product of labour obtained by differentiating this production function *viz.*

$$(8.1) \quad \frac{\partial y}{\partial L} = \alpha \frac{y}{L}$$

and we adopt as well the downward sloping demand function of the product and the upward sloping supply function of the production factor labour as described in the same chapter, then, under profit maximization, it can be derived that

$$(8.2) \quad \frac{\partial y}{\partial L} = \frac{p_l}{p_y} \frac{(1+1/e_L)}{(1+1/e_y)}.$$

In an equilibrium situation the physical marginal product of labour equals the ratio of the 'corrected' wage rate and the 'corrected' price level of production. However, this equilibrium between supply and demand of labour does not necessarily mean that it is a full employment equilibrium. Later on we will elaborate this point. Substitution of equation (8.2) in

---

1. See PHILLIPS (1958), p.284.
2. For example LIPSEY (1960), KUH (1967), SCHULTZE and TYRON (1965), PERRY (1966), VERDOORN (1967), DICKS MIREAUX (1961), VAN DER WERF (1971), PHELPS (1968).

equation (8.1) yields the following well known relationship between the real wage and 'corrected' labour productivity:

(8.3) $\quad \dfrac{p_l}{p_y} = \alpha \dfrac{y}{L} \dfrac{(1+1/e_y)}{(1+1/e_L)}.$

8.3. THE ROLE OF IMPERFECT COMPETITION

Before considering some institutional aspects of wage determination we should pay attention to the role and measurement of imperfect competition. It will be remembered that the price elasticity of demand for products (e_y) and the price elasticity of labour supply (e_L) express this phenomenon in equation (8.3). Analogous to chapter III we approximate the term including the price elasticity of labour supply as

(8.4) $\quad (1 + 1/e_L) = q_L^{-\xi_4} c_1 .$

As concerns the price elasticity of demand we adopt the suggestion of Evans that the elasticity of demand varies with shifts of the demand curve except when the curve shifts so that it is iso-elastic: that is, when the elasticity at any given price remains unchanged. He concludes then that: 'If consumers (and) producers are less price conscious at higher income (and output) levels and more price conscious at lower levels, then the parallel shift of the demand curve has greater validity.[3] He formalizes his hypothesis by postulating a positive relation between the elasticity of demand and the utilization rate of productive capacity. In terms of chapter III, where the total capacity utilization rate was discussed, this means that we arrive at the following approximation for the term including the elasticity of demand:

(8.5) $\quad (1 + 1/e_y) = q_y^{-\theta_1} c_2$

Interpreting again the equations on macro economic level we have now obtained the following, quite static, log-linear wage equation:

(8.6) $\quad \ln p_l = \ln p_y + \ln \dfrac{y}{L} + \xi_4 \ln q_L - \theta_1 \ln q_y + \ln \alpha - \ln c_1 + \ln c_2 .$

Substitution of the relationship between the total capacity utilization rate

---

3. EVANS (1969), p. 296. See also EVANS and KLEIN (1967), p. 34.

and the utilization rate of the labour force as determined in Chapter III[4], viz.:

(8.7) $\quad \ln q_y = \theta_2 \ln q_L + c_3$

in equation (8.6) and after applying a first difference transformation, yields

(8.8) $\quad \Delta \ln p_l = \Delta \ln p_y + \Delta \ln \frac{y}{L} + (\xi_4 - \theta_1 \theta_2) \Delta \ln q_L.$

It is not *a priori* clear whether the impact of the change of the utilization rate of labour on the change of wages is negative or positive. Although θ_2 is greater than unity, and ξ_4 and θ_1 smaller than unity, it may be that $(\xi_4 - \theta_1 \theta_2)$ is positive because the role of unemployment in the supply of labour equation is rather important so that $\xi_4 > \theta_1 \theta_2$.[5]

As it stands, the appearance of the labour utilization rate in this relationship is due to imperfectly organized markets. Apart from other possible considerations it can be seen as a justification of the appearance of the rate of change of the unemployment ratio with a negative sign in equations determining the rate of change of wages as used, for instance, by VERDOORN (1967), VAN DER WERF (1971) and PHILLIPS (1958). On the contrary, LIPSEY (1960) has found a significant positive influence of such a variable which he attributed to '... varying degrees of sectoral inequalities in the distribution of unemployment'.[6]

8.4. INSTITUTIONAL FACTORS

In the real labour market we almost always find deviations between the actual and the desired wage, and as a consequence of these deviations adjustment mechanisms to balance this disequilibrium will be triggered off. It is the analysis of these disequilibria which is fundamental for the empirical investigation of wage determination either on a micro or on a macro level. In connection herewith we have to consider at least two aspects.

Thus far we have been analyzing the wage rate – the wage per worker – resulting from a supply and demand process under certain assumptions. Changes in supply and/or demand were at once resulting in a new wage level

---

4. On page 52 it was derived that $\ln q_y = (\alpha + \beta \xi_6 + \iota \xi_7) \ln q_L + \beta c_4 + \iota c_5$. For reasons of simplicity we replace that complicated formulation by $\ln q_y = \theta_2 \ln q_L + c_3$.
5. See the labour supply equation on page 46.
6. See LIPSEY (1960), p. 23 note 2. These ideas have further been tested by ARCHIBALD (1969).

in accordance with the changed market circumstances. Actually, wages are determined in a negotiation procedure between demanders and suppliers of labour resulting in a contract in which a certain wage rate is agreed upon for a certain period.[7] Usually such a contract contains agreements on what is called secondary labour conditions.

It is obvious that the parties concerned with wage negotiations – usually unions of employers and employees – must formalize their respective expectations about the future development of all relevant factors. Previous analysis has shown that particularly the development of prices and labour productivity are strategic variables in this context.

A second aspect which deserves attention is the fact that, at least over a longer period, the wage sum per worker is rising faster than might have been expected from the changes in wages agreed upon in contracts (either collective wage contracts or uniform wage increases), and changes in social security premiums paid by employers. This difference is usually called incidental wage increase or wage drift. As we will discuss later the existence of this phenomenon depends, among others, on the fact that during the usual period between the revision of contracts, relevant factors have changed. So we are concerned with reactions on an unforeseen disequilibrium situation which has in the meantime arisen. An additional argument in favour of a separate treatment of wage drift is that the theory developed thus far is only related to time wages and normal piece rates, whereas the incidental wage component includes by definition piece wage rises arising from productivity increases above the contractually agreed percentage change in the production per worker.

8.5. WAGE DRIFT

Wage drift has several causes.[8] They can be split up into structural causes, cyclical influences and incidental factors.

To the first group of causes belong changes in the relative composition of the working population as to age, sex and level of training. Furthermore it includes changes in renumeration systems.

Dependent on the business cycle is the wage drift caused by the payments of higher wages than has been agreed upon in contracts (black wages), changes in extra payments (a 13th month salary for instance), changes in the

---

7. We disregard, the sometimes important, wage increases on the basis of general wage rounds. The wage round aspect has been analysed by ECKSTEIN and WILSON (1962).
8. See also PHELPS BROWN (1962) on wage drift.

possibility to differentiate wages per firm and a changing utilization in the providing of facultative allowances. Obviously, an important part of factors varying with the cyclical situation, depends on the labour market situation. During times of a tight labour market, firms are willing to do almost anything to get labour and keep it. Therefore wages are paid and workers let themselves wages be paid which sometimes substantially exseed their contract level. The labour market situation may as well lead to extra allowances for getting hold of and keeping workers. Also closely connected with the situation on the labour market are the payments for overtime, which are included in wage drift by definition. Finally there is a relationship between piece rates occurring in the wage drift component and labour productivity.

In conclusion we have obtained the following explanatory factors for the existence of wage drift: the deviation between contract wages and the desired wage on the basis of the actual price and productivity development, tension in the labour market, labour productivity, overtime, and structural factors.

If we assume that this latter group of influences changes gradually over time and can be approximated by an exponential function, we arrive at the following wage drift equation:

$$(8.9) \quad \Delta \ln p_{lw} = +\theta_3 (\Delta \ln p_l^* - \Delta \ln p_l) + \theta_4 \ln q_L + \theta_5 \Delta \ln \frac{h_w}{h_c} + \theta_6 \Delta \ln \frac{y}{L} + c_4$$

where Δp_{lw} is the change in the wage sum per worker due to wage drift, Δp_l is the actual change in the contract wage level, Δp_l^* is the desired change in the contract wage level, q_L is the labour utilization rate, h_w is hours worked, h_c is contractual working time, y is production and L is employment.

As concerns the desired change in contract wages we postulate that it is a function of the wage rate change in a situation of full utilization of labour ($\Delta \ln \hat{p}_l$) corrected for the actual under-utilization[9]:

$$(8.10) \quad \Delta \ln p_l^* = \Delta \ln \hat{p}_l + \theta_7 \Delta \ln q_L.$$

So, when labour is fully utilized, e.g. $q_L = 1$, the desired change of contract wages is equal to the change of contract wages under full employment. Let

---

9. An alternative formulation is that desired contract wages are revised on the basis of the employment situation.

us postulate this variable to be determined by the sum of the trend of price and labour productivity changes, (c_5). We then obtain:

(8.11) $\quad \Delta \ln \hat{p}_l = c_5.$

After substitution of the thus adjusted equation (8.10) in relationship (8.9) we have:

(8.12) $\quad \Delta \ln p_{lw} = -\theta_3 \Delta \ln p_l + \theta_4 \ln q_L + \theta_5 \Delta \ln \frac{h_w}{h_c} +$

$$+ \theta_6 \Delta \ln \frac{y}{L} + \theta_3 \theta_7 \Delta \ln q_L + c_6,$$

where $c_6 = c_4 + \theta_3 c_5$.

The presented theory with respect to changes in the wage sum per worker due to wage drift implies that in a situation of full employment, given the composition of the working population, there is no other wage drift than the one arising from changes in piece rates or performance rates. In that case wage drift is a function of the trend of labour productivity and other trending elements.

8.6. THE BASIC WAGE EQUATION

Combination of equations concerning contract wages (8.8) and wage drift (8.12) yields an aggregate relationship for the wage sum per worker (w) which includes by definition social premiums paid by the employer (p_{ls}) as well:

(8.13) $\quad \Delta \ln w = (1-\theta_3) \Delta \ln p_y + (1-\theta_3+\theta_6) \Delta \ln \frac{y}{L} +$

$$+ \{(1-\theta_3)(\xi_4 - \theta_1\theta_2) + \theta_3\theta_7\} \Delta \ln q_L + \theta_4 \ln q_L +$$

$$+ \theta_5 \Delta \ln \frac{h_w}{h_c} + \Delta \ln p_{ls} + c_6.$$

In conclusion, changes in the wage sum per worker are in our line of thought determined by changes in the general price level and labour productivity, the level and the change in the utilization rate of labour and the change in overtime.

It should be borne in mind that actually the general price level is not the relevant variable in wage determination and wage policy but the price level of private consumption.[10] It seems therefore significant to include this variable in the basic equation. When the relationship between both price variables is

(8.14) $\Delta \ln p_y = \theta_9 \Delta \ln p_c + c_7$

then the first term of equation (8.13) can be written as

(8.15) $\Delta \ln w = (1-\theta_3)\theta_9 \Delta \ln p_c + \ldots$

Finally we should consider the dynamic aspects of wage determination. It is reasonable to suppose that the agreed wage level is based upon the expected price and productivity development and the expected labour market situation. With respect to payments due to overtime we do not introduce a lag at all, but for the remaining variables unknown lag distributions are introduced to represent imperfect foresight

$$(8.16) \quad \Delta \ln w = (1-\theta_3)\theta_9 \frac{G(L)_1}{H(L)_1} \Delta \ln p_c + (1-\theta_3+\theta_6) \frac{G(L)_2}{H(L)_2} \Delta \ln \frac{y}{L} +$$

$$+ \{(1-\theta_3)(\xi_4 - \theta_1\theta_2) + \theta_3\theta_7\} \frac{G(L)_3}{H(L)_3} \Delta \ln q_L +$$

$$+ \theta_4 \frac{G(L)_4}{H(L)_4} \ln q_L + \theta_5 \Delta \ln \frac{h_w}{h_c} + \Delta \ln p_{ls} + c_8,$$

where $c_8 = c_6 + (1+\theta_3)c_7$.

A few remarks can be made in advance on the long run values of the parameters in this specification. According to empirical experience with annual data the coefficient θ_3 is much smaller than unity, *viz.* about .20 à .30. Furthermore, the elasticity coefficient between production price changes and consumption price changes (θ_9) varies over any given period, and is sometimes above but mostly below unity. The range of possible values of both parameters θ_3 and θ_9 suggests the long run coefficient of the change in the price level of consumption in the wage equation to be mostly below unity.

An elasticity below unity can be expected as well for the labour productivity variable. One of the reasons is that the coefficient θ_6 is very small, so that $(1-\theta_3+\theta_6) < 1$. In addition it should be borne in mind that the market organisation plays its part in wage determination. On the one hand we have

---

10. An exception was the period 1954:4 – 1959:2 when the labour share in national income was central in wage negotiations and wage policy.

imperfect competition (monopolistic and oligopolistic competition) both for products and labour, and on the other hand markets with more or less perfect competition. In this connection it does not seem unrealistic to expect the trend of labour productivity to play a role in wage determination, at least partly, because as far as oligopolistic firms are concerned, they seem to consider trends of variables rather than actual values.[11] In regression equations we may therefore expect an even lower elasticity coefficient than $(1-\theta_3+\theta_6)$ for labour productivity and a correspondingly higher constant term. Another consequence of this amendment on basic specification (8.16) may be that the coefficient of the variable $\Delta \ln q_L$, which was meant to determine the impact of market imperfections, will be reduced. If we consider the coefficient of this variable in equation (8.16) it may be concluded that it will probably be positive, but its effect relatively small. The considerations above make it all the more uncertain whether its influence can be determined at all.

On the magnitude of other variables in basic specification (8.16) we cannot comment extensively. It seems doubtful whether the constant term is really constant during the sample period because the trends of some of the variables included were changing. This is a reason to investigate whether it suffices to estimate one wage equation over the sample period. But another and much more important reason is that the Netherlands had an intensive and changing wage policy during the years under consideration, which gives rise to *a priori* doubt for one and the same wage equation for different periods of wage policy.[12] So, we have estimated as well four separate wage equations, one for each period.

One final remark must be made before the empirical analysis starts. The basic wage equation presented above is derived in a rather mechanical way just like the other basic specifications in the model. But especially in the case of wage formation this may lead to an incomplete evaluation of the real facts since the influence of non-economic factors – such as sociological and psychological ones – on wage determination are not considered.[13] Such experiments have not been carried out but what we have been trying, however, is to determine the impact of shifting. When premiums for social insurance to be paid by employees are raised, they may try to shift this burden to the employer by bargaining more wage for compensation. The same

---

11. See also chapter IX, section 9.2.
12. Alternatively one can estimate one wage equation with a changing set of explanatory variables. This has been done for the Netherlands for the years 1950–1962 by VAN DEN BELD (1965a).
13. See for instance the study of HINES (1964), where he analyses the influence of trade unions on wage determination in the United Kingdom.

thing may occur when direct taxes are raised. Obviously the pressure on wages will be lower when either direct taxes and/or social premiums are lowered. For these reasons basic equation (8.16) has been estimated after adding a variable representing the change in wage and income tax tariffs plus social premiums paid by employees as a per cent of the wage sum per worker.[14]

8.7. EMPIRICAL RESULTS: THE WHOLE PERIOD 1951:1 – 1968:4

In order to compare the results with the estimations of separate periods of wage policy we have first estimated a wage equation for the whole sample period enlarged with twelve quarters.[15] As concerns lag structures we have postulated an infinite distributed lag on the price level of consumption, viz. $G(L)_1 = 1-\lambda$ and $H(L)_1 = 1-\lambda L$ and finite lags on the other variables, except the overtime variable where a simultaneous response is posited. Furthermore social premiums paid by employers were considered as predetermined and subtracted from the wage sum per worker. Actually we have estimated:

$$(8.17) \quad (\Delta \ln w - \Delta \ln p_{ls}) - \lambda(\Delta \ln w - \Delta \ln p_{ls})_{-1} =$$
$$= (1 - \theta_3)\theta_9(1-\lambda)\Delta \ln p_c +$$
$$+ (1-\theta_3+\theta_6)\left[\sum_{i=0}^{m}\gamma_i \Delta \ln\left(\frac{y}{L}\right)_{t-i} - \lambda \sum_{i=1}^{m+1}\gamma_{i-1}\Delta \ln\left(\frac{y}{L}\right)_{t-i}\right] +$$
$$+ \{(1-\theta_3)(\xi_4-\theta_1\theta_2)+\theta_3\theta_7\}\left[\sum_{i=0}^{n}\gamma_i \Delta \ln q_{L_{t-i}} - \lambda \sum_{i=1}^{n+1}\gamma_{i-1}\Delta \ln q_{L_{t-i}}\right] +$$
$$+ \theta_4\left[\sum_{i=0}^{s}\gamma_i \ln q_{L_{t-i}} - \lambda \sum_{i=1}^{s+1}\gamma_{i-1}\ln q_{L_{t-i}}\right]+$$
$$+ \theta_5\left[\Delta \ln\frac{h_w}{h_c} - \lambda \Delta \ln\left(\frac{h_w}{h_c}\right)_{-1}\right] + (1-\lambda)c_6.$$

Instead of regressing one quarter differences of logarithms, four-quarter differences are used. This was done in order to avoid the explanation of a

---

14. Such a variable is also included in the most recent version of the annual model of the CPB.
15. Viz. from 1966:1 up to 1968:4.

very erratic time series. It is furthermore of importance to note that the wage sum per worker series has been corrected for autonomous wage changes, *viz.* lump sum payments in 1956:2, 1965:2 and 1965:4.

According to the rules for acceptance described in chapter II the 'best' wage equation for the period 1951:1 – 1968:4 appeared to be (see figure 8.1).

(8.18) $\quad \ln w - \ln w_{-4} = .3(\ln w_{-1} - \ln w_{-5}) +$
$\phantom{(8.18) \quad \ln w - \ln w_{-4} = .}(-)$

$$+ .553 \sum_{0}^{-1} \gamma_6 (\ln p_c - \ln p_{c-4}) +$$
(11.4%)

$$+ .437 \left[\sum_{-1}^{-4} \gamma_{16} \{(\ln y - \ln L) - (\ln y_{-4} - \ln L_{-4})\} \right.$$
(21.2%)

$$\left. - .3 \sum_{-2}^{-5} \gamma_{16} \{(\ln y - \ln L) - (\ln y_{-4} - \ln L_{-4})\} \right] +$$

$$+ .743 \left[\sum_{0}^{-1} \gamma_6 \ln q_L - .3 \sum_{-1}^{-2} \gamma_6 \ln q_L \right] +$$
(23.9%)

$$+ .211 \left[\{(\ln h_w - \ln h_c) - (\ln h_{w-4} - \ln h_{c-4})\} \right.$$
(62.7%)

$$\left. - .3 \{(\ln h_{w-1} - \ln h_{c-1}) - (\ln h_{w-5} - \ln h_{c-5})\} \right] +$$

$$+ 1.000 [SPE - 3. SPE_{-1}] +$$
$(-)$

$$+ .372 [TSPW - .3 \, TSPW_{-1}] +$$
(40.7%)

$$+ .037 \, Dum_5 -$$
(26.5%)

$$- .022 \, Dum_6 +$$
(41.8%)

$$+ .031$$
(13.9%)

$$\bar{R}^2 = .815$$
$$NR = 1.88$$

where w = wage sum per worker in enterprises, excluding lump sum payments in 1956:2, 1965:2 and 1965:4, 1963 = 100;

p_c = price level of consumption, 1963 = 100;
y = production in enterprises, in 1963 prices;
L = employment in enterprises;
q_L = utilization rate of labour;
h_w = hours worked, 1963 = 100;
h_c = contractual labour time, 1963 = 100;
$TSPW$ = four quarter change in autonomous income tax changes plus social premiums paid by employees as percentage of the wage sum per worker;
SPE = four quarter change in social premiums paid by employers as percentage of the wage sum per worker;
Dum_5 = dummy variable representing the introduction of a new national insurance system in 1957;
Dum_6 = dummy variable for delay in wage negotiations due to discussions on a new wage policy in 1959;
γ_6 = .50, .50;
γ_{16} = .30, .45, .20, .05.

Figure 8.1. Actual and computed four-quarter changes in the wage sum per worker excluding lump sum payments (whole period) according to equation (8.18)

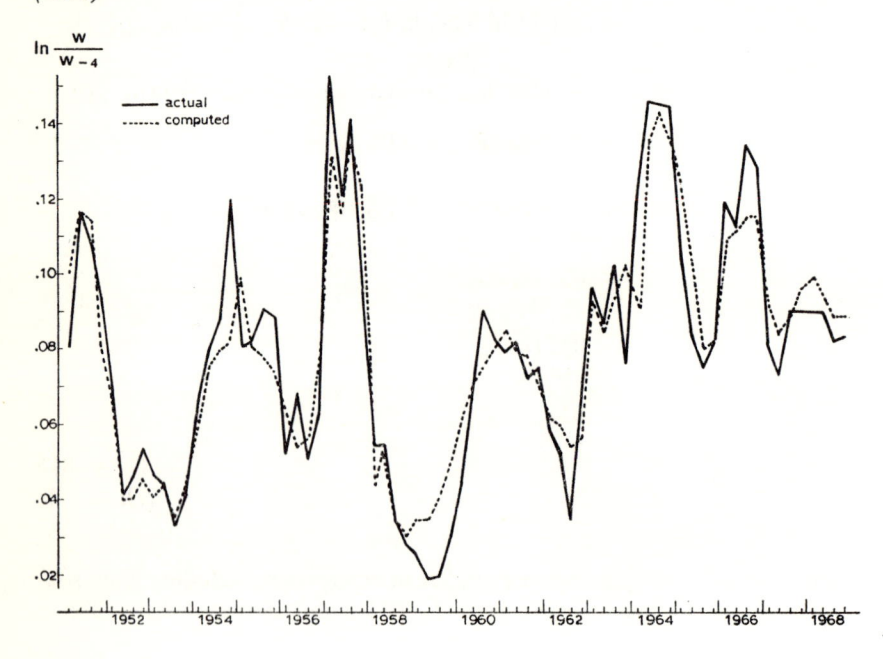

This wage equation, including nearly all theoretical variables, gives a fairly good picture of actual wage rate movements. The long run elasticity with respect to consumer prices is .790. This value does not contradict the hypothesized long run elasticity. The productivity variable has a much smaller elasticity than unity because the productivity trend comes to expression in the constant term, which amounts 4.43 per cent. Remarkable from an economic policy point of view is the elasticity coefficient of .372 found for the shifting of autonomous income tax changes and social premiums paid by employees.[16] The trade off between wage rate changes and the level of unemployment is relatively weak and of a linear nature.[17] As expected a contribution of the relative change of the utilization rate of labour could not be determined. Table 8.1 below shows that generally the average lags are rather short.

Table 8.1. Average lags of variables explaining changes in the wage sum per worker: whole period (equation 8.18)[a]

Variable	Number of quarters
	0 1 2 3 4 5 6
1. Change in price level of consumption	× ×
2. Change in labour productivity	×
3. Utilization rate of labour	× ×
4. Change in overtime	×
5. Changes in autonomous taxes and social premiums	×

a. A mark in two columns indicates an average lag between the respective quarters.

8.8. SHORT SUMMARY OF WAGE POLICY IN THE NETHERLANDS

Before investigating whether the basic wage equation is as valuable for periods with each a different wage policy, we give a short review of the character and contents of this wage policy. Up to 1968 wage determination

---

16. In the most recent wage equation of the annual model of the Central Planning Bureau the coefficient of this variable amounts .310.
17. For a rejection of the hegemony of the unemployment rate as a determinant of changes in wages, See KUH (1967).

in the Netherlands has been a product of explicitly recognized national wage policy implemented via legal provisions and institutional arrangements specifically designed for the purpose. The two main features of this system are:[18]

a. the government's influence on the general wage level, obtained through direct participation in the negotiations, and used as an integral part of overall economic policy and

b. the policy of 'wage co-ordination' aimed at creating a wage structure based primarily on the nature of the work rather than on the employers' ability to pay.

As mentioned, targets of wage policy have not been the same throughout the years. The following is a short view on each period.[19] Institutional aspects can be found in the literature.[20]

Period 1951:1–1954:3 Controlled nation wide wage increases based on increased costs of living

Till October 1954 wage policy mainly aimed at a constant real wage per worker.[21] On the whole wage increases were uniform during this period and meant to compensate for the rising cost of living. Incidentally some wage contracts had a larger increase than the average in order to compensate for existing wage differentials. Wage policy in the years 1951–1954 aimed at the redress of the balance of payments disequilibrium and the acceleration of the growth rate by restraining the share of consumption in national income.

Period 1954:4–1959:2 Controlled nation-wide wage increases based on the share of wages in national income

Due to the improved economic situation and diverging from the system of uniform wage rounds, wage increases in the second period were also based on labour productivity increases. An increase of wages was possible to the extent that a comparison of per capita wages in industry with the national income per head of active working population indicated a lag of wages. So, after 1954 the share of wages in national income has been used as a criterion but the connection with the cost of living index was partially maintained,

---

18. Quotation from FELLNER, GILBERT, HANSEN, KAHN, LUTZ, DE WOLFF (1961), p. 359.
19. The following 'one sentence' characteristics for each period have been adopted from HESSEL (1965).
20. See among others FELLNER *et. al.* (1961) and HAAS (1960).
21. In the years before 1951 wage policy had this character as well. We here restrict ourselves to the sample period.

since uniform wage compensations were given, for example, for the raise in rents. During this period there was also the possibility, though rather restrained, to differentiate wage increases according to productivity per sector.

Period 1959:3–1962:4 Controlled wage increases based on differences in productivity increases
In the middle of 1959 the wish of the partners in the wage negotiations to have greater differences in wage increases resulted in a new wage political system based on the trend of productivity growth per sector of industry. When productivity of a sector rose faster than the general average, wages could rise faster, although the productivity gain had to be expressed in product prices. An important condition for the practical execution of this type of wage policy is an adequate price control to assure that productivity gains will influence the level of prices.

Period 1963:1–1968:4 Controlled wage increases based on a yearly target for the national average wage increases
This form of wage policy was a reaction to practical difficulties with the system of differentiated wage determination. The productivity trends as a fundamental criterion for the negotiations were superseded by the expected macro economic possibilities in terms of the realisation of economic policy targets like sufficient foreign exchange reserves, balance of payments equilibrium, price stability and a high and stable level of employment. The role of the government was less predominant in this system but it was always possible to intervene in wage determination.

Although it is beyond the scope of this study we should like to point out that this wage system has since been replaced by a system of free wage negotiations without central control. There is, however, a wage law enabling the government to intervene in wage determination when wage increases are not in line with economic policy targets.

8.9. EMPIRICAL RESULTS: THE PERIOD 1951:1–1954:3

Estimating the basic specification yields as its best result (see figure 8.2.a)

$$\text{(8.19)} \quad \ln w - \ln w_{-4} = \underset{(-)}{.3} (\ln w_{-1} - \ln w_{-5}) +$$

$$+ \underset{(13.6\%)}{.549} (\ln p_c - \ln p_{c-4}) +$$

$$+ \underset{(32.5\%)}{.484} \left[\sum_{-1}^{-4} \gamma_{16} \{(\ln y - \ln L) - (\ln y_{-4} - \ln L_{-4})\} - \right.$$

$$\left. - .3 \sum_{-2}^{-5} \gamma_{16} \{(\ln y - \ln L) - (\ln y_{-4} - \ln L_{-4})\} \right] +$$

$$+ \underset{(29.2\%)}{1.441} \left[\{(\ln h_w - \ln h_c) - (\ln h_{w-4} - \ln h_{c-4})\} - \right.$$

$$\left. - .3 \{(\ln h_{w-1} - \ln h_{c-1}) - (\ln h_{w-5} - \ln h_{c-5})\} \right] +$$

$$+ \underset{(-)}{1.000} [SPE - .3\, SPE_{-1}] +$$

$$+ \underset{(66.2\%)}{.541} [TSPW - .3\, TSPW_{-1}] +$$

$$+ \underset{(57.9\%)}{.011}$$

$$\bar{R}^2 = .942$$
$$NR = 2.96$$

The most striking result of this equation is that both labour market variables do not appear, because their influence could not be determined with the appropriate sign. Note that this result confirms the conclusion of LIPSEY and PARKIN (1970), *viz.* that there is no significant trade off between inflation and unemployment in 'policy-on' periods in Great Britain.[22] The long run coefficient of the price variable is .784. This does not contradict the main target of wage policy during this period – a constant real wage – because there was a relatively large wage drift. Obviously this was not due to effects arising from a disequilibrium between the desired and actual wage level, because wage policy had prevented these by the system of uniform wage rounds. As can be seen in the estimation result wage drift was mainly the consequence of overtime and extra productivity increases. The latter phenomenon explains the still high coefficient found for this variable, which has furthermore a distributed lag slightly different from the overall equation. The estimating result suggests that wage policy in the period before 1954:3

---

22. A policy-on period is a period with wage (and price) policy in contradiction to policy-off periods. See also PARKIN (1970) on further results.

Figure 8.2.a. Actual and computed four-quarter changes in the wage sum per worker excluding lump sum payments (period 1951:1–1954:3) according to equation (8.19)

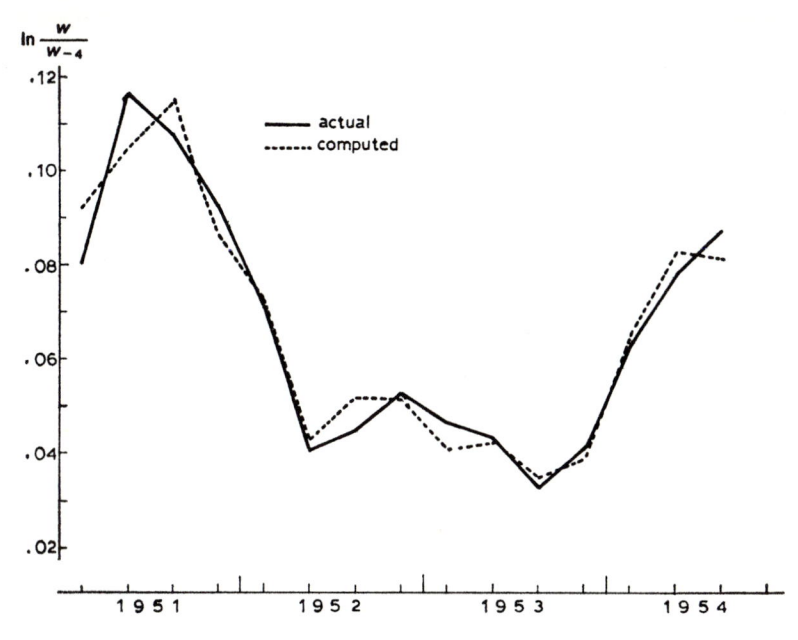

Figure 8.2.b. Comparison of sub-period and whole period residuals 1951: 1–1954:3

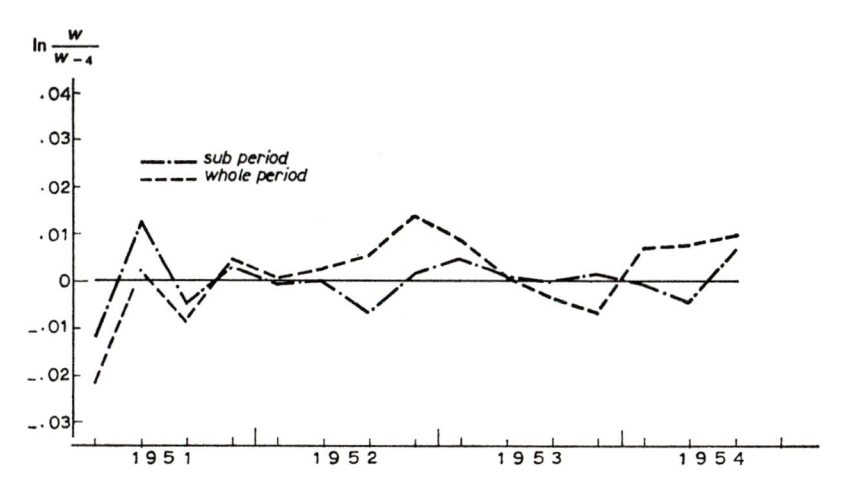

was not only restricted to the determination of the timing of wage rate changes but that it did also significantly influence their size by eliminating the effect of the labour market situation. This conclusion is supported by the comparison of the residuals of the sub-period equation with the corresponding residuals of the wage relationship covering the whole period 1951–1968 as in figure 8.2.b. The root mean square residuals and the inequality coefficients (see definitions on page 185) are respectively:

Table 8.2. Comparison of sub-period and whole period wage equation residuals 1951:1–1954:3

	Sub-period equation	Whole period equation
Root mean square residual	.56%	.88%
Inequality coefficient	.08	.12

8.10. EMPIRICAL RESULTS: THE PERIOD 1954:4 – 1959:2

Estimating the basic specification yields as its best result (see figure 8.3.a):

(8.20) $\quad \ln w - \ln w_{-4} = .2(\ln w_{-1} - \ln w_{-5}) +$
$\qquad\qquad\qquad\qquad (-)$

$$+ .739 \sum_{0}^{-1} \gamma_6 (\ln p_c - \ln p_{c-4}) +$$
$\qquad (31.5\%)$

$$+ .636 \left[\sum_{-1}^{-4} \gamma_{16} \{(\ln y - \ln L) - (\ln y_{-4} - \ln L_{-4})\} - \right.$$
$\qquad (35.1\%)$

$$\left. - .2 \sum_{-2}^{-5} \gamma_{16} \{(\ln y - \ln L) - (\ln y_{-4} - \ln L_{-4})\} \right] +$$

$$+ .049 \, Dum_5 -$$
$\qquad (29.6\%)$

$$- .025 \, Dum_6 +$$
$\qquad (45.5\%)$

$$+ 1.000 [SPE - .2\, SPE_{-1}] +$$
$$(-)$$

$$+ .149 [TSPW - .2\, TSPW_{-1}] +$$
$$(192.1\%)$$

$$+ .028$$
$$(29.0\%)$$

$$\bar{R}^2 = .818$$
$$NR = 2.58$$

Figure 8.3.a. Actual and computed four-quarter changes in the wage sum per worker excluding lump sum payments (period 1954:4–1959:2) according to equation (8.20)

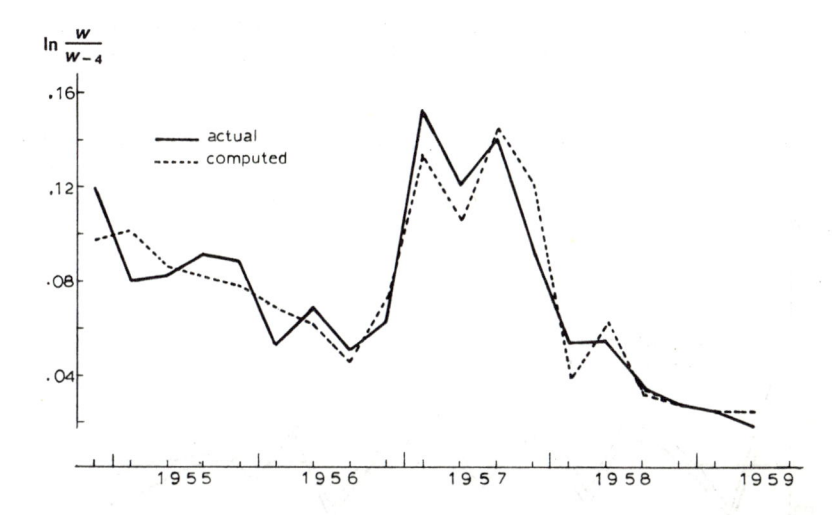

In this period of nation-wide controlled wage increases we did not find any acceptable influence of the labour market variables as well. The long term elasticity coefficient for prices is now higher .924. This is roughly in agreement with the wage policy target during this period, *viz.* a growth of contract wages parallel to changes in the wage share in national income. Using arguments given earlier the elasticity coefficient of labour productivity seems not therefore in contradiction to the actual wage policy during the years under consideration. Compared to the first period its value is greater thus expressing the increasing importance of labour productivity in wage determination. Note that the influence of labour productivity first rises and then declines, just like the impact of prices.

Furthermore the equation shows a relatively low shifting of autonomous taxes and social premiums and two dummy variables. The first one (Dum_5) represents the effect of an overall increase in wages to offset the introduction of a new insurance premium in the first quarter of 1957. The second one (Dum_6) was introduced to represent the lowering effect on wages in 1959:1 and 1959:2 awaiting proposals for a new wage policy. The result suggests that wage policy in the period 1954:4–1959:2 has been able to eliminate the direct effects of the labour market situation on wages. It has furthermore influenced the timing of wage increases as can be read from the residuals and from the dummy variable. Similar to the first period of wage policy there is some evidence that autonomous tax changes and social premiums paid by workers have led to additional wage changes.

Comparison of the residuals of the sub-period equation with corresponding residuals of the overall relationship (see figure 8.3.b.) shows root mean square residuals and inequality coefficients in favour of the sub-period equation.

Figure 8.3.b. Comparison of sub-period and whole period residuals (1954: 4–1959:2)

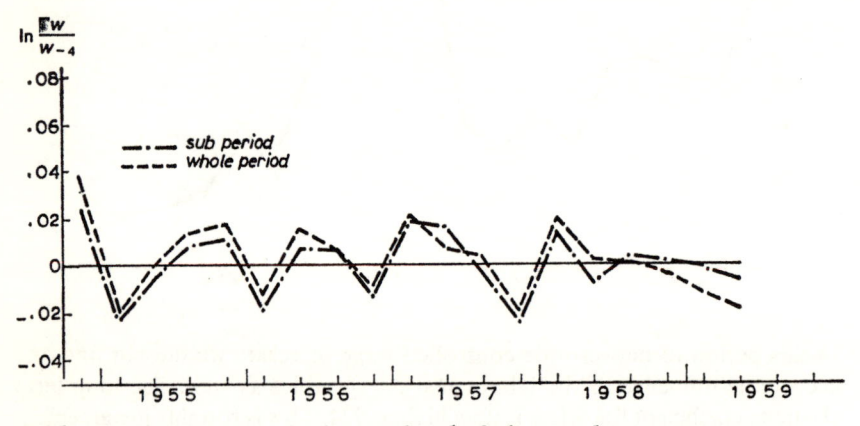

Table 8.3. Comparison of sub-period and whole period wage equation residuals 1954:4–1959:2

	Sub-period equation	Whole period equation
Root mean square residual	1.39%	1.56%
Inequality coefficient	.17	.19

8.11. EMPIRICAL RESULTS: THE PERIOD 1959:3–1962:4

Estimating the basis specification yielded as its best result (see figure 8.4.a.):

$$(8.21) \quad \ln w - \ln w_{-4} = + .900 \sum_{0}^{-1} \gamma_6 (\ln p_c - \ln p_{c-4}) +$$
$$(-)$$

$$+ .667 \sum_{-1}^{-4} \gamma_{16} \{(\ln y - \ln L) - (\ln y_{-4} - \ln L_{-4})\} +$$
$$(20.4\%)$$

$$+ 2.854 \sum_{-1}^{-2} \gamma_6 \ln q_L + .008 \, Dum_6 +$$
$$(15.5\%) \qquad\qquad (41.8\%)$$

$$+ 1.000 \, SPE + .773 \, TSPW +$$
$$(-) \qquad\quad (75.1\%)$$

$$+ .042$$
$$(16.0\%)$$

$$\bar{R}^2 = .787$$
$$NR = 2.07$$

Figure 8.4.a. Actual and computed four-quarter changes in the wage sum per worker excluding lump sum payments (period 1959:3–1962:4) according to equation (8.21)

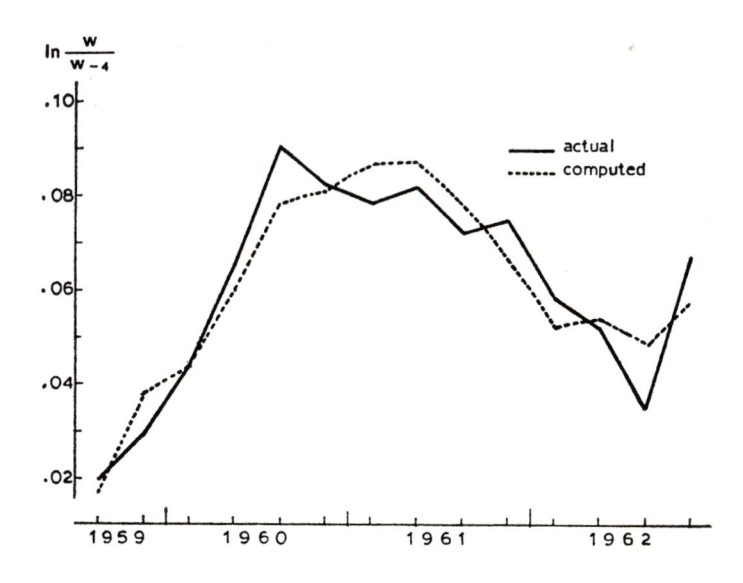

Different from the two preceding equations is the significant contribution of the level of the labour utilization rate with a relatively strong influence. It should be borne in mind that during this sample period the labour force was nearly fully utilized, which explains the high pressure on wages. It is furthermore striking that the coefficient of the price variable had to be fixed *a priori*. During the period under consideration the price level of consumption has almost increased with a constant percentage so that ordinary estimates yielded no significant influence for consumer prices at all, but a very high constant term. From a point of view of causality it was desirable to express the price influence separately. Thus we have applied an iterative procedure to determine the impact of consumer prices an wage rate changes. In accordance with the predominant role of labour productivity we have found a rather high coefficient of this variable and a substantial constant term. Again a wage policy dummy was necessary.

The comparison of sub-period and corresponding whole period residuals is again in favour of the sub-period specification (see figure 8.4.b.).

Figure 8.4.b. Comparison of sub-period and whole period residuals (1959: 3–1962:4)

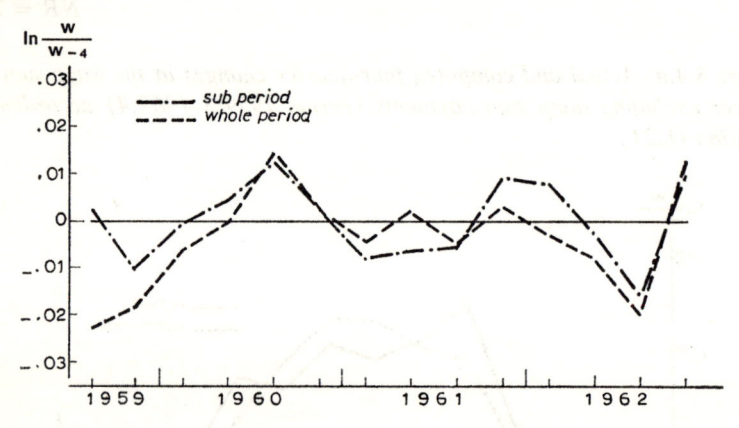

Table 8.4. Comparison of sub-period and whole period wage equation residuals 1959:3–1962:4

	Sub-period equation	Whole period equation
Root mean square residual	.82%	1.14%
Inequality coefficient	.13	.18

8.12. EMPIRICAL RESULTS: THE PERIOD 1963:1–1968:4

Estimating the basic specification yields as its best result (see figure 8.5.a.)

$$(8.22) \quad \ln w - \ln w_{-4} = \underset{(21.7\%)}{+ 1.239} \sum_{0}^{-1} \gamma_6 (\ln p_c - \ln p_{c-4}) +$$

$$\underset{(45.8\%)}{+ .378} \sum_{-1}^{-3} \gamma_{17} \{(\ln y - \ln L) - (\ln y_{-4} - \ln L_{-4})\} +$$

$$\underset{(87.9\%)}{+ .590} \sum_{0}^{-1} \gamma_6 \ln q_L +$$

$$\underset{(-)}{+ 1.000} SPE + \underset{(213.3\%)}{.153} TSPW +$$

$$\underset{(41.2\%)}{+ .030}$$

$$\bar{R}^2 = .769$$
$$NR = 2.22$$

Figure 8.5.a. Actual and computed four-quarter changes in the wage sum per worker excluding lump sum payments (period 1963:1–1968:4) according to equation (8.22)

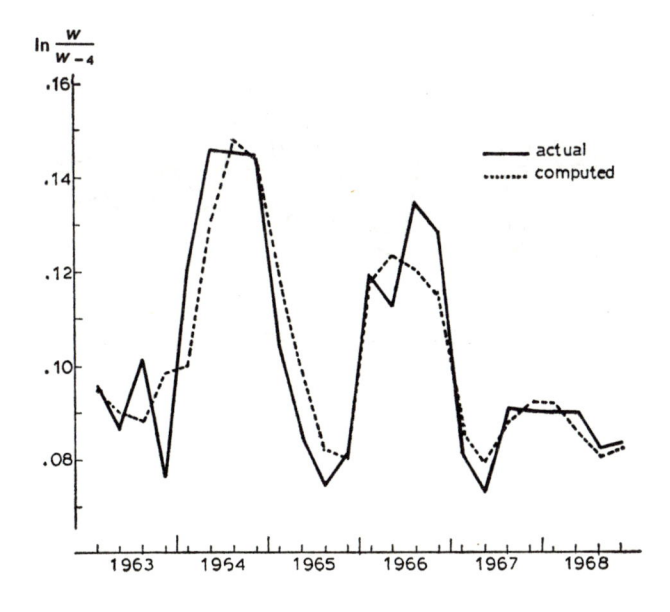

This time we could hardly determine a distributed lag of consumer prices. This does not seem very astonishing as average price rises were larger than in years before 1963 and people seem to anticipate on expected inflation nowadays. Herein may lie the relatively high price elasticity coefficient as well, although it is possible that this is partly the reflection of the fact that the wage explosion in 1964 – wages were rising with about 15 per cent – was included in the sample period. In addition, the influence of labour productivity, the utilization rate of labour and the shift variable could be determined. Summarizing, this sub-period equation does not show specific characteristics of wage policy. However, it expresses the strong inflationary forces in the Netherlands' economy as it contains an accelerating wage-price movement. This element is absent in the whole period equation and so this specification is again not as good in generating the actual movement of wages in the years 1963–1968, as can be seen from figure 8.5.b.

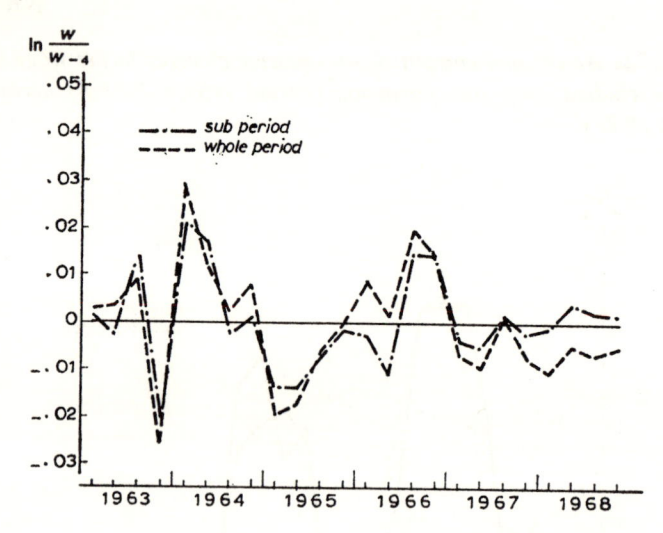

Figure 8.5.b. Comparison of sub-period and whole period residuals (1963: 1–1968:4)

Table 8.5. Comparison of sub-period and whole period wage equation residuals 1963:1–1968:4

	Sub-period equation	Whole period equation
Root mean square residual	1.01%	1.24%
Inequality coefficient	.10	.12

Finally we summarize the average lag of variables in sub-period equations in table 8.6.

Table 8.6. Average lags of variables explaining changes in the wage sum per worker: sub-periods (equations 8.19, 8.20, 8.21 and 8.22)[a]

Variable	Number of quarters
	0 1 2 3 4 5 6

Equation 8.19
1. Change in price level of consumption — — × — — — —
2. Change in labour productivity — — — × — — —
3. Change in overtime × — — — — — —
4. Change in autonomous taxes and social premiums × — — — — — —

Equation 8.20
1. Change in price level of consumption × × — — — — —
2. Change in labour productivity — — × — — — —
3. Change in autonomous taxes and social premiums × — — — — — —

Equation 8.21
1. Change in price level of consumption × × — — — — —
2. Change in labour productivity — — × — — — —
3. Utilization rate of labour — — × × — — —
4. Change in autonomous taxes and social premiums × — — — — — —

Equation 8.22
1. Change in price level of consumption × × — — — — —
2. Change in labour productivity — — × × — — —
3. Utilization rate of labour × × — — — — —
4. Change in autonomous taxes and social premiums × — — — — — —

a. A mark in two columns indicates an average lag between the respective quarters.

8.13. CONCLUSIONS

The foregoing analysis of wage determination and wage policy in the Netherlands, which has resulted in the inclusion of four wage equations in the model, gives rise to some tentative conclusions:

i. there seems to be an increasing influence of consumer prices on wages in the period considered;
ii. the lag between changes in the price level of consumption and changes in the wage rate seems to become shorter;
iii. for the period 1951:1–1959:2 the Phillips curve – the relationship between wage rate changes and the level of unemployment – could not be determined; this might be due to the character of wage policy during these years;
iv. for the period 1959:3–1968:4 there is evidence for an unemployment-inflation trade off, though on the whole the level of unemployment had a minor influence on wage rate changes, and finally
v. wage policy has sometimes significantly influenced the timing of wage increases.

IX. Price formation

9.1 INTRODUCTION

In four of five equations describing final demand components their prices appear. These prices, as well as those of autonomous expenditures, are truly endogenous variables in the system and consequently our model should explain them. For this purpose a specification has been developed which fits in the general approach followed till now. The price equations are therefore price fixation equations in line with the hypothesis of the imperfectness of competition.

To arrive at specifications for prices several methods have been used in econometric model building. One is to add an input-output system to the model but this procedure is beyond the scope and scale of our present approach.[1] Another is to explain one or more value added prices and to translate these into market prices of final goods. This approach was used in the Brookings-model.[2] A third possibility, which is actually used, is the straightforward explanation of the prices of final demand components. This procedure is in our view the most acceptable one in an aggregate model.

9.2. THEORY OF PRICE FORMATION

In the previous chapters we have repeatedly introduced the profit maximizing firm under conditions of imperfect competition. When markets of products and production factors are imperfectly organized and the supply

---

1. See for example AGARWALA and GOODSON (1970).
2. See SCHULTZE and TYRON (1965) on prices and wages in the Brookings model (pp. 281–311).

129

and demand functions used in chapter III are valid, prices are fixed on a level where marginal costs equal marginal revenues. If p_{yj} is the price of final demand component j and MC is marginal cost of production, we have in an equilibrium position [3]:

$$(9.1) \quad p_{yj} = MC \left(\frac{1}{1+1/e_{yj}} \right)$$

Furthermore, if total costs are expressed in terms of labour and capital costs

$$(9.2) \quad TC = p_{lj} L_j + p_{kj} K_j$$

we arrive at a specification for marginal costs as a function of prices of production factors, their supply elasticities and marginal productivities.[4]

$$(9.3) \quad MC = p_{lj}\left(1 + 1/e_{Lj}\right) \bigg/ \frac{\partial y_j}{\partial L_j} + p_{kj}\left(1 + 1/e_{Kj}\right) \bigg/ \frac{\partial y_j}{\partial K_j}$$

Substitution of equation (9.3) in equation (9.1) yields a specification for the product price in the same variables plus the price elasticity of demand:

$$(9.4) \quad p_{yj} = p_{lj} \left(\frac{1+1/e_{Lj}}{1+1/e_{yj}} \right) \bigg/ \frac{\partial y_j}{\partial L_j} + p_{kj} \left(\frac{1+1/e_{Kj}}{1+1/e_{yj}} \right) \bigg/ \frac{\partial y_j}{\partial K_j}$$

If marginal labour and marginal capital productivity are written as a function of average labour and capital productivity respectively. (see Chapter III equation (3.16) and (3.17)) and the shares of labour and capital costs in the product price are represented by ζ_1 and ζ_2 we obtain the following first difference price equation:

$$(9.5) \quad \Delta \ln p_{yj} = \zeta_1 \Delta \ln p_{lj} - \zeta_1 \Delta(\ln y_j - \ln L_j) + \zeta_2 \Delta \ln p_{kj} -$$

$$- \zeta_2 \Delta(\ln y_j - \ln K_j) + \zeta_1 \Delta \ln \left(\frac{1+1/e_{Lj}}{1+1/e_{yj}} \right) + \xi_2 \Delta \ln \left(\frac{1+1/e_{Kj}}{1+1/e_{yj}} \right)$$

In fact the weighting factors ζ_1 and ζ_2 may shift over time, but for practical reasons we assume that they are fixed parameters and we add a constant term to represent the effects of structural shifts.

---

3. Compare Chapter III, p. 28.
4. See also FERGUSON (1969), pp. 176–179.

Thus far we have ignored imports as a factor of production. If these are included we must extend equation (9.5) with additional cost elements, *viz.* import prices and import productivity.[5]

(9.6) $\quad \Delta \ln p_{vj} = \zeta_1 \Delta \ln p_{lj} - \zeta_1 \Delta (\ln y_j - \ln L_j) + \zeta_2 \Delta \ln p_{kj} -$

$- \zeta_2 \Delta (\ln y_j - \ln K_j) + \zeta_3 \Delta \ln p_{mj} - \zeta_3 \Delta \ln (\ln y_j - \ln m_j) +$

$+ \zeta_1 \Delta \ln \left(\dfrac{1+1/e_{Lj}}{1+1/e_{yj}} \right) + \zeta_2 \Delta \ln \left(\dfrac{1+1/e_{Kj}}{1+1/e_{yj}} \right) + \zeta_3 \Delta \ln \left(\dfrac{1}{1+1/e_{yj}} \right) + c_1$

This specification cannot be used for estimation because it contains a great number of unobservable elements. Hence the general hypothesis has to be made that variables specifically relevant for demand component *j* are approximated by their macro economic equivalents. In other words, factor prices and productivities relevant for producing demand component *j* are supposed to be linear functions of aggregate factor prices and aggregate productivities. The changed character of equation (9.6) is expressed by introducing a new parameter Ψ. When, furthermore, the terms representing imperfect competition are replaced by their equivalents in terms of the utilization rate of labour as in previous chapters, the average productivity of capital is assumed to have a constant rate of growth, import productivity is assumed to be constant and when, finally, the variable p_l is replaced by the wage sum per worker (w), we obtain:

(9.7) $\quad \Delta \ln p_{vj} = \Psi_1 \Delta \ln w + \Psi_2 \Delta \ln p_k + \Psi_3 \Delta \ln p_m -$
$\quad\quad\quad - \Psi_4 \Delta (\ln y - \ln L) + \Psi_5 \Delta \ln q_L + c_2$

This equation says nothing more than that the relative change in the price of demand component *j* is related to relative changes in the wage rate, the user cost of capital, import prices, labour productivity and the labour utilization rate.

The above price relationship holds under conditions of static equilibrium: supply and demand stay in continuous balance through instantaneous price changes. This, however, is an exception: disequilibrium, either in the form of excess supply or excess demand is the more common situation. Foresight of demand is imperfect as well as the estimation of costs and the equilibrium between demand and supply for establishing maximum short run profits will therefore be but rarely attained. This again emphasizes that the hypothesis of the profit maximizing firm is a long run equilibrium concept rather than a reflection of short run market behaviour.

5. It is remembered that the supply of imported goods is assumed to be independent of prices ($e_{mj} = \infty$). Because imports are included the symbol p_{vj} is used in the following.

It will be clear that these disequilibria arising from unanticipated situations will have their influence on price fixation. We hypothesize most of these phenomena to be a function of utilization rates. When, for instance, demand is low and excess capacity comes into existence, firms will reduce prices as they seek to boost sales in order to raise capacity utilization and profits. Reversely, when demand is high utilization rates will be high. This situation will usually be associated with delays in deliveries, non-price terms of transactions, shortages, etc. In general, these phenomena will lead to price increases. Apart from more specific disequilibria, such as imbalances between actual and desired levels of stocks, which are especially relevant for firms selling from stocks, and unfilled orders, which are especially relevant for firms delivering on order, we may add on the foregoing considerations the *level* of the utilization of productive capacity to the basic relationship. In a near full employment economy this will usually be the utilization rate of labour. We then obtain:

(9.8) $\quad \Delta \ln p_{vj} = \Psi_1 \Delta \ln w + \Psi_2 \Delta \ln p_k + \Psi_3 \Delta \ln p_m -$
$\quad\quad\quad - \Psi_4 \Delta (\ln y - \ln L) + \Psi_5 \Delta \ln q_L + \Psi_6 \ln q_L + c_3$

It will be understood that the overall labour utilization rate is only an approximation for the utilization rate in specific industries. This procedure is, therefore, rather poor but can be somewhat improved upon by the following modification. Let us assume the situation that the aggregative utilization rate does not change but that the composition of demand shifts. In this situation, especially when supply cannot easily be adjusted as is usually the case in a near full employment economy, the price level of the growing demand component tends to rise relative to the price level of the declining one. Price equation (9.8) can therefore be improved by adding a new variable defined as the difference between the rate of change in the relevant final demand category j and the rate of change in aggregate demand (v),

(9.9) $\quad \Delta \ln p_{vj} = \Psi_1 \Delta \ln w + \Psi_2 \Delta \ln p_k + \Psi_3 \Delta \ln p_m - \Psi_4 \Delta (\ln y - \ln L) +$
$\quad\quad\quad + \Psi_5 \Delta \ln q_L + \Psi_6 \ln q_L + \Psi_7 \Delta (\ln v_j - \ln v) + c_4.$

It has been argued earlier in this study that relationships based on the theory of imperfect competition only are just as unrealistic as those exclusively based on the assumption of perfect competition. Furthermore, we should remember that oligopolistic competition is a frequently occurring market form. Oligopolistic firms are subject to relative great uncertainty because of the interdependent reactions of competitors. They are therefore likely to consider the long term aspects of their decisions. In connection with price fixation this will presumably lead to rather rigid prices especially downwards. The emphasis lies on long term security, on stability of market share and on a steady expansion rather than on short run profit maximization. Although even large oligopolistic firms incidentally price some products on a competitive short-run basis, oligopolistic pricing is characteristically based on a mark up over standard or normal unit variable costs. These firms do not consider the very short run cost changes which occur from quarter but they relate prices to costs which are expected to be more lasting in nature.[6]

We follow the literature[7] in order to make the concept of normal costs or standard costs operational and assume that

i. changes in the wage rate and the user cost of capital are mainly considered to be permanent changes in costs;
ii. the trend of changes in labour productivity is predominantly relevant;
iii. the trend of changes in import prices is predominantly relevant and that
iv. temporary deviations from the normal capacity utilization are not considered.

Actual pricing behaviour, however, is a mixture of competitive, monopolistic and oligopolistic pricing. In a competitive market prices respond to the difference between demand and supply, and assuming profit maximization, the variables of the price relationship developed sofar will provide a satisfactory explanation for competitive pricing.[8] This implies that the classical model of price determination requires the actual changes in the wage rate, user costs of capital,[9] import prices, labour productivity and utilization rate rather than their 'normal' changes to play their part.

Acceptation of these considerations leads to a reformulation of our price equation in which actual as well as 'normal' changes, especially in labour productivity and import prices, will occur. The long term character of the following specification can be seen from the fact that variables have an asterisk in order to express their expected nature. To express the changed character of the specification we use new parameters.

---

6. See ECKSTEIN (1964) on the theory of pricing in modern industries.
7. See ECKSTEIN and FROMM (1968) and SCHULTZE and TYRON (1965).
8. When supply of production factors would also take place in a competitive market the reasoning concerning the supply elasticities must be adjusted and the specification would slightly change.
9. ECKSTEIN and FROMM (1968) argue that the classical theory of the firm calls for no direct influence of the size of the capital stock on short run, profit maximizing, price-output decisions. They do not agree with this theory and posit that the capacity utilization rate reflects the influence of the cost of capital.

$$(9.10) \quad \Delta \ln p_{vj}^* = \Psi_8 \Delta \ln w^* + \Psi_9 \Delta \ln p_k^* + \Psi_{10} \Delta \ln p_m^* + \Psi_{11} \overline{\Delta \ln p_m} -$$
$$- \Psi_{12} \Delta(\ln y - \ln L)^* - \Psi_{13} \overline{\Delta(\ln y - \ln L)} +$$
$$+ \Psi_{14} \Delta \ln q_L^* + \Psi_{15} \ln q_L^* + \Psi_{16} \Delta(\ln v_j - \ln v)^* + c_5$$

where a bar over a variable indicates a standard or normal value of this variable. In addition we assume that these standard costs have constant exponential growth rates, viz. $\overline{\Delta(\ln y - \ln L)} = c_6$ and $\overline{\Delta \ln p_m} = c_7$. Then, after the introduction of unknown lag distributions we obtain as basic specification for price changes of final demand components:

$$(9.11) \quad \Delta \ln p_{vj} = \Psi_8 \frac{G(L)_1}{H(L)_1} \Delta \ln w + \Psi_9 \frac{G(L)_2}{H(L)_2} \Delta \ln p_k +$$
$$+ \Psi_{10} \frac{G(L)_3}{H(L)_3} \Delta \ln p_m - \Psi_{12} \frac{G(L)_4}{H(L)_4} \Delta(\ln y - \ln L) +$$
$$+ \Psi_{14} \frac{G(L)_5}{H(L)_5} \Delta \ln q_L + \Psi_{15} \frac{G(L)_6}{H(L)_6} \ln q_L +$$
$$+ \Psi_{16} \frac{G(L)_7}{H(L)_7} \Delta(\ln v_j - \ln v) + c_8$$

where $c_8 = c_5 - c_6 + c_7$.

A characteristic of this equation is the separation of the impact of wages and labour productivity. This is rather unusual in empirical work on price formation since most investigators consider labour unit costs (or standard labour unit costs, or the difference between actual and standard labour unit costs) as the most appropriate variable.[10] However, when it is recognized that different market forms exist the conclusion must be that the coefficients of the wage variable and the labour productivity variable are different.

However, it remains to be seen whether for *statistical* reasons a separate estimation of the wage and the labour productivity variable is preferable. Anyway, the elasticity coefficient of labour productivity tends to be lower than the elasticity coefficient of the wage rate.

Another characteristic of specification (9.11) is that three variables representing supply and demand tensions occur. One is connected with the

10. See, for instance, SCHULTZE and TYRON (1965), VERDOORN (1967), VAN DEN BELD (1968), ECKSTEIN and FROMM (1968).

frequently used excess demand variable, here represented by the *level* of the labour utilization rate.[11] Another is connected with the impact of imperfect competition and represented by the change in the labour utilization rate.

Finally, the difference between the rate of change in the relevant final demand category and the rate of change in aggregate demand represents specific tensions in specific industries producing the relevant demand component.

The price relation (9.11) allows direct estimation provided a decision about the lags is taken. As a first general approach it is assumed that import prices react with an infinite lag. It should, furthermore, be noted that basic relationship (9.11) is a very general one, and it may be necessary to add specific variables in each of the equations explaining the price of private consumption, gross fixed investment, autonomous expenditures, exports of goods and exports of services respectively.

9.3. THE PRICE OF PRIVATE CONSUMPTION

As variable to explain has been chosen the endogenous consumption price. Autonomous influences, caused by changes in indirect taxes, rents, subsidies etc. have been eliminated in advance. This procedure implies a unitary elasticity of these items with respect to the consumption price which seems plausible.

Experiments with the basic specification yielded acceptable results but on statistical grounds it was necessary to estimate a combined wage-productivity variable, in which the wage rate variable had a weight two and the half times the weight of the labour productivity variable. This ratio was found after experimentation with several weighting schemes. The explanation of the changes in the endogenous consumption price could be improved by adding the deviation of desired stocks from their actual level as an explanatory variable. This confirms the results of other investigators, such as VAN DEN BELD (1968) and COURCHENE (1969). All other things being equal producers of consumer goods lower their prices when stocks overshoot their desired mark and the other way round. It is clear that such an influence will not be found when commodities are mainly sold on order and not from existing stocks.[12]

In contrast to the basic specification we ultimately have adopted a Koyck lag on the disequilibrium between actual and desired stocks. Such a lag

---

11. See SAMUELSON (1948) p. 263. Furthermore, see NEILD (1963), RUSHDY and LUND (1967) and MCCALLUM (1970) for a discussion of the effect of demand on manufacturing prices in Great Britain.

12. Average lags of the price equations are presented on page 146.

can also be found for import prices, as postulated, but the results can be somewhat improved when import prices are weighted in advance according to a thus obtained implicit weighting scheme.

The equation included in the model, with a very weak influence of the imperfect competition variable, is the following

(9.12) $\quad \ln p_{c\,end} - \ln p_{c\,end-4} = .6(\ln p_{c\,end-1} - \ln p_{c\,end-5}) +$
$\phantom{(9.12) \quad \ln p_{c\,end} - \ln p_{c\,end-4} = } (-)$

$$+ .239 \left[\sum_{0}^{-1} \gamma_{18}(\ln w - \ln w_{-4}) - .6 \sum_{-1}^{-2} \gamma_{18}(\ln w - \ln w_{-4}) \right] +$$
(29.7%)

$$+ .014 \left[\sum_{-3}^{-5} \gamma_{4}(\ln p_k - \ln p_{k-4}) - .6 \sum_{-4}^{-6} \gamma_{4}(\ln p_k - \ln p_{k-4}) \right] +$$
(272.4%)

$$+ .194 \left[\sum_{0}^{-2} \gamma_{12}(\ln p_{mg-sa} - \ln p_{mg-sa-4}) - \right.$$
(21.7%)

$$\left. - .6 \sum_{-1}^{-3} \gamma_{12}(\ln p_{mg-sa} - \ln p_{mg-sa-4}) \right] -$$

$$- .096 \left[\sum_{0}^{-2} \gamma_{17} \{(\ln y - \ln L) - (\ln y - \ln L)_{-4}\} - \right.$$
(29.7%)

$$\left. - .6 \sum_{-1}^{-3} \gamma_{17} \{(\ln y - \ln L) - (\ln y - \ln L)_{-4}\} \right] +$$

$$+ .238 \left[\sum_{0}^{-2} \gamma_{4}(\ln q_L - \ln q_{L-4}) - .6 \sum_{-1}^{-3} \gamma_{4}(\ln q_L - \ln q_{L-4}) \right] +$$
(211.4%)

$$+ .209 \left[\sum_{0}^{-2} \gamma_4 \ln q_L - .6 \sum_{-1}^{-3} \gamma_4 \ln q_L \right] +$$
(110.1%)

$$+ .092 \left[\sum_{-2}^{-5} \gamma_7 \{(\ln c - \ln v) - (\ln c - \ln v)_{-4}\} - \right.$$
(55.8%)

$$\left. - .6 \sum_{-3}^{-6} \gamma_7 \{(\ln c - \ln v) - (\ln c - \ln v)_{-4}\} \right] +$$

$+ .008 \{(n_d - n_{-1}) - (n_d - n_{-1})_{-4}\} +$
(33.5%)

$+ .006$ $ \bar{R}^2 = .889$
(44.1%) $ NR = 1.62$

where $p_{c\,end}$ = price level of private consumption excluding autonomous influences, 1963 = 100;
w = wage sum per worker in enterprises excluding lump sum payments, 1963 = 100;
p_k = user cost of capital, 1963 = 100;
p_{mg-sa} = price level of imports of goods excluding ships and airplanes, 1963 = 100;
y = production of enterprises, in 1963 prices;
L = employment in enterprises;
q_L = utilization rate of labour;
c = private consumption, in 1963 prices;
v = total expenditures, less inventory formation, government wages, exports of services and factor incomes received from abroad, in 1963 prices;

Actual 9.1. Actual and computed four-quarter changes in the endogenous price level of consumption according to equation (9.12)

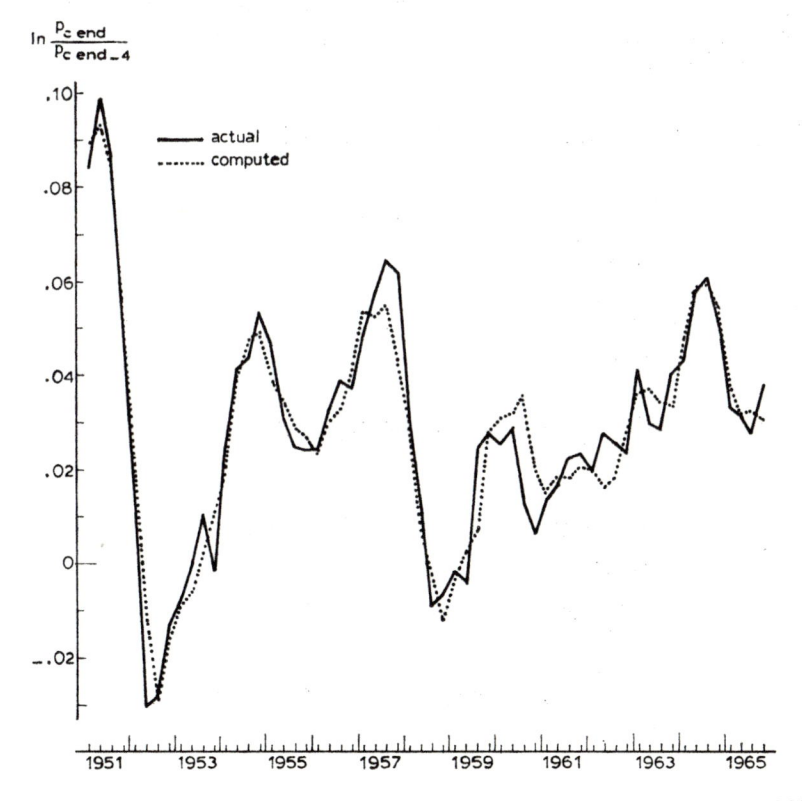

n_d = desired level of stocks, in 1963 prices;
n = level of stocks, in 1963 prices;
γ_4 = .33, .34, .33;
γ_7 = .25, .25, .25, .25;
γ_{12} = .70, .20, .10;
γ_{17} = .60, .30, .10;
γ_{18} = .80, .20.

9.4. THE PRICE OF GROSS FIXED INVESTMENT IN ENTERPRISES

Apart from an influence of the level of the utilization rate, all variables theoretically specified in advance could be found. The failure of the utilization rate variable may be due to the fact that the impact of demand is unimportant relative to the role of supply. This time the influence of imperfect competition could be significantly determined. As in the equation for consumer prices the influence of short run fluctuations in capital costs is negligible. The final equation, in which wages, labour productivity and import prices have been simultaneously estimated by imposing an infinite lag structure, is

$$(9.13) \quad \ln p_{i-sa} - \ln p_{i-sa_{-4}} = \underset{(-)}{.7}(\ln p_{i-sa_{-1}} - \ln p_{i-sa_{-5}}) +$$

$$+ .144 \sum_{-1}^{-2} \gamma_{18}(\ln w - \ln w_{-4}) +$$
(20.8%)

$$+ .031 \left[\sum_{-2}^{-3} \gamma_6(\ln p_k - \ln p_{k-4}) - .7 \sum_{-3}^{-4} \gamma_6(\ln p_k - \ln p_{k-4}) \right] +$$
(187.8%)

$$+ .144 \sum_{0}^{-1} \gamma_6(\ln p_{mg-sa} - \ln p_{mg-sa_{-4}}) -$$
(20.8%)

$$- .058 \sum_{-1}^{-3} \gamma_{17} \{(\ln y - \ln L) - (\ln y - \ln L)_{-4}\} +$$
(20.8%)

$$+ .972 [(\ln q_{L-2} - \ln q_{L-6}) - .7(\ln q_{L-3} - \ln q_{L-7})] +$$
(51.0%)

$$+ .065 \left[\sum_{-3}^{-5} \gamma_{12} \{(\ln i_{-sa} - \ln v) - (\ln i_{-sa} - \ln v)_{-4}\} - \right.$$
(77.0%)

$$-.7 \sum_{-4}^{-6} \gamma_{12} \left\{(\ln i_{-sa} - \ln v) - (\ln i_{-sa} - \ln v)_{-4}\right\} \Bigg] -$$

$$-.001$$
$$(350.2\%)$$

$$\bar{R}^2 = .819$$
$$NR = 2.32$$

where p_{i-sa} = price level of gross fixed investment in enterprises excluding housing, ships and airplanes, 1963 = 100;
w = wage sum per worker in enterprises excluding lump sum payments, 1963 = 100;
p_k = user cost of capital, 1963 = 100;
p_{mg-sa} = price level of imports of goods excluding ships and airplanes, 1963 = 100;
y = production of enterprises, in 1963 prices;
L = employment in enterprises;

Figure 9.2. Actual and computed four-quarter changes in the price level of gross fixed investment excluding housing, ships and airplanes according to equation (9.13)

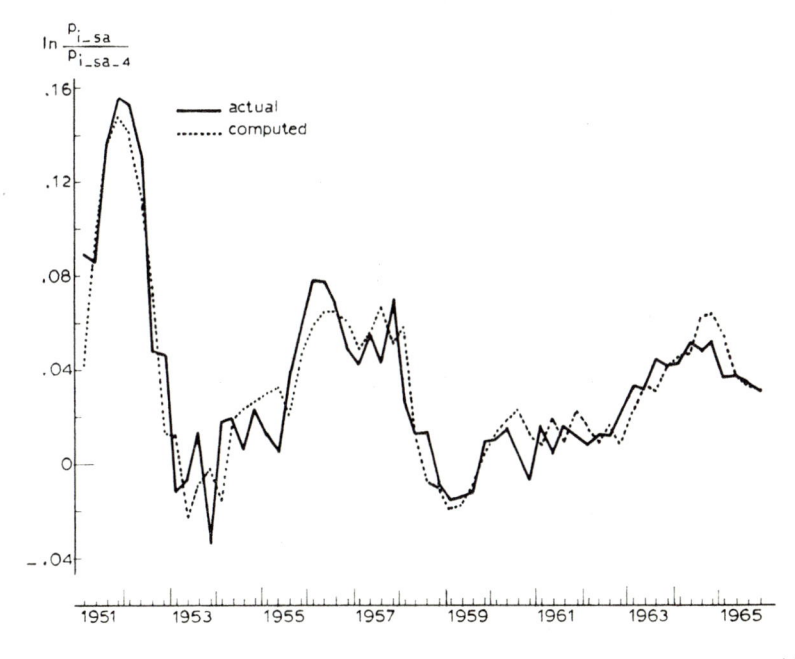

q_L = utilization rate of labour;
i_{-sa} = gross fixed investment in enterprises excluding housing, ships and airplanes, in 1963 prices;
v = total expenditures, less inventory formation, government wages, exports of services and factor incomes received from abroad, in 1963 prices;
γ_6 = .50, .50;
γ_{12} = .70, .20, .10;
γ_{17} = .60, .30, .10;
γ_{18} = .80, .20.

9.5. THE PRICE OF AUTONOMOUS EXPENDITURES

The price equation of autonomous expenditures was obtained with a Koyck lag on import prices only. Furthermore the influence of all theoretical variables, except the user cost of capital, could be determined with the appropriate sign, albeit not always with low standard errors. The lacking of the user cost of capital is not astonishing as a labour intensive industry – the building industry – is predominant here. The model equation is

(9.14) $\quad \ln p_x - \ln p_{x-4} = .7(\ln p_{x-1} - \ln p_{x-5}) +$
$\qquad\qquad\qquad\quad (-)$

$\qquad + .248 \left[\sum_0^{-1} \gamma_{18}(\ln w - \ln w_{-4}) - .7 \sum_{-1}^{-2} \gamma_{18}(\ln w - \ln w_{-4}) \right] +$
$\qquad\quad (63.5\%)$

$\qquad + .236(\ln p_{mg-sa} - \ln p_{mg-sa_{-4}}) -$
$\qquad\quad (15.8\%)$

$\qquad - .099 \left[\sum_0^{-2} \gamma_{17} \{(\ln y - \ln L) - (\ln y - \ln L)_{-4}\} - \right.$
$\qquad\quad (63.5\%)$

$\qquad\qquad\left. - .7 \sum_{-1}^{-3} \gamma_{17} \{(\ln y - \ln L) - (\ln y - \ln L)_{-4}\} \right] +$

$\qquad + .968 \left[\sum_{-1}^{-3} \gamma_4(\ln q_L - \ln q_{L-4}) - .7 \sum_{-2}^{-4} \gamma_4(\ln q_L - \ln q_{L-4}) \right] +$
$\qquad\quad (65.3\%)$

$\qquad + .721 \left[\sum_0^{-2} \gamma_4 \ln q_L - .7 \sum_{-1}^{-3} \gamma_4 \ln q_L \right] +$
$\qquad\quad (82,8\%)$

$$+ .093 \left[\sum_{-3}^{-5} \gamma_4 \{(\ln x - \ln v) - (\ln x - \ln v)_{-4}\} - \right.$$
(80.5%)
$$\left. - .7 \sum_{-4}^{-6} \gamma_4 \{(\ln x - \ln v) - (\ln x - \ln v)_{-4}\} \right] +$$
$$+ .008$$
(60.9%)

$$\bar{R}^2 = .894$$
$$NR = 1.85$$

Figure 9.3. Actual and computed four-quarter changes in the price level of antonomous expenditures according to equation (9.14)

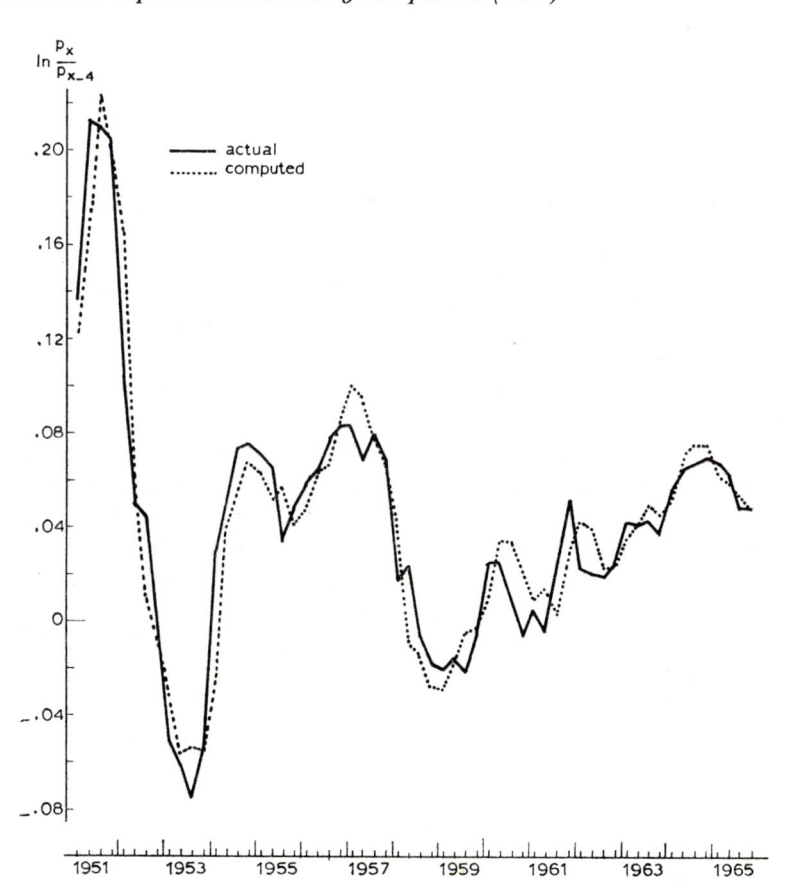

where p_x = price level of autonomous expenditures, 1963 = 100;
  w = wage sum per worker in enterprises excluding lump sum payments, 1963 = 100;
  p_{mg-sa} = price level of imports of goods excluding ships and airplanes, 1963 = 100;
  y = production of enterprises, in 1963 prices;
  L = employment in enterprises;
  q_L = utilization rate of labour;
  x = autonomous expenditures (government consumption, investment in housing and net-investment of the government);
  v = total expenditures, less inventory formation, government wages, exports of services and factor incomes received from abroad, in 1963 prices;
  γ_4 = .33, .34, .33;
  γ_{17} = .60, .30, .10;
  γ_{18} = .80, .20.

9.6. THE PRICE OF EXPORTS OF MANUFACTURED GOODS

In the equation of the export price of manufactured goods excluding ships and airplanes, the impact of import prices, wages and labour productivity is estimated simultaneously. The weights have been determined according to the accumulated shares of labour costs and imports in exports of goods. In addition to the theoretical basic specification we have experimented with export prices of competitors as explanatory variable. As far as Dutch exporters follow prices on the world market and wish to maintain their market share we may expect a significant influence of such a variable. Finally, some influence of the acceleration or deceleration of world import demand could be determined as well. It should be noted that the following equation has a negative constant term representing the larger increase in labour productivity in relatively capital intensive exporting firms relative to macro economic productivity. The role of capital appears as well from the relatively high coefficient of the user cost of capital.

(9.15) $\quad \ln p_{bf-sa} - \ln p_{bf-sa-4} = \underset{(-)}{.4} (\ln p_{bf-sa-1} - \ln p_{bf-sa-5})$

$$+ .121 \sum_{0}^{-1} \gamma_{18} (\ln w - \ln w_{-4})$$
$\quad\quad (23.2\%)$

$$+ .100 \left[\sum_{-1}^{-2} \gamma_6 (\ln p_k - \ln p_{k-4}) - .4 \sum_{-2}^{-3} \gamma_6 (\ln p_k - \ln p_{k-4}) \right] +$$
(73.4%)

$$+ .283 (\ln p_{mg-sa} - \ln p_{mg-sa-4}) -$$
(23.2%)

$$- .048 \sum_{0}^{-2} \gamma_{17} \{(\ln y - \ln L) - (\ln y - \ln L)_{-4}\} +$$
(23.2%)

$$+ 1.524 \left[(\ln q_{L-1} - \ln q_{L-5}) - .4 (\ln q_{L-2} - \ln q_{L-6}) \right] +$$
(31.9%)

$$+ 1.179 \left[\sum_{-1}^{-4} \gamma_7 \ln q_L - .4 \sum_{-2}^{-5} \gamma_7 \ln q_L \right] +$$
(38.9%)

$$+ .449 \left[\sum_{-2}^{-4} \gamma_4 \{(\ln b_{f-sa} - \ln v) - (\ln b_{f-sa} - \ln v)_{-4}\} - \right.$$
(26.7%)

$$\left. - .4 \sum_{-3}^{-5} \gamma_4 \{(\ln b_{f-sa} - \ln v) - (\ln b_{f-sa} - \ln v)_{-4}\} \right] +$$

$$+ .260 \left[\sum_{-1}^{-4} \gamma_7 (\ln p_{bgw} - \ln p_{bgw-4}) - \right.$$
(34.4%)

$$\left. - .4 \sum_{-2}^{-5} \gamma_7 (\ln p_{bgw} - \ln p_{bgw-4}) \right] +$$

$$+ .210 \left[\sum_{-1}^{-3} \gamma_{19} \Delta (\ln m_w - \ln m_{w-4}) - \right.$$
(61.9%)

$$\left. - .4 \sum_{-2}^{-4} \gamma_{19} \Delta (\ln m_w - \ln m_{w-4}) \right] -$$

$$- .012$$
(43.3%)

$$\bar{R}^2 = .918$$
$$NR = 1.98$$

Figure 9.4. Actual and computed four-quarter changes in the price level of exports of manufactured goods excluding ships and airplanes according to equation (9.15)

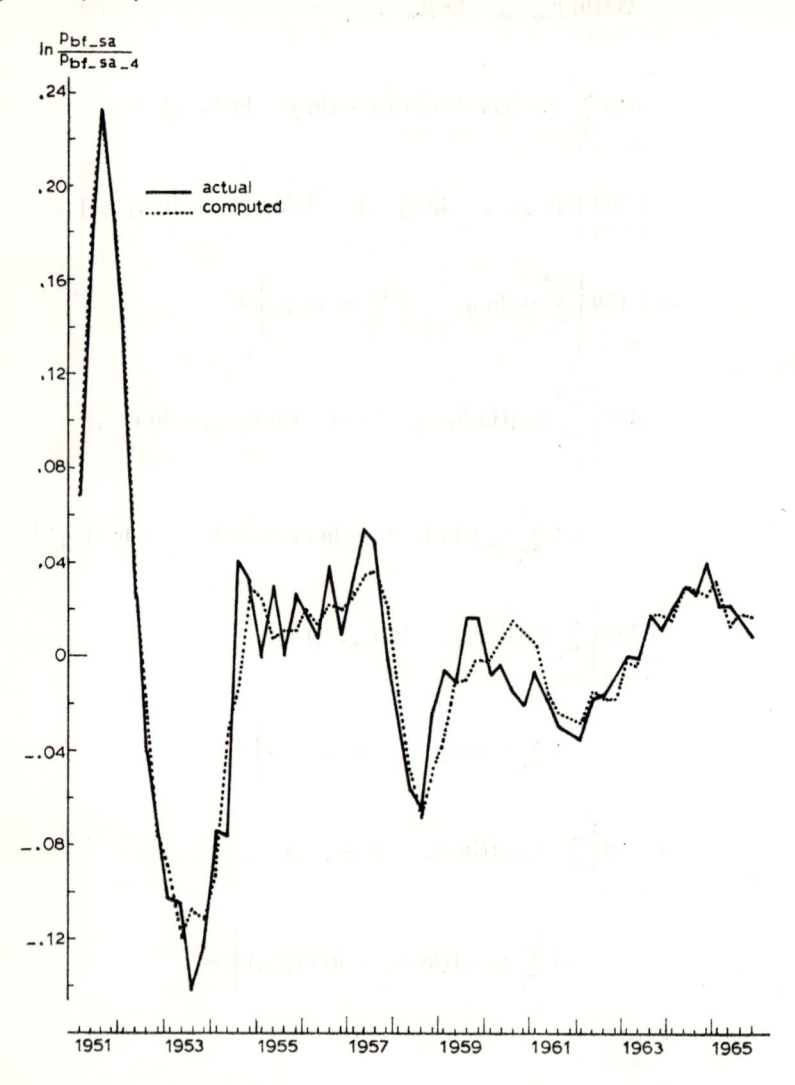

where p_{bf-sa} = price of exports of manufactured goods excluding ships and airplanes, 1963 = 100;
w = wage sum per worker in enterprises excluding lump sum payments, 1963 = 100;
p_k = user cost of capital, 1963 = 100;
p_{mg-sa} = price level of imports of goods, excluding ships and airplanes, 1963 = 100;
y = production of enterprises, in 1963 prices;
L = employment in enterprises;
q_L = utilization rate of labour;
b_{f-sa} = exports of manufactured goods excluding ships and airplanes, in 1963 prices;
v = total expenditures, less inventory formation, government wages, exports of services and factor incomes received from abroad, in 1963 prices;
p_{bgw} = price of exports of competitors reweighted according to relative importance as competitor, 1963 = 100;
m_w = world imports of goods, reweighted according to the geographical distribution of Dutch exports of goods, 1963 = 100;
γ_4 = .33, .34, .33;
γ_6 = .50, .50;
γ_7 = .25, .25, .25, .25;
γ_{17} = .60, .30, .10;
γ_{18} = .80, .20;
γ_{19} = .50, .30, .20.

9.7. THE PRICE OF EXPORTS OF SERVICES

The explanation of the export price of services does not originate with specific demand and supply factors. The approach is therefore a technical and not an analytical one. Again we base ourselves on the division of exports of services in three broad items, tourism, transportation and other services. In addition, we assume that the price of the receipts from tourism is represented by the price index of private consumption, that transportation receipts can be deflated with the price of sea transport (a weighted index of liner, tramp and tanker freight rates) and that the price of other services shows a development parallel to that of the export price of commodities.[13]

13. For an econometric analysis of ocean freight rates, see DRIEHUIS (1970a, 1971).

In this way we arrive at the following equation:

(9.16) $\ln p_{bs-t} - \ln p_{bs-t-4} = +.3(\ln p_{bf-sa} - \ln p_{bf-sa-4}) +$
$+ .3(\ln p_c - \ln p_{c-4}) + .4(\ln p_f - \ln p_{f-4})$

where
- p_{bs-t} = price level of exports of services, excluding receipts from transit trade, 1963 = 100;
- p_c = price level of private consumption, 1963 = 100;
- p_{bf-sa} = price level of exports of manufactured goods excluding ships and airplanes, 1963 = 100;
- p_f = ocean freight rates, (weighted average of liner, tramp and tanker rates), 1963 = 100.

Table 9.1. *Average lags of variables explaining changes in final demand prices*[a]

Variable	Number of quarters						
	0	1	2	3	4	5	6
Equation 9.12							
1. Change in wage sum per worker	x	x					
2. Change in user cost of capital				x			
3. Change in price of imports	x	x					
4. Change in labour productivity	x	x					
5. Change in utilization rate of labour			x				
6. Utilization rate of labour			x				
7. Change in ratio c/v				x	x		
8. Change in discrepancy desired/actual stocks			x	x			
Equation 9.13							
1. Change in wage sum per worker				x	x		
2. Change in user cost of capital			x	x			
3. Change in price of imports			x	x			
4. Change in labour productivity				x	x		
5. Change in utilization rate of labour			x				
6. Change in ratio i_{-sa}/v				x	x		
Equation 9.14							
1. Change in wage sum per worker	x	x					
2. Change in price of imports			x	x			
3. Change in labour productivity	x	x					
4. Change in utilization rate of labour			x				
5. Utilization rate of labour			x				
6. Change in ratio x/v					x		
Equation 9.15							
1. Change in wage sum per worker	x	x					
2. Change in user cost of capital			x	x			
3. Change in price of imports	x	x					
4. Change in labour productivity			x	x			
5. Change in utilization rate of labour			x				
6. Utilization rate of labour				x	x		
7. Change in ratio b_{g-sa}/v					x		
8. Change in export prices competitors			x	x			
9. Second difference in world imports			x	x			

a. A mark in two columns indicates an average lag between the respective quarters.

X. Government receipts and expenditures

10.1. INTRODUCTION

In the model the government sector is represented by no more than three equations, *viz.* three tax revenue equations. Government expenditure as well as other revenues are treated as exogenous as a result of the decision to limit the scale of the government sector in the model by including as endogenous variables only those which heavily depend on other already occuring endogenous variables.

All government expenditures are treated as exogenous policy variables. In fact this is not entirely realistic where wages of civil servants are concerned because these follow enterprise wages with a lag. Actually government wages are raised in the beginning of the year by a percentage determined by the Cabinet, after consultation with representatives of government employees. This percentage is usually taken on the cautious side because the government endeavours to avoid becoming a wage leader. After the middle of the year people receive a 'trend payment' to adjust the development of government wages to private wages. This adjustment is based on the wage increase in a specific group of enterprises during the year ending June 30th. This procedure is rather complicated and seems therefore not suited for a quarterly model specification.

---

1. Investment in housing is on the whole Government controlled in the Netherlands although nowadays there is a tendency to liberalize the housing market. The choice to make autonomous expenditures exogenous in current prices is made to have a link with the Government's budget philosophy. However, for investment in housing this approach in current prices is less suited.

147

Furthermore, government consumption and gross public investment, plus investment in housing are combined in one exogenous variable, called autonomous expenditures, in current prices.[1] The price deflator of these expenditures is an endogenous variable which we have already discussed in the previous chapter. Consequently real autonomous expenditures are endogenous to the model. Income transfers are treated as predetermined variables because they are less dependent on the current level of economic activity.[2]

10.2. INSTITUTIONAL ASPECTS OF TAXATION

Before the tax equations in the model are discussed in detail a short review of the institutional aspects of taxation is necessary. National taxes in the Netherlands can be divided into three broad groups: taxes based on income and profits, taxes based on capital and taxes based on sales or turnover. The third category is also denoted as indirect taxes, whereas the first two groups can be called direct taxes. Taxes based on capital are neglected in the model, we therefore concentrate on the other two groups.

Taxes based on income or profits can be divided into income tax, company tax and dividend tax. Income tax is payable by individuals on total income per calender year. The taxable profits of traders or partnerships are also subject to income tax. In the case of wages, salaries and similar payments tax is withhold at source and credited against final income tax liability. A number of income tax-payers is required to make advance payments on the basis of a provisional assessment of their taxable income. Corporate tax is levied on the profits of corporations. Basis of assessment is the profit in the tax year. Companies are required to make tax payments in advance. At the end of the tax year and during subsequent years a return of taxes has to be made on the basis of the final assessment of taxable profits.

Taxes on sales or turnover are payable on deliveries and services rendered in the Netherlands in the course of trade and imports.[3] Tax is due at the time the invoice is rendered and is payable monthly or quarterly.

For practical reasons we have constructed three equations describing tax payments on cash basis in the model. These equations are chosen in such a way that the dependent variables can be easily related to independent

---

2. This is not true for unemployment transfers which should be treated as an endogenous variable. This has not been done so far.
3. This is true for the sample period. In 1969 the Netherlands changed to the value added tax.

variables already appearing in the model, *viz.* income variables in connection with taxes on income and profits and an expenditure variable in connection with taxes on sales (expenditures).

These relationships have been formulated in first difference form relating the endogenous change in tax revenues to the change in the independent variables. When we add the autonomous change in tax revenues arising from changes in tariffs, changes in the cashing pattern etc. we arrive at the total change in tax receipts. It should be noted that in the following taxes are considered on cash rather than on transaction basis because this seems most relevant for the impact of taxes on expenditures.

10.3. WAGE AND INCOME TAX

The first tax revenue equation relates the change in wage and income taxes on cash basis to the change in wage income and to autonomous changes in these taxes due to alterations of tariffs, changes in cashing patterns and the like.[4] In the previous section we saw that in the case of wages and salaries taxes are paid when incomes are earned. A part of the individuals pays only wage tax whereas another part, which has an income above a certain level or more than one source of income, is subjected to income tax. For these people the paid wage tax, and also the dividend tax, is credited against the final amount of income tax. The equation for wage and income taxes must therefore consist of these elements.

Taking into account as well what has been empirically found in this field on an annual basis for the Netherlands, we have constructed and not estimated the following equation in which the change in wage and income tax is dependent on a weighted average of

i. the unlagged change in wage income representing the wage tax element and
ii. the lagged and weighted change in wage income representing the income tax element, split up into an advance payment and a payment resulting from the definite assessment of taxable income.[5]

$$(10.1) \quad \Delta T_W = [\pi_W] \left\{ (1 - [v_W]) \Delta W_T + [v_W] \left(.60 \sum_{-1}^{-4} \gamma_7 \Delta W_T + \right. \right.$$
$$\left. \left. + .40 \sum_{-6}^{-10} \gamma_{20} \sum_{0}^{-3} \gamma_7 \Delta W_T \right) \right\} + \Delta T_{W\ aut}$$

---
4. The term wage income includes wages, salaries, transfers etc.
5. A coefficient between square brackets is changing over time.

where T_W = direct taxes on wage income (cash basis);
W_T = wage income;
T_{Waut} = autonomous taxes on wage income (cash basis);
π_W = marginal tax quota of wage income;
v_W = share of income tax payments by individuals in total income tax;
γ_7 = .25, .25, .25, .25,;
γ_{20} = .35, .30, .20, .10, .05.

10.4. TAXES ON NON-WAGE INCOME

Taxes on non-wage income consist of two parts: income tax paid by self employed and tax paid by corporations (including government enterprises). As far as income tax is concerned the considerations mentioned in the previous section are valid. Corporation tax for a certain year is paid in advance. During the subsequent year these advance payments are accounted for in the final assessment of corporate profits.

The equation below relates, apart from an autonomous term, the change in taxes on non-wage income to a weighted average of

i. the lagged and weighted change in non-wage income representing the corporate tax element (the weighting scheme represents the institutional cashing pattern) and

ii. the lagged and weighted change of non-wage income representing the income tax element, split up into an advance payment element and a definite assessment of taxable income element.

$$(10.2) \quad \Delta T_Z = [\pi_Z] \left\{ (1 - [v_Z]) \sum_{-2}^{-8} \gamma_{21} \sum_{0}^{-3} \gamma_7 \Delta Z + \right.$$
$$\left. + [v_Z] \left(.60 \sum_{-1}^{-4} \gamma_7 \Delta Z + .40 \sum_{-6}^{-10} \gamma_{20} \sum_{0}^{-3} \gamma_7 \Delta Z \right) \right\} + \Delta T_{Z\,aut}$$

where T_Z = direct taxes on non-wage income (cash basis);
Z = non-wage income (including corporate profits);
$T_{Z\,aut}$ = autonomous taxes on non-wage income (cash basis);
π_Z = marginal tax quota of non-wage income;
v_Z = share of income tax payments by self employed in total income tax;
γ_7 = .25, .25, .25, .25;
γ_{20} = .35, .30, .20, .10, .05;
γ_{21} = .60, .95, .10, .10, $-$.45, $-$.25, $-$.05.

10.5. TAXES ON SALES

The third tax equation is very simple. Apart from an autonomous term, the changes in taxes on sales (indirect taxes) are related to aggregate sales excluding the rent component in private consumption expenditures.

(10.3) $\quad \Delta T_K = [\pi_K] \Delta(V - CHR) + \Delta T_{K\,aut}$

where
- T_K = indirect taxes (cash basis);
- V = total expenditures, excluding government wages, inventory formation, exports of services and factor incomes received from abroad, in current prices;
- CHR = rent component in private consumption expenditures, in current prices;
- $T_{K\,aut}$ = autonomous indirect taxes;
- π_K = marginal indirect tax quota.

XI. Monetary phenomena

11.1. INTRODUCTION

Thus far we have used two monetary variables in the expenditure equations: the nominal interest rate and the liquidity ratio. The interest rate was a determinant of private consumption, gross fixed investment, labour demand and inventory formation. The model thus clearly includes the *IS* schedule of the well-known Hicksian diagram.[1] The liquidity ratio plays a part in explaining private consumption, gross fixed investment and the demand for labour. Although the influence of both the interest rate and the liquidity ratio was rather moderate, indicating that monetary policy will probably be not so important as some economists want us to believe, we consider monetary phenomena as endogenous.

Quite in line with the aggregative character of this study we have only analysed the two mentioned monetary variables. The result is a synthesis of Keynes' theory of liquidity preference and Fisher's ideas of the role of anticipated inflation on the one hand and money supply theory on the other.

11.2. DETERMINANTS OF THE INTEREST RATE

The basic Keynesian liquidity preference theory posits a relation between the quantity of money, the level of income and the interest rate. This is the so-called demand for money equation.[2] Following Keynes, demand for money consists of demand for transaction, precautionary and speculative

---

1. See HICKS (1937).
2. For a review of demand for money equations see MELTZER (1963).

purposes.[3] The demand for transactions money is dependent on the number and the value of transactions, usually measured by the level of income or total expenditures, as well as on the interest rate.[4]

The parameter describing the relationship with expenditures may be considered as being inversely proportional to the velocity of circulation. This parameter need not to be a constant as the velocity of circulation is determined by the number of transactions, the value per transaction, the organization of markets, payment habits, the organization of payments, etc, factors which are gradually changing over time, although not all in the same direction.

The demand for precautionary balances arises mainly from the endeavour to minimize the inconvenience of cash shortage at some future time. Therefore, this part of money demand is certainly dependent on the (expected) level of transactions and the (expected) rate of interest. But in addition typical cyclical circumstances may play a part. For instance, when people expect a slackening of economic development, accompanied by increasing unemployment the economic future is highly uncertain and they may feel the need for more cash.

Finally, the speculative demand arises from the fact that if the rate of interest is expected to rise an owner of cash may do better not to buy securities but to wait until these securities can be bought at a lower price. The higher the 'normal' level of interest relative to the actual interest rate the lower will be the loss of interest in not investing at once. The greater too will be the demand for money to hold as speculative balances, because the actual interest rate tends to the normal interest rate.

In a way this line of thought is partial because it is based on the assumption that the only possibility of investing funds is in securities. One might object that the long term interest rate is representative for all alternatives to idle balances but this presupposes, in its turn, a fixed structure of interest rates. That is to say interest rates are assumed to differ only according to factors like risk, time period of investment, degree of liquidity, costs of transaction etc.

Let us assume the situation that the actual long term interest rate equals the normal rate, but that short term rates differ more – or less – from long term rates than might normally be expected on the basis of differences in the above mentioned aspects. It seems to us that in this case too people's demand of balances for speculative purposes is influenced. For instance, in the case of a greater than normal difference between short term and long

3. See KEYNES (1936), Chapter 13.
4. See TOBIN'S (1956) article on the interest elasticity of demand for transactions money.

term rates this may lead to the expectation that long term rates will decline in the near future and consequently to a reduction in money holdings for speculative purposes.[5]

We have now arrived at the following set of, still static, demand for money equations:

(11.1) $$\frac{L_T}{p_v} = \tau_1 \frac{V}{p_v} - \tau_2 \left(r^r . \frac{V}{p_v}\right) + c_1 \frac{V}{p_v}$$

(11.2) $$\frac{L_P}{p_v} = \tau_3 \frac{V}{p_v} - \tau_4 \left(r^r . \frac{V}{p_v}\right) - \tau_5 \left(q_L . \frac{V}{p_v}\right) + c_2 \frac{V}{p_v}$$

(11.3) $$\frac{L_S}{p_v} = \tau_6 \left\{(r^{r*} - r^r)\frac{V}{p_v}\right\} + \tau_7 \left\{[r_s^r - (r^r - \tau_8)]\frac{V}{p_v}\right\} + c_3 \frac{V}{p_v}$$

(11.4) $$\frac{L_D}{p_v} = \frac{L_T}{p_v} + \frac{L_P}{p_v} + \frac{L_S}{p_v}$$

Equation (11.1) relates real demand for transactions balances $\left(\frac{L_T}{p_v}\right)$ positively to real expenditures $\left(\frac{V}{p_v}\right)$ and negatively to the real long term rate of interest (r^r). The coefficient of the latter being adjusted for the growth of expenditures in order to have the same intensity of reaction for each level of expenditures.

Real demand for precautionary purposes $\left(\frac{L_P}{p_v}\right)$ (equation 11.2) is related to real expenditures $\left(\frac{V}{p_v}\right)$, the real rate of interest (r^r) and the utilization rate of labour (q_L), with (q_L) acting as representative for the general conjunctural situation. In other words precautionary balances are a percentage of transaction balances fluctuating with the business cycle. Here again the variables are multiplied by the level of real expenditures.

Equation (11.3) explains real demand for speculative money $\left(\frac{L_S}{p_v}\right)$ from

---

5. An alternative formulation is $r^r - r_s^r = (r^{re} - r^r) + c$ where r^{re} is the expected long term interest rate. This is a formalization of MALKIEL's (1966) hypothesis on the term structure of interest rates.

the difference between the normal real rate of interest (r^{r*}) and the real long term rate (r^r) as well as from the difference between the real short term rate (r_s^r) and the real long term rate (r^r). The normal difference between long and short term rates is taken into account by including a constant term τ_8. Finally we have a definition equation in order to arrive at aggregate real demand for money. After substitution of equations (11.1), (11.2) and (11.3) into equation (11.4) and rewriting terms, real aggregate money demand is determined as follows:

(11.5) $$\frac{L_D}{p_v} = (\tau_1 + \tau_3) \frac{V}{p_v} - (\tau_2 + \tau_4)\left(r^r \frac{V}{p_v}\right) +$$

$$+ \tau_6 \left\{(r^{r*} - r^r)\frac{V}{p_v}\right\} + \tau_7 \left\{[r_s^r - (r^r - \tau_8)]\frac{V}{p_v}\right\} -$$

$$- \tau_5 \left(q_L \frac{V}{p_v}\right) + c_4 \frac{V}{p_v}$$

where $c_4 = c_1 + c_2 + c_3$.

This equation can be easily simplified by dividing all terms by real expenditures. We then obtain a relationship for the demand for money (liquidity) ratio:

(11.6) $$\frac{L_D}{V} = -(\tau_2 + \tau_4) r^r + \tau_6(r^{r*} - r^r) + \tau_7 [r_s^r - (r^r - \tau_8)]$$

$$- \tau_5 q_L + c_5$$

where $c_5 = c_4 + \tau_1 + \tau_3$.

It is to be noted that in the steady rate $r^{r*} = r^r$, $(r^r - \tau_8) = r_s^r$ and $q_L = 1$. Equation (11.6) then simplifies to

(11.7) $$\frac{L_D}{V} = -(\tau_2 + \tau_4) r^r + c_5 - \tau_5$$

When demand for money equals supply of money, assuming the total quantity of money to be predetermined, the parameters in equation (11.7) determine the slope of the other schedule of the Hicksian diagram, the LM curve. Reasoning in this way implies, however, that we have implicitly arrived at an alternative approach of the liquidity preference function as defining the interest rate at which investors are content to hold the predetermined money supply. We have adopted this approach as realistic in a quarterly analysis of monetary phenomena. Some other researchers who think along these lines are STEVERS (1963), VAN DEN BELD (1968) and FELDSTEIN and ECKSTEIN (1970). The interest rate equation thus obtained is:

$$(11.8) \quad r^r = -\frac{1}{\tau_9}\frac{L_D}{V} + \frac{\tau_6}{\tau_9}r^{r*} + \frac{\tau_7}{\tau_9}r_s^r - \frac{\tau_5}{\tau_9}q_L + \frac{c_5 + \tau_7\tau_8}{\tau_9}$$

where $\tau_9 = \tau_2 + \tau_4 + \tau_6 + \tau_7$.

The real rate of interest, either long term or short term, is not an observable variable. Following the lines developed by FISHER (1930) we define the real rate of interest as the nominal rate of interest minus the expected change in the price level:

$$(11.9) \quad r^r = r^n - \tau_{10} \Delta \ln p_v^*$$

where r^n is the nominal interest rate and $\Delta \ln p_v^*$ is the expected change in the general price level.[6] So, if expectations of the same rate of inflation persist, interest rates will also remain the same. They will rise or decline again if the inflation is expected to accelerate or decelerate. In other words, a stable rate of moderate inflation will generally be associated with a moderate interest rate, and rising rates of inflation with rising interest rates, all other things being unchanged.

It should be kept in mind that this reasoning is especially valid when τ_{10} is unity as Fisher originally proposed. This assumption, however, has not been justified by empirical evidence. Fisher himself, for example, suggested that the adjustment of money interest rates was only partial: 'Men are unable or unwilling to adjust at all accurately and promptly the money interest rates to changed price levels.'[7] Furthermore the results of SARGENT (1969), FELDSTEIN and ECKSTEIN (1970) and FELDSTEIN (1970) support this opinion. In addition, MUNDELL (1963) argued that under certain theoretical assumptions the money rate of interest will rise by less than the expected rate of inflation.

---

6. This is not exactly Fisher's relationship. His formulation was $r^r = r^n - \tau_{10} \Delta \ln p_v^* + r^n \Delta \ln p_v^*$, where he originally assumed that $\tau_{10} = 1$. We have omitted the last term in our specification as is usual in the explanation of real interest rates. See SARGENT (1969), FELDSTEIN and ECKSTEIN (1970), MUNDELL (1963) and FELDSTEIN (1970).

7. FISHER (1930), p. 415.

For the time being we rewrite equation (11.8) in nominal terms as

$$(11.10) \quad r^n = -\frac{1}{\tau_9}\frac{L_D}{V} + \frac{\tau_6}{\tau_9}(r^n - \tau_{10} \Delta \ln p_v^*)^* +$$

$$+ \frac{\tau_7}{\tau_9} r_s^n + \left(\tau_{10} - \frac{\tau_7 \tau_{11}}{\tau_9}\right) \Delta \ln p_v^* -$$

$$- \frac{\tau_5}{\tau_9} q_L + \frac{c_5 + \tau_7 \tau_8}{\tau_9}$$

where we have used

$$(11.11) \quad r_s^r = r_s^n - \tau_{11} \Delta \ln p_v^*.$$

It can be seen that the coefficient of anticipated inflation for the real short term interest rate (τ_{11}) is assumed to be different from the analogous coefficient in the formulation for the real long term interest rate (equation 11.9) because there is no *a priori* reason why they should be identical.[8]

This static interest rate equation finally needs some sort of dynamization. We shall appeal again to the concept of permanentness of a variable: on the whole people are more likely to consider and react to normal or permanent components of variables rather than to consider transitory components as well. Unknown rational distributed lag functions are therefore added to the liquidity ratio variable, the expected nominal rate of interest and the expected change in the price level. The short term interest rate is assumed to react with no lag at all due to its role in a speculative context. So we have

$$(11.12) \quad r^n = -\frac{1}{\tau_9}\frac{G(L)_1}{H(L)_1}\frac{L_D}{V} + \frac{\tau_6}{\tau_9}\frac{G(L)_2}{H(L)_2}\left(r^n - \tau_{10}\frac{G(L)_3}{H(L)_3}\Delta \ln p_v\right) + \frac{\tau_7}{\tau_9} r_s^n +$$

$$+ \left(\tau_{10} - \frac{\tau_7 \tau_{11}}{\tau_9}\right)\frac{G(L)_3}{H(L)_3} \Delta \ln p_v - \frac{\tau_5}{\tau_9}\frac{G(L)_4}{H(L)_4} q_L + c_6$$

where $c_6 = (c_5 + \tau_7 \tau_8)/\tau_9$.

Before discussing the estimating results we should consider the impact of phenomena which may be summarized under the term scale factors: the influence of changes in payment habits and the payment process as well as changes that are due to vertical integration or desintegration of enterprises

---

8. Results of SARGENT (1969) p. 136, suggest τ_{11} to be greater than τ_{10}.

which influence the development of the liquidity ratio or time.[9] We have assumed, following BAKHOVEN (1971), that the effect of these factors can be approximated by a hyperbolic trend.

11.3. EMPIRICAL RESULTS

Basic specification (11.12) has in first instance been estimated with an infinite lag on the liquidity ratio corrected for its decreasing trend.[10] Therefore $G(L)_1 = 1 - \lambda$ and $H(L)_1 = 1 - \lambda L$. In addition we have assumed $G(L)_2$, $G(L)_3$, $G(L)_4$ to be finite lag distributions and $H(L)_{2,3,4} = 1$. A specific problem is the value of τ_{10}, which can be estimated in different ways. We have chosen the following procedure.[11] In the second term of equation (11.12) we have assumed τ_{10} to be unity and have added the unknown difference $\frac{\tau_6}{\tau_9}(1 - \tau_{10}) \frac{G(L)_3}{H(L)_3} \Delta \ln p_v$ to the existing price variable term. For the sake of simplicity we have neglected the additional lag $\frac{G(L)_2}{H(L)_2}$. In this way we obtain the following equation for estimating.

$$(11.13) \quad r^n - \lambda r^n_{-1} = \tau_{12}(1 - \lambda)\frac{L_q}{V} + \frac{\tau_6}{\tau_9} \sum_{j=0}^{k} \gamma_j \left[\left(r^n_{t-j} - \sum_{i=0}^{m} \gamma_i \Delta \ln p_{v_{t-i-j}} \right) \right.$$

$$\left. - \lambda \left(r^n_{t-j-1} - \sum_{i=1}^{m+1} \gamma_{i-1} \Delta \ln p_{v_{t-i-j}} \right) \right] + \frac{\tau_7}{\tau_9} [r^n_s - \lambda r^n_{s-1}] +$$

$$+ \tau_{13} \left[\sum_{i=0}^{m} \gamma_i \Delta \ln p_{v_{t-i}} - \lambda \sum_{i=1}^{m+1} \gamma_{i-1} \Delta \ln p_{v_{t-i}} \right] -$$

$$- \frac{\tau_5}{\tau_9} \left[\sum_{i=0}^{s} \gamma_i q_{L_{t-i}} - \lambda \sum_{i=1}^{s+1} \gamma_{i-1} q_{L_{t-i}} \right] + (1 - \lambda) c_6$$

where τ_{12} is a new parameter for the liquidity ratio adjusted for its decreasing trend $\left(\frac{L_q}{V}\right)$ and $\tau_{13} = (\tau_{10}\tau_9 + \tau_6 - \tau_{10}\tau_6 - \tau_7\tau_{11})/\tau_9$.

We have experimented with several lag distributions for the expected rate of inflation. In contrast with CAGAN (1956), FELDSTEIN (1970), SARGENT (1969),

9. See also FRIEDMAN (1970).
10. The symbol L_D is therefore replaced by L_q.
11. For an alternative estimating procedure and a discussion of related statistical problems, see FELDSTEIN (1970).

FELDSTEIN and ECKSTEIN (1970), we have found that a relative short lag structure is valid. An average of the rate of change in the preceding four quarters seems to determine the expected inflation rate in the Netherlands. Although the theoretical analysis takes into account the change in the general price level (p_v), we have also used as an explanatory variable the change in the consumer price level, because it is an index actually known to the subjects concerned. This may of course somewhat change the empirical value of the coefficients. In addition, the total amount of liquidities is 'deflated' by the value of expenditures as defined by definition equation (48) of the complete model which seems a more appropriate variable than total expenditures as such.[12] Finally, we represented short term interest rates by the official discount rate. The best equation according to the rules of selection mentioned in chapter II is

$$(11.14) \quad r = .8\, r_{-1} - 7.565\, \frac{L_q}{V} +$$
$$ (-) \quad\quad (19.2\%)$$

$$+ .525 \sum_{-1}^{-10} \gamma_2 \left[\left(r - \sum_{0}^{-3} \gamma_7\, 100\, \Delta \ln p_c \right) - \right.$$
$$(20.4\%)$$
$$\left. - .8 \left(r_{-1} - \sum_{-1}^{-4} \gamma_7\, 100\, \Delta \ln p_c \right) \right] +$$

$$+ .090 \left[\sum_{0}^{-3} \gamma_7\, 100\, \Delta \ln p_c - .8 \sum_{-1}^{-4} \gamma_7\, 100\, \Delta \ln p_c \right] +$$
$$(72.9\%)$$

$$+ .267\, [r_k - .8\, r_{k-1}] + 5.590 \left[\frac{q_{L-2}}{\sum_{-3}^{-6} \gamma_7\, q_L} - .8\, \frac{q_{L-3}}{\sum_{-4}^{-7} \gamma_7\, q_L} \right]$$
$$ (34.7\%) \phantom{[r_k - .8\, r_{k-1}] +} (158.9\%)$$

$$+ .285$$
$$(54.0\%)$$

$$\bar{R}^2 = .917$$
$$NR = 1.93$$

where r = long term interest rate;

$\frac{L_q}{V}$ = liquidity ratio, after correction for its decreasing trend;

p_c = price level of consumption, 1963 = 100;
r_k = discount rate;

12. See appendix A, p. 238.

q_L = utilization rate of labour;
γ_2 = .21, .17, .15, .12, .10, .08, .06, .05, .04, .02;
γ_7 = .25, .25, .25, .25.

Figure 11.1. Actual and computed long term interest rate according to equation (11.14)

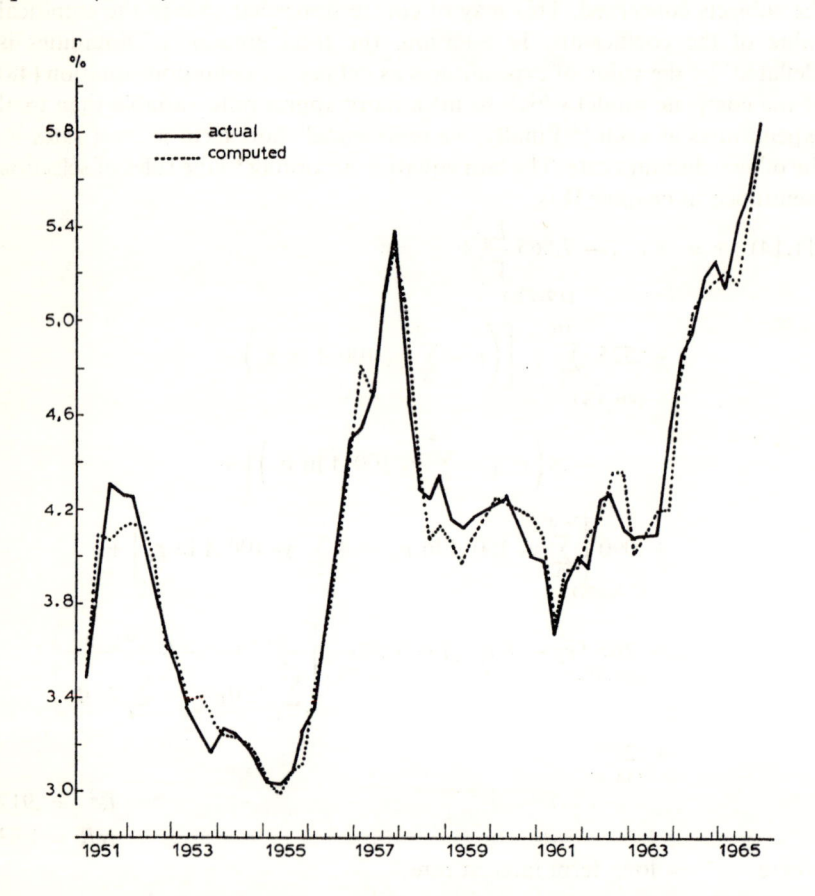

The rate of interest appears to be influenced by the liquidity ratio with a rather long lag. (See table 11.1). In general, consumer prices performed better than the price level of expenditures. Furthermore the small coefficient of the expected change in the consumer price level indicates that the influence of the expected inflation rate τ_{10} is smaller than unity in the original formulation of the real interest rate equation. This indicates rather substantial money illusion in interest rate determination. The coefficient of the discount rate is furthermore smaller than the coefficient of the real rate of interest variable and this was to be expected. Finally, we could only find the right sign for the conjunctural variable when it was formulated as the two quarters lagged utilization rate of labour in deviation from its four quarter average. The standard error of the coefficient is nevertheless very high.

Table 11.1. Average lags of variables explaining the long term interest rate (equation 11.14)[a]

Variable	Number of quarters						
	0	1	2	3	4	5	6
1. Liquidity ratio						×	
2. Real interest rate					×	×	
3. Change in price level of consumption			×	×			
4. Discount rate	×						
5. Utilization rate of labour					×		

a. A cross in two columns indicates an average lag between the respective quarters.

11.4. SUPPLY OF MONEY THEORY

The analysis of money supply is based upon a methodology used by VAN DEN BELD (1968) in his model of cyclical growth.[13] He distinguishes between the origin of money supply *viz.* creation of liquidities by the banking system, by the balance of payments and by the government. Rather than estimating three money supply equations separately, however, we maintain the aggregative character of the analysis and estimate one money supply relationship.[14] The underlying line of thought is the following.

We start from the assumption that the banking system is prepared to meet demand for money except when monetary authorities try to prevent this or their own liquidity position imposes restrictions on the expansion of supply. So, supply of liquidities by banks is assumed to be perfectly elastic at the going interest rate and inelastic in the case of restrictions and/or a relatively narrow liquidity position of banks. When demand is represented

13. See also VAN DEN BELD (1964).
14. An additional reason is the lack of sufficient appropriate quarterly money supply data for the whole observation period.

161

by the set of variables already used in the previous section, we postulate the following money supply function of the banking system. By analogy it is written in real terms:

$$(11.15) \quad \frac{M_B^s}{p_v} = \omega_1 \frac{V}{p_v} - \omega_2 \left(r^r \frac{V}{p_v}\right) + \omega_3 \left\{(r^{r*} - r^r) \frac{V}{p_v}\right\} +$$

$$+ \omega_4 \left\{[r_s^r - (r^r - \omega_5)] \frac{V}{p_v}\right\} - \omega_6 \left(q_L \frac{V}{p_v}\right) - \omega_7 \left(C_{rr} \frac{V}{p_v}\right) +$$

$$+ \omega_8 \left(L_B \frac{V}{p_v}\right) + c_1 \frac{V}{p_v}$$

where, apart from symbols already used in this chapter, M_B^s is money supply by the banking system, C_{rr} stands for credit restrictions by the central bank and L_B is liquidity position of banks.

The second origin of liquidities is the balance of payments. Creation of liquidities by the balance of payments (ΔM_F^s) is here by definition equal to the sum of the balance on current account (E_L) and capital account (E_K). In real terms therefore:

$$(11.16) \quad \frac{\Delta M_F^s}{p_v} = \frac{E_L + E_K}{p_v}$$

Creation of liquidities by the government (ΔM_G^s) is assumed to be endogenous. This is not the exact state of affairs and the implication is that the autonomous part of government liquidity creation brings about residuals in the ultimate money supply equation.[15] The creation of liquidities by the government is, firstly, assumed to neutralize to a certain extent liquidity creation from abroad. Secondly, it is assumed to be lower when the rate of change of the price level is high as compared to its normal or average rate of change and the other way around. Thirdly, it will be higher when unemployment is high in order to stimulate economic activity. Finally, all these reactions will be modified when the initial liquidity position of the public deviates from its normal or average liquidity position. Generally speaking, it would be unreasonable to expect that the government is prepared to neutralize completely a relative liquidity narrowing arising from a shortage of the balance of payments when the economy is near its full utilization of produc-

---

15. Future research should also include the balance of government receipts and expenditures as a determinant of government liquidity creation.

tion factors and existing liquidity positions are tight. In doing so the government would prevent the endogenous monetary mechanism to work.

In summary we postulate the following relationship for government liquidity creation in real terms:

$$(11.17) \quad \frac{\Delta M_G^s}{p_v} = -\omega_9 \left(\frac{E_L+E_K}{p_v}\right) - \omega_{10}\left(q_L \cdot \frac{V}{p_v}\right) -$$

$$- \omega_{11}[\Delta \ln p_v^* - \overline{\Delta \ln p_v}]\frac{V}{p_v} - \omega_{12}\left[\left(\frac{L_q}{V}\right)_{-1} - \left(\overline{\frac{L_q}{V}}\right)\right] +$$

$$+ c_2 \frac{V}{p_v}$$

where a bar over a variable indicates an average value. Substitution of equations (11.15), (11.16) and (11.17) in the definition

$$(11.18) \quad M^s = M_B^s + \Delta M_F^s + \Delta M_G^s + \sum_{-1}^{-\infty} \Delta M_F^s + \sum_{-1}^{-\infty} \Delta M_G^s$$

and dividing by real expenditures $\left(\frac{V}{p_v}\right)$, yields the aggregate real money supply equation:

$$(11.19) \quad \frac{M^s}{V} = \omega_1 - \omega_2 r^r + \omega_3(r^{r*} - r^r) + \omega_4[r_s^r - (r^r - \omega_5)] -$$

$$- \omega_6 q_L - \omega_7 C_{rr} + \frac{\sum_{-1}^{-\infty} \Delta M_F^s + \sum_{-1}^{-\infty} \Delta M_G^s}{V} +$$

$$+ \omega_8 L_B - \omega_{10} q_L - \omega_{11}[\Delta \ln p_v^* - \overline{\Delta \ln p_v}] -$$

$$- \omega_{12}\left(\frac{p_v}{V}\right)\left[\left(\frac{L_q}{V}\right)_{-1} - \left(\overline{\frac{L_q}{V}}\right)\right] + (1-\omega_9)\frac{E_L+E_K}{V} + c_3$$

where $c_3 = c_1 + c_2$.

The term following ω_{12} is so small that it can be neglected in the remaining analysis.

JONGMAN (1960) has shown that in the Netherlands the free liquidities with the banking system are negatively correlated with short term interest rates, especially the discount rate.[16] When this relationship is substituted in equation (11.19), real interest rate variables are written analogous to the previous section (equations 11.9 and 11.11) and when the average price increase is replaced by a constant term c_5, we obtain after rearranging terms:

$$(11.20) \quad \frac{M^s}{V} = -(\omega_2 + \omega_3 + \omega_4)(r^n - \Delta \ln p_v^*) + \omega_3 (r^n - \Delta \ln p_v^*)^* +$$

$$+ (\omega_4 - \omega_8 \omega_{13}) r_s^n - (\omega_6 + \omega_{10}) q_L + (1 - \omega_9) \frac{E_L + E_K}{V} -$$

$$- \omega_7 C_{rr} + \frac{\sum_{-1}^{-\infty} \Delta M_F^s + \sum_{-1}^{-\infty} \Delta M_G^s}{V} + \omega_{14} \Delta \ln p_v^* + c_6$$

where $\omega_{14} = \{-\omega_{11} - (\omega_2 + \omega_4)(1 - \tau_{10}) - \tau_{11}\omega_4\}$ and $c_6 = \omega_1 + \omega_4 \omega_5 + \omega_8 \omega_4 + \omega_{11} c_5 + c_3$

Figure 11.2 Cumulated liquidity creation by the government and via the balance of payments as per cent of expenditures (1951–1969)

16. Therefore we have assumed in the following $L_B = -\omega_{13} r_s^n + c_4$.

This condensed money supply equation allows direct estimation provided the variable $\dfrac{\sum\limits_{-1}^{-\infty} \Delta M_F^s + \sum\limits_{-1}^{-\infty} \Delta M_G^s}{V}$ is known. This term is not observable. However, its recent development over time can be illustrated by considering the cumulated values of ΔM_F^s and ΔM_G^s over a more restricted period. The result is here presented for the years 1951–1969.

It is not our task to analyse and explain the decreasing trend in the considered time series, but we accept this fact and use it for the analysis of money supply. What we do is replacing the cumulated liquidity creation via the balance of payments and the government by a hyperbolic trend and the utilization rate of labour as proxy for cyclical deviations from this trend.

Finally, as far as money supply by banks is concerned, we must add the already mentioned decreasing trend arising from scale factors in money demand. It will be clear that, *ex post*, the two mentioned trend factors on the aggregate supply side must be equal to the trend influence on the aggregate demand side. Consequently we must have the following *ex post* equilibrium condition

$$(11.21) \quad \frac{L_q}{V} = \frac{M^s}{V} - \frac{\omega_{15}}{t+\omega_{16}}$$

where $\dfrac{L_q}{V}$ is the liquidity ratio after correction for its decreasing trend and where the hyperbolic trend represents the same phenomenon in aggregate money supply.

11.5. EMPIRICAL RESULTS

Thus far we only had a static specification of the money supply relationship. A dynamic version can be obtained by postulating appropriate lag distributions. We suppose the government's monetary reaction on a deficit or surplus on the balance of payments to be rather gradual and assume an infinite lag structure. Lag distributions for other variables are assumed to be finite. When, as far as interest rate variables are concerned, lag distributions similar to the interest rate equation of the previous section are used, then the following money supply equation must be estimated.

$$(11.22) \quad \frac{L_q}{V} - \lambda \left(\frac{L_q}{V}\right)_{-1} = (1 - \omega_9)(1 - \lambda) \frac{E_L + E_K}{V} -$$

$$- (\omega_2 + \omega_3 + \omega_4) \left[\left(r^n - \sum_{i=0}^{m} \gamma_i \Delta \ln p_{v-i} \right) - \right.$$

$$\left. - \lambda \left(r^n_{-1} - \sum_{i=1}^{m+1} \gamma_{i-1} \Delta \ln p_{v-i} \right) \right] +$$

$$+ \omega_3 \left[\sum_{j=0}^{p} \gamma_j \left(r^n_{-j} - \sum_{i=0}^{m} \gamma_i \Delta \ln p_{v-i-j} \right) - \right.$$

$$\left. - \lambda \sum_{j=1}^{p+1} \gamma_{j-1} \left(r^n_{-j} - \sum_{i=0}^{m} \gamma_i \Delta \ln p_{v-i-j} \right) \right] +$$

$$+ (\omega_4 - \omega_8 \omega_{13}) [r^n_s - \lambda r^n_{s-1}] -$$

$$- (\omega_6 + \omega_{10}) \left[\sum_{i=0}^{k} \gamma_i q_L - \lambda \sum_{i=1}^{k+1} \gamma_{i-1} q_L \right] -$$

$$- \omega_7 \left[\sum_{i=0}^{r} \gamma_i C_{rr} - \lambda \sum_{i=1}^{r+1} \gamma_{i-1} C_{rr} \right] +$$

$$+ \omega_{14} \left[\sum_{i=0}^{s} \gamma_i \Delta \ln p_v - \lambda \sum_{i=1}^{s+1} \gamma_{i-1} \Delta \ln p_v \right] +$$

$$+ (1 - \lambda) c_6$$

Estimation of this specification results in a model equation which gives an acceptable description of reality. It is not possible to determine a clear influence of the quantitative credit restrictions imposed by the central bank. It must be kept in mind, furthermore, that the theoretical specification does not give a judgement about the sign of the rate of price change variable and the short term interest rate. The greater part of our results shows a negative sign for the price variable indicating the domination of the parameter ω_{11}, which represents the negative influence of inflationary financing by the government when prices are expected to rise and *vice versa*. On the contrary, the sign of the short term interest variable is mostly found to be positive, indicating that the coefficient ω_4 is predominant. Finally, the specification of the balance of payments variable is not satisfactory since this variable must have a greater unlagged effect on the liquidity ratio.

$$(11.23) \quad \frac{L_q}{V} = .3 \left(\frac{L_q}{V}\right)_{-1} + .364 \sum_{0}^{-2} \gamma_4 \frac{E_L + E_K}{V} -$$
$$\underset{(-)}{} \qquad \underset{(21.6\%)}{}$$

$$- .016 \left[\left(r_{-1} - \sum_{-1}^{-4} \gamma_7 \, 100 \, \Delta \ln p_c \right) - \right.$$
$$\underset{(35.8\%)}{}$$
$$\left. - .3 \left(r_{-2} - \sum_{-2}^{-5} \gamma_7 \, \Delta \, 100 \ln p_c \right) \right] +$$

$$+ .014 \sum_{-1}^{-10} \gamma_2 \left[\left(r - \sum_{0}^{-3} \gamma_7 \, 100 \, \Delta \ln p_c \right) - \right.$$
$$\underset{(28.6\%)}{}$$
$$\left. - .3 \left(r_{-1} - \sum_{-1}^{-4} \gamma_7 \, 100 \, \Delta \ln p_c \right) \right] +$$

$$+ .008 \, [r_{k-1} - .3 \, r_{k-2}] -$$
$$\underset{(68.1\%)}{}$$

$$- .007 \left[\sum_{-1}^{-8} \gamma_{22} \, C_{rr} - .3 \sum_{-2}^{-9} \gamma_{22} \, C_{rr} \right] -$$
$$\underset{(163.5\%)}{}$$

$$- .152 \left[\sum_{0}^{-1} \gamma_6 \, q_L - .3 \sum_{-1}^{-2} \gamma_6 \, q_L \right] - .015 \left[\sum_{-1}^{-4} \gamma_7 \, 100 \, \Delta \ln p_c - \right.$$
$$\underset{(133.0\%)}{}$$
$$\left. - .3 \sum_{-2}^{-5} \gamma_7 \, 100 \, \Delta \ln p_c \right] + .267$$
$$\underset{(51.4\%)}{}$$

$$\bar{R}^2 = .856$$
$$NR = 2.08$$

where $\dfrac{L_q}{V}$ = liquidity ratio, after correction for its decreasing trend;
E_L = balance of payments on current account;
E_K = balance of payments on capital account;
V = total expenditures, less inventory formation, government wages, exports of services and factor incomes received from abroad, in current prices;
r = long term interest rate;
p_c = price level of consumption, 1963 = 100;
r_k = discount rate;
C_{rr} = quantitative credit restrictions by the central bank during 1962:1–1965:4;

q_L = utilization rate of labour;
γ_2 = .21, .17, .15, .12, .10, .08, .06, .05, .04, .02;
γ_4 = .33, .34, .33;
γ_6 = .50, .50;
γ_7 = .25, .25, .25, .25;
γ_{22} = .40, .24, .15, .09, .06, .03, .02, .01.

Figure 11.3. Actual and computed liquidity ratio after correction for its decreasing trend according to equation (11.23)

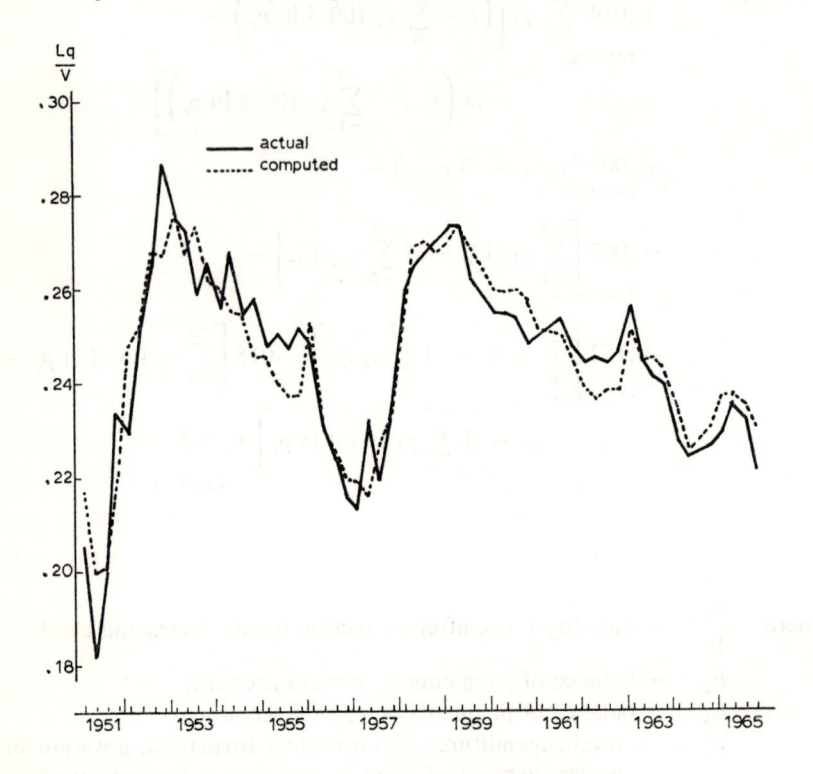

As concerns average lags (table 11.2) relatively short lags could be determined for the creation of liquidities via the balance of payments, the real interest rate and the short term interest rate. The impact of quantative credit restrictions seems to take place within a relatively short period of time, 2–3 quarters, as well.

Table 11.2. Average lags of variables explaining the liquidity ratio (equation 11.23)[a]

Variable	Number of quarters
	0 1 2 3 4 5 6
1. Balance of payments on current and capital account	× ×
2. Real interest rate (+sign)	× ×
3. Real interest rate (−sign)	×
4. Discount rate	×
5. Credit restrictions	× ×
6. Utilization rate of labour	× ×
7. Change in the price level of consumption	× ×

a. A mark in two columns indicates an average lag between the respective quarters.

XII. The complete model

12.1. INTRODUCTION

Having considered all the individual equations of the model it seems useful to obtain a full understanding of the complete set of equations and to consider its economic content. For that purpose we summarize the reaction equations estimated in the previous chapters and add a number of definition equations so as to arrive at the complete model. For reasons of simplification we have dropped all the lags and the dummy variables in the relationships. Thus we arrive at a static version of the complete system. The full dynamic version is given in appendix A. Compared with this appendix we have combined a number of equations and re-arranged their sequence somewhat in order to promote the understanding of how the working of the economy is represented by the model[1]. We have furthermore reformulated the consumption function in volume terms and we have neglected the aspect of overlapping quarterly changes. A bar over a variable indicates an average value of a variable.[2] Exogenous variables are underlined. The list of symbols can be found in appendix B.

---

[1]. As a consequence the static and reduced version has 46 equations whereas the dynamic one consists of 68 equations.
[2]. For the sake of simplicity separate definition equations for average values are omitted.

12.2. STATIC AND REDUCED VERSION OF THE MODEL

I. *Labour market and capacity utilization*

1. $\ln L = .800 \ln y + .267 (\ln p_k - \ln w) + .712 q_L +$
$+ .040 \ln \dfrac{L_q}{V} + .061 \{\ln(Z - T_z) - \ln p_{i-sa}\} -$
$- .742 \ln \underline{h_c} - .215 \ln i_{-sa} + 1.325$

2. $\Delta \ln P_S = .917 \Delta \ln \underline{P_{ST}} + .071 \{(\Delta \ln w - \Delta \ln p_c) -$
$- \overline{(\Delta \ln w - \Delta \ln p_c)}\} + .208 \Delta q_L + .162 \Delta^2 q_L -$
$- .002$

3. $q_L = \dfrac{L}{P_S - \underline{L_g} - \underline{L_s} - .01} + .006$

4. $U = P_S - L - \underline{L_g} - \underline{L_s}$

II. *Domestic expenditures*

5. $\ln i_{-sa} = .704 \Delta \ln y - .730 (\Delta \ln p_k - \Delta \ln w) + 6.384 q_L +$
$+ 2.103 \Delta q_L + .613 \dfrac{L_q}{V} + .245 \{\ln(Z - T_z) -$
$- \ln p_{i-sa}\} + .012 \underline{t} - .722 \Delta \ln \underline{h_c} + .026 \underline{T_c} - 4.665$

6. $\ln c = .837 \varphi \ln W_D + .308 (1 - \varphi) \ln Z_D + .668 \Delta \ln p_c -$
$- 1.000 \ln p_c - .003 r + .184 \dfrac{L_q}{V} +$
$+ 1.238 \Delta q_L + \ln 100 + .932$

7. $\Delta n = .372 \Delta v + .754 (n_d - n) + .006 \Delta \underline{p_{mg-sa}} -$
$- .312 \Delta r + .284$

8. $n = n_{-1} + .25\,\Delta n$

9. $n_d = (.390 - .127\,t/100)\,v$

10. $x = \dfrac{X}{p_x}\,100$

11. $v = c + i_{-sa} + b_{f-sa} + \underline{b_{g\,aut}} + x$

12. $V = (c\,p_c) + (i_{-sa}\,p_{i-sa}) + (b_{f-sa}\,p_{bf-sa}) + \underline{B_{g\,aut}} + (x\,p_x)$

13. $\ln v_{mg} = .420 \ln c + .170 \ln i_{-sa} + .080 \ln x + .300 \ln b_{f-sa} +$
                   $+ .030 \ln b_{s-t}$

14.[3] $\ln v_{ms} = [.430] \ln c + .045 \ln i_{-sa} + .065 \ln x +$
                   $+ .160 \ln b_{f-sa} + [.300] \ln b_{s-t}$

III. *Balance of payments on current account*

15. $\ln b_{f-sa} = .930 \ln \underline{m_w} - 2.045(\ln \underline{p_{bf-sa}} - \ln \underline{p_{bgw}}) -$
                   $- .554 \ln q_L - 1.555$

16. $\ln b_{s-t} = 1.126 \ln \underline{y_w} - .568(\ln \underline{p_{bs-t}} - \ln \underline{p_{bsw}}) -$
                   $- 1.628\,\Delta \ln q_L - .024 \ln \underline{U_G} - 3.444$

17. $\ln m_{g-sa} = 1.009 \ln v_{mg} + .365\,\Delta \ln v_{mg} + .031\,\Delta n -$
                   $- .700(\ln \underline{p_{mg-sa}} - \ln p_{vmg}) + 1.684\,q_L +$
                   $+ .850\,\Delta \ln p_v - 1.559$

18. $\ln m_s = .973 \ln v_{ms} + .421\,\Delta \ln v_{ms} - .954(\Delta \ln \underline{p_{ms}} -$
                   $- \Delta \ln p_{vms}) + 2.155\,\Delta q_L - 1.582$

3. A coefficient between square brackets does not have a constant value for the sample and extrapolation periods. See appendix F.

19. $\quad E_L \quad = (b_{f-sa}\, p_{bf-sa}) + \underline{B_{g\,aut}} + (b_{s-t}\, p_{bs-t}) + \underline{B_{s\,aut}} +$
$\qquad\qquad\quad + \underline{B_p} - (m_{g-sa}\, \underline{p_{mg-sa}}) - \underline{M_{sa}} - (m_s\, \underline{p_{ms}}) - \underline{M_p} + \underline{D_s}$

IV. Wages and prices

20a. $\quad \Delta \ln w \quad = .785\, \Delta \ln p_c + .484(\Delta \ln y - \Delta \ln L) +$
$\qquad\qquad\qquad + 1.441(\Delta \ln \underline{h_w} - \Delta \ln \underline{h_c}) + 1.000\, \underline{SPE} +$
$\qquad\qquad\qquad + .541\, \underline{TSPW} + .016$

20b. $\quad \Delta \ln w \quad = .924\, \Delta \ln p_c + .636(\Delta \ln y - \Delta \ln L) +$
$\qquad\qquad\qquad + 1.000\, \underline{SPE} + .149\, \underline{TSPW} + .035$

20c. $\quad \Delta \ln w \quad = .900\, \Delta \ln p_c + .667(\Delta \ln y - \Delta \ln L) +$
$\qquad\qquad\qquad + 2.854 \ln q_L + 1.000\, \underline{SPE} + .773\, \underline{TSPW} + .042$

20d. $\quad \Delta \ln w \quad = 1.239\, \Delta \ln p_c + .378(\Delta \ln y - \Delta \ln L) +$
$\qquad\qquad\qquad + .590 \ln q_L + 1.000\, \underline{SPE} + .153\, \underline{TSPW} + .030$

21. $\quad \Delta \ln p_{c\,end} = .239\, \Delta \ln w + .014\, \Delta \ln p_k + .194\, \Delta \ln \underline{p_{mg-sa}} -$
$\qquad\qquad\qquad - .096(\Delta \ln y - \Delta \ln L) + .238\, \Delta \ln q_L +$
$\qquad\qquad\qquad + .209 \ln q_L + .092(\Delta \ln c - \Delta \ln v) +$
$\qquad\qquad\qquad + .020(\Delta n_d - \Delta n) + .015$

22. $\quad \Delta \ln p_{i-sa} = .480\, \Delta \ln w + .031\, \Delta \ln p_k + .480\, \Delta \ln \underline{p_{mg-sa}} -$
$\qquad\qquad\qquad - .193(\Delta \ln y - \Delta \ln L) + .972\, \Delta \ln q_L +$
$\qquad\qquad\qquad + .065(\Delta \ln i_{-sa} - \Delta \ln v) - .003$

23. $\quad \Delta \ln p_x \quad = .248\, \Delta \ln w + .787\, \Delta \ln \underline{p_{mg-sa}} -$
$\qquad\qquad\qquad - .099(\Delta \ln y - \Delta \ln L) + .968\, \Delta \ln q_L +$
$\qquad\qquad\qquad + .721 \ln q_L + .093(\Delta \ln x - \Delta \ln v) + .027$

24. $\Delta \ln p_{bf-sa} = .202 \Delta \ln w + .100 \Delta \ln p_k + .472 \Delta \ln \underline{p_{mg-sa}} -$
$- .080(\Delta \ln y - \Delta \ln L) + 1.524 \Delta \ln q_L +$
$+ 1.179 \ln q_L + .449(\Delta \ln b_{f-sa} - \Delta \ln v) +$
$+ .260 \Delta \ln p_{bgw} + .210 \Delta^2 \ln \underline{m_w} - .020$

25. $\Delta \ln p_{bs-t} = .300 \Delta \ln p_{bf-sa} + .300 \Delta \ln p_c + .400 \Delta \ln \underline{p_f}$

26. $\ln p_c = \ln \underline{p_{c\,end}} + \ln \underline{p_{c\,aut}} - \ln 100$

27. $\ln p_k = \ln p_{i-sa} + \ln r - \ln \{1 - (1 + .01\,r)^{-20}\} +$
$+ \ln \underline{I_a} - \ln 7.488 - \ln 100$

28. $\ln p_{vmg} = .420 \ln p_{c\,end} + .170 \ln p_{i-sa} + .080 \ln p_x +$
$+ .300 \ln p_{bf-sa} + .030 \ln p_{bs-t}$

29.[4] $\ln p_{vms} = [.430] \ln p_{c\,end} + .045 \ln p_{i-sa} + .065 \ln p_x +$
$+ .160 \ln p_{bf-sa} + [.300] \ln p_{bs-t}$

30. $p_v = \dfrac{V}{v} 100$

31. $p_y = \dfrac{Y}{y} 100$

32. $p_{gnp} = \dfrac{Y_{gnp}}{y_{gnp}} 100$

V. Taxes

33.[4] $\Delta T_W = [\pi_W] \Delta W_T + \Delta \underline{T_{W\,aut}}$

34.[4] $\Delta T_Z = [\pi_Z] \Delta Z + \Delta \underline{T_{Z\,aut}}$

35[4]. $\Delta T_K = [\pi_K] \Delta(V - \underline{CHR}) + \Delta \underline{T_{K\,aut}}$

[4]. A coefficient between square brackets does not have a constant value for the sample period and the extrapolation periods. See appendix F.

VI. Monetary phenomena

36. $\quad r \quad = -37.825 \dfrac{L_q}{V} + .525\overline{(r - 100 \, \Delta \ln p_c)} +$

$\quad\quad\quad\quad\quad + .090(100 \, \Delta \ln p_c) + .267 \, \underline{r_k} + 5.590 \dfrac{q_L}{\bar{q}_L} + 1.425$

37. $\quad \dfrac{L_q}{V} \quad = .520 \dfrac{E_L + \underline{E_K}}{V} - .016(r - 100 \, \Delta \ln p_c) +$

$\quad\quad\quad\quad\quad + .014\overline{(r - 100 \, \Delta \ln p_c)} + .008 \, \underline{r_k} -$

$\quad\quad\quad\quad\quad - .105(100 \, \Delta \ln p_c) - .007 \, \underline{C_{rr}} - .152 \, q_L + .381$

VII. Incomes

38. $\quad y \quad = v + \underline{i_{sa}} + \Delta n + b_{s-t} + \underline{b_{s\,aut}} - m_{g-sa} - \underline{m_{sa}} - m_s - \underline{r_g}$

39. $\quad y_{gnp} \quad = y + \underline{w_g} + \underline{r_g} + \underline{c_{gl}} + \underline{f_g} + \underline{b_p} - m_p$

40. $\quad Y \quad = V + \underline{I_{sa}} + \left(\Delta n \, \dfrac{p_{\Delta n}}{100}\right) + (b_{s-t} \, p_{bs-t}) + \underline{B_{s\,aut}} -$

$\quad\quad\quad\quad\quad - (m_{g-sa} \, \underline{p_{mg-sa}}) - \underline{M_{sa}} - (m_s \, \underline{p_{ms}}) - \underline{R_g}$

41. $\quad Y_{gnp} \quad = Y + (\underline{w_g} \, \underline{L_g}) + \underline{R_g} + \underline{C_{gl}} + \underline{F_g} + \underline{B_p} - M_p$

42^{a}. $\quad W_T \quad = \{(w + \underline{w_{aut}}) L\} / 14.0618 + (\underline{w_g} \, \underline{L_g})$

43^{a}. $\quad Z \quad = Y - \{(w + \underline{w_{aut}}) L\} / 14.0618 - \underline{F} - T_K + \underline{S}$

44. $\quad W_D \quad = W_T - T_W - \underline{O_W}$

45. $\quad Z_D \quad = Z - T_Z - \underline{O_Z}$

46. $\quad \varphi \quad = \dfrac{W_D}{W_D + .25 \, Z_D}$

a. See note on p. 239

12.3. WORKING OF THE MODEL

The working of the model can be easily understood by studying its most essential relationships. For that purpose we first consider aggregate expenditures in volume terms. Aggregate expenditures can be divided into domestic expenditures and foreign expenditures. Domestic expenditures can be split up into an *endogenous* and an *exogenous* part (autonomous expenditures). The endogenous part is determined by:

i. production or disposable income variables;
ii. price or relative price variables (including the wage rate);
iii. a utilization rate variable, and
iv. monetary variables.

Taking into account the lags involved in the system the conclusion is that the volume of aggregate domestic expenditures is predominantly determined by lagged values of the above mentioned categories of variables and unlagged exogenous expenditures.

In addition, *foreign* expenditures are explained in the model by exogenous variables such as demand and prices abroad and endogenous variables such as the own export prices and the utilization rate, both mainly lagged.

The income-expenditure sequence of the model will now be clear. With prices, the utilization rate and the monetary situation known, production (income) in the past determines expenditures at present. The distribution of these expenditures over domestic production and imports depends on technical circumstances, the degree of capacity utililization and the ratio of domestic prices to import prices. The price (wage) variables, the utilization rate variable and the monetary variables are the regulating factors of the system. They must bring about that actual production does not exceed production possibilities.

Let us briefly consider these three groups of regulating variables. Prices and wages are in part simultaneously determined but furthermore dependent on

i. lagged endogenous variables, such as labour productivity and the utilization rate of labour and
ii. exogenous variables which are determined abroad, especially import prices.

The utilization rate is, with labour supply given, mainly dependent on demand for labour which is, in its turn, determined by lagged production, lagged relative factor prices and the lagged utilization rate. The value of monetary variables is determined recursively. Once the autonomous part of money supply is fixed: the interest rate influences the liquidity ratio which in its turn explains the rate of interest in the next period. Relevant too are lagged values of the 'normal' interest rate, the short term interest rate and the rate of change of the price level.

Although each of the reaction equations, which together describe the working of the Netherlands' economy, may give a satisfactory picture of the phenomenon they explain, there is no *a priori* garantee that the equations as an interdependent system do so. For this purpose, we have to undertake a number of simulation and extrapolation experiments. But before these experiments are discussed we pay attention to a classification of endogenous and exogenous variables and to a classification of target and instrument variables.

12.4. CLASSIFICATION OF ENDOGENOUS VARIABLES

In addition to the listing of the endogenous variables, as given in section 12.2, they can be classified in another way. This classification is related to the way in which the results of the forecasting are usually summarized, *viz.* in an account of resources and expenditures. Such an account can be found in nearly every publication of the Central Planning Bureau. Experience has

Table 12.1. Classification of endogenous variables

Group 1	Group 2	Group 3
Resources	Expenditures	Labour utilization
$L, w_s, W_T, Z, y, Y, y_{gnp},$ $Y_{gnp}, p_y, p_{gnp}, T_K, m_g,$ M_g, m_s, M_s	$c, C, i, I, \Delta n, \Delta N, x, b_g,$ $B_g, b_s, B_s, p_c, p_i, p_x, p_{bg},$ p_{bs}	P_S, U, U_p, q_L
Group 4	Group 5	Group 6
Monetary variables	Disposable incomes and direct taxes	Other variables
$r, \dfrac{L_q}{V}, E_L$	$W_D, Z_D, T_W, T_Z, \varphi$	$v, V, V', v_{mg}, v_{ms}, n, n_d,$ $p_v, p_{vmg}, p_{vms}, p_k$

177

Table 12.2. *National Resources and Expenditures 1968 (in billions of Dfl and percentage changes)*
(□ *is exogenous*)

	1967 at 1967 prices	Changes in volume	1968 at 1967 prices	Price changes	1968 at 1968 prices		1967 at 1967 prices	Changes in volume	1968 at 1967 prices	Price changes	1968 at 1968 prices
National product at factor cost attributable to: enterprises	34.89	1.6	35.44	8.9	38.58	Private consumption	47.52	6.9	50.81	2.3	51.99
wages	22.36		24.77		24.77	Public consumption:					
non-wage income	9.82		10.21		10.70	a. net expenditure on goods and services	3.90	2.5	4.00	3.3	4.13
government	.70		.42		.46	b. wages and salaries	9.43	2.2	9.63	6.7	10.28
net factor incomes						Total public consumption	13.33	2.3	13.63	5.7	14.41
Net national product at factor cost	67.77				74.51	Total consumption	60.85	5.9	64.44	3.0	66.40
Indirect taxes	8.80				10.21	Gross investment by enterprises in:					
Subsidies	−.73				−.79	a. housing	4.57	9.0	4.98	4.0	5.18
Net national product at market prices	75.84	6.4	80.72	4.0	83.93	b. other fixed assets	12.71	10.4	14.03	.4	14.08
Depreciation by:						Inventory information	.74		.64	−1.6	.63
a. enterprises	6.65		7.09		7.12	Gross public investment	4.05	15.0	4.66	3.4	4.82
b. government	.51		.63		.63	Total gross investment	22.07	10.1	24.31	1.6	24.71
Total depreciation	7.16		7.72		7.75						
Gross national product at market prices	83.00	6.6	88.44	3.7	91.68	Total national expenditure	82.92	7.0	88.75	2.7	91.11
Imports:						Exports:					
a. goods c.i.f.	30.78	12.6	34.67	−2.9	33.68	a. goods f.o.b.	27.02	14.8	31.01	−1.0	30.69
b. services	4.87	15.6	5.63	−2.7	5.48	b. services	8.01	6.8	8.56	.2	8.58
c. factor incomes	2.05	22.1	2.50	−2.8	2.43	c. factor incomes	2.75	6.1	2.92	−1.0	2.89
Total imports	37.70	13.5	42.80	−2.8	41.59	Total exports	37.78	12.5	42.49	−.8	42.16
Total	120.70	8.7	131.24	1.5	133.27	Total	120.70	8.7	131.24	1.5	133.27
Transfer payments to foreign countries	.51		.50		.49	Trade balance	.08		−.31		.57
Balance of payments (current account)	−.25				.27	Transfer payments from abroad	.18		.19		.19
Total	.26				.76	Total	.26				.76

shown this type of account to be a very useful summary of economic developments. In the Netherlands discussions on economic planning in organizations and committees often take this account as their starting point. Apart from the resources and expenditures we distinguish four other groups of endogenous variables which are, more or less, grouped around these two categories. The classification we have in mind is given in table 12.1.

What do the endogenous variables of the first two groups actually cover of the account of resources and expenditures? This is illustrated in table 12.2, which presents such a consolidated account for the year 1968. It is evident that the same type of account can be made for quarters. When the year 1967 is taken as the base-year the table shows which resources and expenditures, either in constant and/or in current prices are treated as exogenous. It can be seen that the government sector, both its expenditures and its production, is nearly completely exogenous. This need not to be so in the future when this sector can be made endogenous in the system.[5]

12.5. CLASSIFICATION OF EXOGENOUS VARIABLES

The exogenous variables in the model can be divided into four main groups.[6] The first group contains variables which are exogenous to the model because they are determined abroad, such as world imports of goods, OECD industrial production, import prices, export prices of competitors, etc. The second group consists of so-called instruments of economic policy; either controlled by the government: tax tariffs, social premiums or by the central bank: discount rate, quantative credit restrictions, etc. The third group contains variables which are exogenous by choice, such as imports and exports of ships and airplanes, the balance on capital account, etc. The last group of exogenous variables consists of real exogenous variables in the sense that they are not explained by economic theory and therefore belong to the data of economic science: temperature, time and working population. Table 12.3 summarizes the exogenous variables according to this classification.

---

5. The government sector is partly endogenous in van den Beld's cyclical growth model for the Netherlands economy. See VAN DEN BELD (1968).
6. We disregard here the initial data.

Table 12.3. Classification of exogenous variables

Group 1	Group 2	Group 3	Group 4
Determined abroad	Instruments of economic policy	By choice	Non economic data
$m_w, y_w, U_G, p_{bgw},$ $p_{bsw}, p_{mg}, p_{ms}, p_f$ p_{mg-sa}	$X, \Delta T_{Waut}, \Delta T_{Zaut},$ $\Delta T_{Kaut}, O_W, O_Z, SPE,$ $TSPW, I_a, p_{caut}, L_g,$ $w_g, w_{aut}, r_k, C_{rr}, h_c$ S, D_s	$E_K, B_p, b_p, M_p, m_p,$ $B_{gaut}, b_{gaut}, B_{saut}, b_{saut},$ $M_{sa}, m_{sa}, I_{sa}, i_{sa},$ $F, F_g, f_g, h_w, p_{\Delta n}, r_g, R_g,$ c_{gl}, C_{gl}, L_s	t, T_c, P_{ST}

12.6. TARGET AND INSTRUMENT VARIABLES

Similar to what is done in most industrialized countries five important targets of economic policy have been formulated in the Netherlands. These targets as well as the main instruments of economic policy to achieve them, are represented in the model.

The major objectives of economic policy in the Netherlands as formulated by the Social Economic Council and endorsed by subsequent governments are[7]:

1. *internal equilibrium*, viz. a high and stable level of employment, in the model represented by the variables: unemployment ratio (U_p) and utilization rate of labour (q_L);
2. *external equilibrium*, viz. a balance of payments on current account that, recognizing the requirements of foreign aid, shows neither substantial surplusses nor deficits, in the model represented by the variable (E_L);
3. *a stable level of prices*, in the model represented by the price of private consumption (p_c), although this target can also be represented by variables like the price level of production of enterprises (p_y), or the price deflator of G.N.P. (p_{gnp});
4. *a stable and satisfactory rate of growth of production*, in the model represented by the variables gross production of enterprises (y) and gross national product (y_{gnp});
5. *an acceptable distribution of income*, particularly with regard to wage and non-wage income, in the model represented by the variables wage income (W_T) and non-wage income (Z) which can be combined as the ratio $W_T/(W_T+Z)$.

7. See 'Advies inzake mogelijkheden ter bestrijding van inflatie' (Publication of the Social Economic Council, nr. 19)

restrictions on money creation by the banking system. Although with varying intensity this instrument has been regularly used by the central bank since the year 1961. It should be noted that with the model we can also evaluate the effects of liquidity creation by the government by adding an autonomous term to the money supply equation.

The equations representing the linkage with foreign economies in the income sphere all contain relative prices. They are therefore suited to give an indication of short and long term effects of *exchange rate policy*.

Furthermore, the model contains a number of *instruments of direct control*. During the sample period the government had a control of rents. General changes in rents are included in the autonomous consumption price variable ($p_{c\,aut}$). This variable also includes effects on prices of measures taken in connection with policies for the agricultural sector such as subsidies, grants etc. Another example of direct control of the government is its control of the building industry, more specifically its influence on investment in housing. These investments are included in the variable autonomous expenditures.

Finally, we mention *wage policy*. The role of this policy in dutch economic policy was important during the sample period as we have shown in chapter VIII. This justifies the insertion of four wage equations in the model, one for each distinct period of wage policy. A policy variable connected herewith is the working time in enterprises. The reduction of contractual working time was part of government policy during the sample period. The variable working time is therefore treated as an exogenous variable, although it has an endogenous component dependent on the level of wages, the utilization rate of labour, etc.

It should be noted that, although there is no specific variable for these purposes in the equations, the model is able to evaluate other forms of direct control by the government. One could think of regulations of working population (immigration), price policy and direct control of imports and exports and an instrument as the selective employment tax.

XIII. Short-term simulations

13.1. INTRODUCTION

The performance of the complete model has been tested in both short- and medium-term simulations. In these experiments, starting from an initial situation and presupposing perfect knowledge of the exogenous variables, the values of the endogenous variables are generated over a certain period of time. These are stringent tests since wrong values of endogenous variables in an early phase, wrong in direction and/or wrong in magnitude, influence the performance of the complete system in subsequent quarters.

In this chapter we present the results of eight quarter simulations, both within and beyond the sample period. Chapter XIV reports on medium-term, i.e. twenty quarter simulations. We have made nine eight-quarter simulations: seven cover the sample period and two are simulated extrapolations. Once the 297 starting values of lagged endogenous variables have been read in, together with 1320 values of 165 exogenous variables, both lagged and unlagged, the UNIVAC 1108 needs 15 seconds for an eight-quarter simulation of the complete model, consisting of 68 equations. As the model is non-linear, we need a procedure for solving such a system. We have used the method developed by VAN DER GIESSEN (1970). This procedure distinguishes between a simultaneous part of the model and a recursive one, the former being solved by eight successive iterations. The method is described in Appendix G.

The results of the simulations are summarized in the following sections in a table and a figure. These are clear in themselves so that we have restricted our verbal comments to a minimum. Two aspects of the simulations are considered, *viz.* the simulation performance in *levels* and in *first differences*. Furthermore separate attention is given to the *quarterly* aspect of the simula-

tions and the implicit *annual* aspect, the latter being important for comparison with the performance of annual models of the netherlands economy in use. The *level and the first difference performance per quarter* becomes apparent from a figure in which the simulations of six important policy variables are shown. These variables are:
i. the unemployment ratio (U_p), i.e. the number of registered unemployed as a percentage of total working population;
ii. the balance of payments on current account (E_L), in billions of Dfl.;
iii. the wage sum per worker (w_s), index 1963 = 100;
iv. the price level of private consumption (p_c), index 1963 = 100;
v. the production of enterprises (y), in billions of 1963 Dfl. and
vi. the gross fixed investment of enterprises excluding housing (i), in billions of 1963 Dfl.

The *level and the first difference performance per year* are shown in a separate table for thirteen variables *viz.*, apart from the six already mentioned:
vii. employment in enterprises (L), in thousand persons;
viii. private consumption (c), in billions of 1963 Dfl.,
ix. exports of goods (b_g), in billions of 1963 Dfl.;
x. imports of goods (m_g), in billions of 1963 Dfl.;
xi. price level of exports of goods (p_{bg}), index 1963 = 100;
xii. the long term interest rate (r) (per cent), and
xiii the liquidity ratio $\left(\dfrac{L_q}{V}\right)$ (per cent).

The first difference performance per year for all thirteen variables is summarized by the so-called inequality coefficient.[1] This coefficient is defined for n years and m variables as

(13.1)
$$\frac{\sqrt{\dfrac{1}{mn}\sum_m\sum_n(\dot{R}-\dot{P})^2}}{\sqrt{\dfrac{1}{mn}\sum_m\sum_n\dot{R}^2}}$$

where $\dot{R}$ is the actual percentage (or absolute) change and $\dot{P}$ is the simulated percentage (or absolute) change. The nominator is the root mean square simulation error for m variables in n periods. This root mean square error is standardized by relating it to the average actual change of the variables. It is clear that when the inequality coefficient is zero the simulated changes are equal to the actual changes which implies a perfect simulation. On the other

1. See VERDOORN and VAN EYK (1958), pp. 59-60.

hand, when the inequality coefficient equals unity the simulation is as bad as a simple 'naive' simulation in the form of an 'average change' simulation.

In the last section we summarize the results of the nine simulation periods and present for each of the selected variables the root mean square error and inequality coefficient over all the simulation periods.

Finally we mention a number of circumstances which have been handled as autonomous influences in the quarters beyond the sample period, i.e. during the period 1966:1 – 1968:4. These circumstances are:

i. the reaction in 1966:1 on the anticipatory consumption and investment outlays in 1965:4;
ii. the extreme rise in imports in 1967:4 (and the reaction in 1968:1) in anticipation to the change in the taxation on imports and exports in connection with the introduction of the value added tax in 1969;
iii. the fact that the increase in indirect taxes in 1967:3 did not have a significant effect on the price level of consumption;
iv. the anticipatory consumption and investment purchases in 1968:4 in relation with the introduction of the value added tax in 1969:1 and
v. the changes in the supply structure of exports of goods on behalf of the exports of natural gaz and the exports of the chemical and oil refining sector.

13.2. SIMULATION 1951:1 – 1952:4

As can be seen from figure 13.1 the simulation gives a fairly good picture of reality, both considered in levels as in first differences. Nevertheless there are several faulty turning points. Another shortcoming, which appears in other simulations as well, is that the simulated fluctuations in the unemployment ratio are too large compared with reality. The explanation is evident since this ratio is the balance of supply and demand for labour which each have their residuals. Other balancing variables, such as the production of enterprises, show the same type of error.

Table 13.1 makes clear that external trade is correctly simulated in volume terms in 1951, but because of an overestimation of export prices the improvement in the terms of trade is exaggerated. Another dificiency is the simulated decrease in production of enterprises in 1952, whereas in fact it was rising with about 1.5 per cent. A reverse situation is found in 1951. As a consequence the demand for labour is underestimated and so is the unemployment ratio.

For the whole period the inequality coefficient for the thirteen variables in table 13.1 is very low, *viz.* 16.

13.3. SIMULATION 1953:1–1954:4

A deficiency of this simulation is the underestimation of the wage level and therefore of the price level of private consumption. Both the unemployment ratio and production are too volatile, but investment is perfectly generated. Although the overestimation of capacity utilization (the unemployment ratio is underestimated) restricts exports, imports are more underestimated and consequently the balance of payments is too favourable at the end of the period.

The simulation is characterized by a low inequality coefficient, *viz.* .19.

13.4. SIMULATION 1955:1–1956:4

Both the levels and the turning points of the policy variables in figure 13.3 are captured rather well. Due to an error in labour supply the unemployment ratio is too low in 1956:4. This is of no great consequence for this short-run simulation, but is more important in the medium term experiment (see section 14.3).

The thirteen variables in table 13.3 have an inequality coefficient of .16.

13.5. SIMULATION 1957:1–1958:4

The recession is simulated too mild. Production is overpredicted in 1958 and so is employment. Unemployment is not high enough in both years for this reason and because labour supply is too large in 1957. This bears consequences particularly for investment. Wages are too low in 1958 due to an underestimation of labour productivity and so are prices. The simulated investment and consumption outlays stimulate imports. The improvement in the balance of payments is therefore less than it should be. Since the liquidity ratio does not enlarge enough the decline in the interest rate does not take place.

The simulation is characterised by a higher inequality coefficient compared with previous periods, *viz.* . 33.

13.6. SIMULATION 1959:1–1960:4

The tensions in the economy are slightly exaggerated in the simulation. Production is too large on the average and so is employment; the unemploy-

Table 13.1. Simulated annual data of selected variables[a] derived from eight quarter simulation 1951:1–1952:4

	Absolute level				Percentage or absolute change[b]			
	1951		1952		1951		1952	
	Actual	Simulated	Actual	Simulated	Actual	Simulated	Actual	Simulated
Employment	2395	2402	2364	2352	1.7	2.0	−1.3	−2.1
Unemployment ratio	2.4	2.2	3.5	3.4	.3	.1	1.1	1.2
Private consumption	18.45	18.50	18.59	18.55	−1.9	−1.6	.8	.3
Gross fixed investment	3.71	3.64	3.34	3.30	−2.6	−4.6	−10.0	−9.2
Exports of goods	6.78	6.76	7.38	7.17	13.4	13.0	8.9	6.1
Imports of goods	8.26	8.23	7.36	7.37	−3.8	−4.2	−10.9	−10.5
Production of enterprises	26.64	26.90	26.99	26.63	2.4	3.4	1.3	−1.0
Price of consumption	75.5	75.0	75.5	76.3	10.6	9.9	−.1	1.6
Wage sum per worker	44.5	44.3	46.9	47.2	10.5	10.0	5.4	6.6
Price of exports of goods	109.9	111.7	109.1	110.3	19.9	21.9	−.8	−1.3
Balance of payments on current account	−.26	.03	1.76	1.71	.86	1.15	2.02	1.68
Interest rate	4.0	3.8	4.0	3.7	.8	.6	0	−.1
Liquidity ratio	20.5	21.4	25.8	26.3	−8.6	−7.7	5.3	4.9

a. For the definitions of the variables see page 185.
b. Variables 2, 11, 12 and 13 are given in absolute changes, the remaining variables in percentage changes.

Figure 13.1. Eight quarter simulation 1951:1–1952:4 (billions of Dfl., index number 1963 = 100 or per cent)

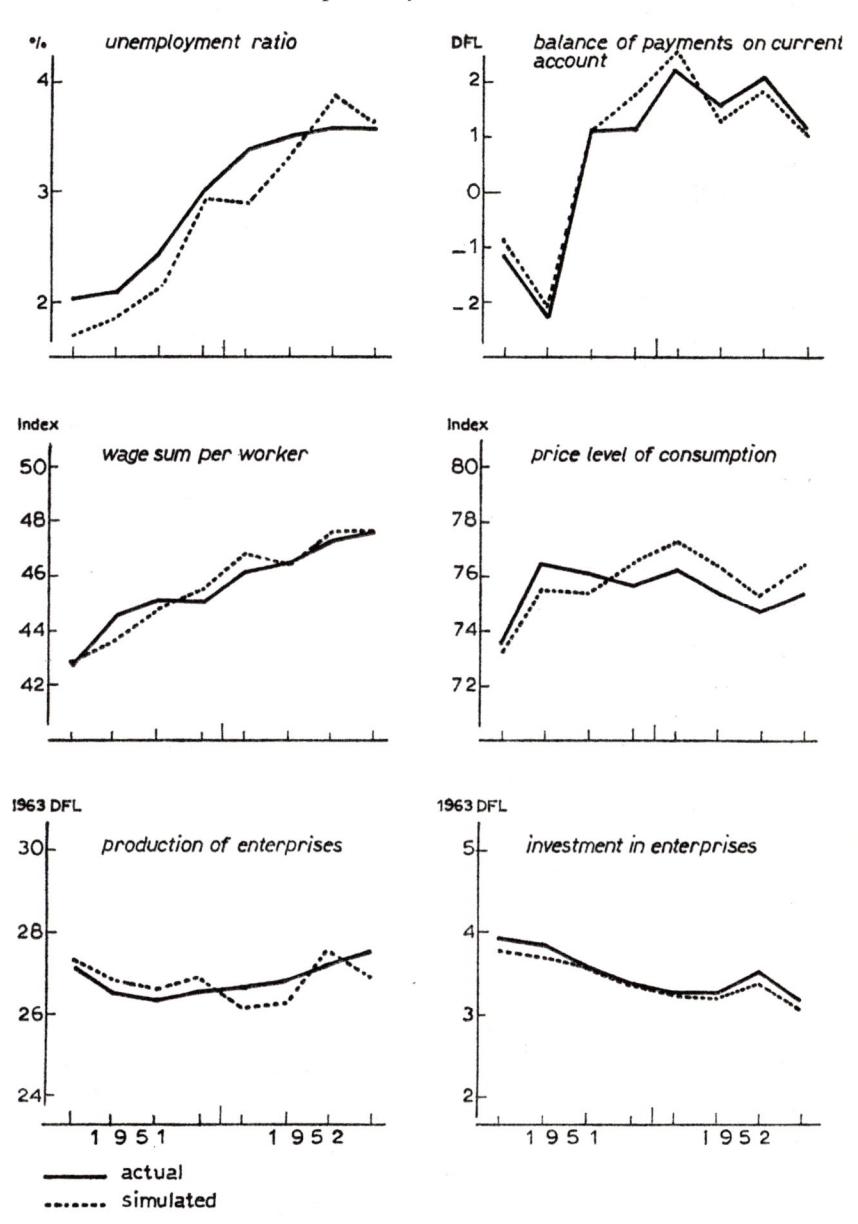

——— actual
······· simulated

Table 13.2. Simulated annual data of selected variables[a] derived from eight quarter simulation 1953:1–1954:4

	Absolute level				Percentage or absolute change[b]			
	1953		1954		1953		1954	
	Actual	Simulated	Actual	Simulated	Actual	Simulated	Actual	Simulated
Employment	2416	2412	2503	2503	2.2	2.0	3.6	3.8
Unemployment ratio	2.6	2.8	1.9	1.7	−.9	−.7	−.7	−1.1
Private consumption	19.69	19.31	20.75	20.61	5.9	3.9	5.4	6.7
Gross fixed investment	3.69	3.67	4.50	4.40	10.5	9.7	22.0	20.0
Exports of goods	8.27	8.15	9.37	8.97	12.1	10.4	13.3	10.1
Imports of goods	8.81	8.73	10.99	10.33	19.7	18.6	24.7	18.3
Production of enterprises	29.32	29.13	31.32	31.08	8.6	7.9	6.8	6.7
Price of consumption	75.2	74.8	78.7	77.3	−.3	−.9	4.7	3.3
Wage sum per worker	48.9	48.1	53.3	51.8	4.2	2.6	9.2	7.8
Price of exports of goods	100.8	102.7	99.0	99.4	−7.6	−5.8	−1.8	−3.2
Balance of payments on current account	1.36	1.51	.23	.65	−.40	−.25	−1.13	−.86
Interest rate	3.3	3.4	3.2	3.2	−.7	−.6	−.1	−.2
Liquidity ratio	26.8	27.8	25.9	26.5	1.0	2.0	−.9	−1.3

a. For the definitions of the variables see page 185.
b. Variables 2, 11, 12 and 13 are given in absolute changes, the remaining variables in percentage changes.

Figure 13.2. Eight quarter simulation 1953:1–1954:4 (billions of Dfl., index number 1963 = 100 or per cent)

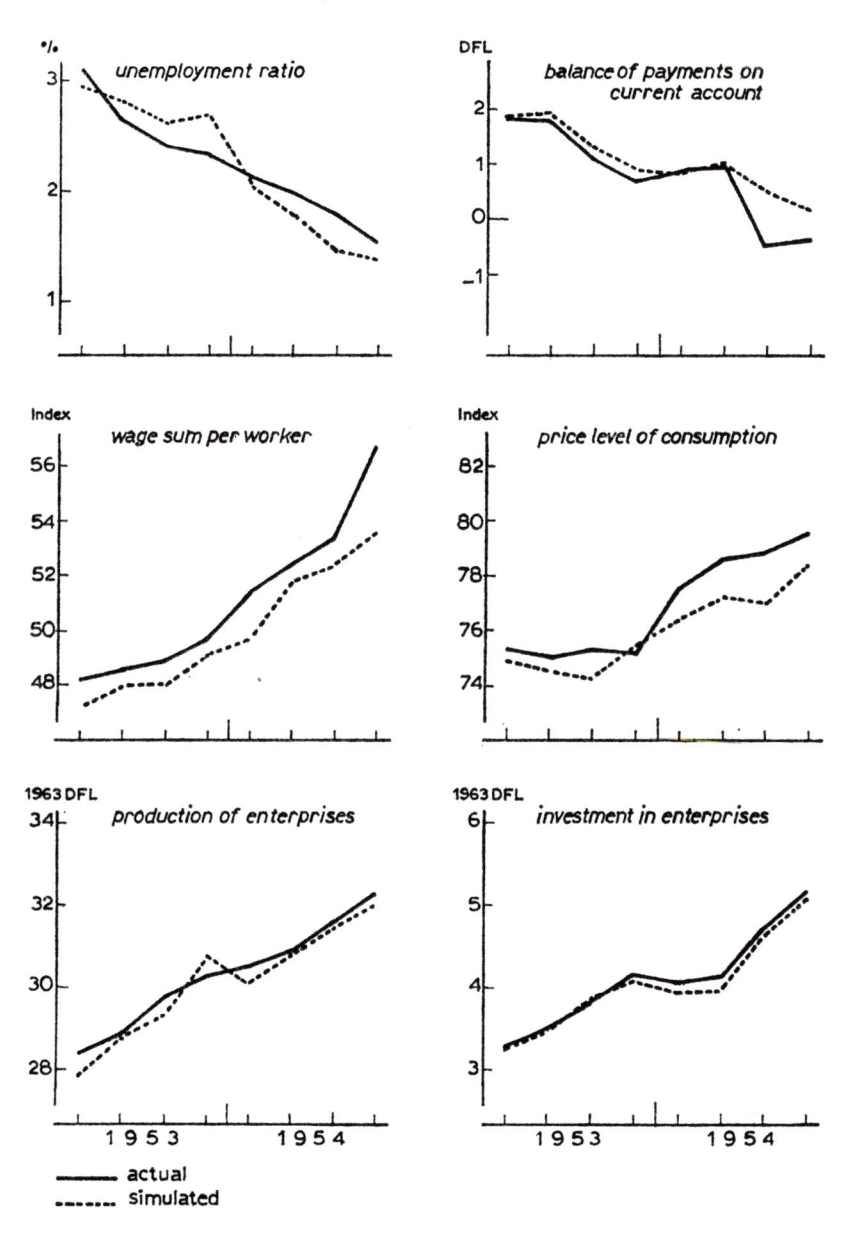

———— actual
------- simulated

Table 13.3. Simulated annual data of selected variables[a] derived from eight quarter simulation 1955:1–1956:4

	Absolute level				Percentage or absolute change[b]			
	1955		1956		1955		1956	
	Actual	Simulated	Actual	Simulated	Actual	Simulated	Actual	Simulated
Employment	2581	2580	2649	2648	3.1	3.1	2.6	2.6
Unemployment ratio	1.3	1.3	1.0	.9	-.6	-.6	-.3	-.4
Private consumption	22.08	22.01	23.73	23.74	6.4	6.1	7.5	7.9
Gross fixed investment	5.55	5.38	6.07	5.82	23.3	19.7	9.4	8.2
Exports of goods	10.35	10.27	10.66	10.80	10.5	9.6	3.0	5.2
Imports of goods	11.87	11.93	13.47	13.20	8.0	8.6	13.5	10.7
Production of enterprises	33.70	33.68	35.31	35.67	7.6	7.5	4.8	5.9
Price of consumption	80.5	80.9	82.5	82.8	2.3	2.8	2.4	2.4
Wage sum per worker	58.1	58.5	63.1	64.0	8.9	9.6	8.6	9.4
Price of exports of goods	100.3	100.1	102.8	103.0	1.3	1.1	2.5	2.9
Balance of payments on current account	.78	.56	-.75	-.37	.55	.33	-1.53	-.93
Interest rate	3.1	3.2	3.9	3.9	-.1	0	.8	.7
Liquidity ratio	24.9	23.7	23.0	23.3	-1.0	-2.2	-1.9	-.4

a. For the definitions of the variables see page 185.
b. Variables 2, 11, 12 and 13 are given in absolute changes, the remaining variables in percentage changes.

Figure 13.3. Eight quarter simulation 1955:1–1956:4 (billions of Dfl., index number 1963 = 100 or per cent)

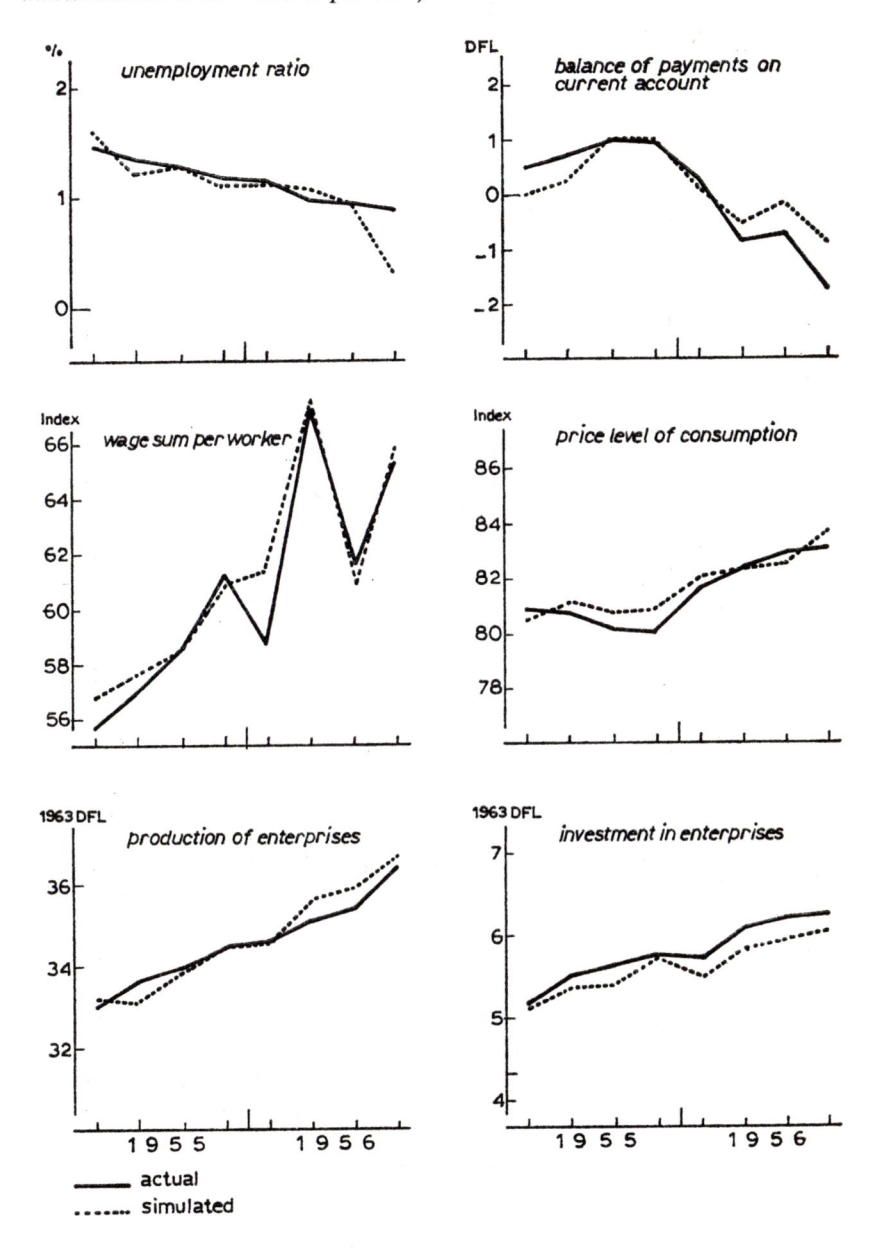

Table 13.4. Simulated annual data of selected variables[a] derived from eight quarter simulation 1957:1–1958:4

| | Absolute level |||| Percentage or absolute change[b] ||||
| | 1957 || 1958 || 1957 || 1958 ||
	Actual	Simulated	Actual	Simulated	Actual	Simulated	Actual	Simulated
Employment	2686	2698	2663	2697	1.4	-.9	-.9	0
Unemployment ratio	1.2	1.1	2.3	2.1	.2	.2	1.1	1.0
Private consumption	23.79	23.65	23.87	24.29	.3	-.6	.3	2.7
Gross fixed investment	6.16	6.41	5.22	5.68	1.5	5.4	-15.3	-11.4
Exports of goods	11.24	11.34	12.37	12.25	5.4	6.3	10.1	8.1
Imports of goods	13.88	13.77	13.05	13.40	3.0	2.2	-6.0	-2.7
Production of enterprises	36.40	36.30	35.98	36.28	3.1	2.8	-1.2	-.1
Price of consumption	87.1	86.9	88.5	86.8	5.7	5.4	1.6	-.2
Wage sum per worker	70.0	69.5	73.0	71.7	10.9	10.1	4.4	3.2
Price of exports of goods	105.8	105.3	101.5	100.9	2.9	2.4	-4.0	-4.2
Balance of payments on current account	-.59	-.80	1.53	.89	.16	-.05	2.12	1.69
Interest rate	4.9	5.2	4.4	5.2	1.0	1.3	-.5	0
Liquidity ratio	22.4	22.0	26.5	25.0	-.6	-1.0	4.1	3.0

a. For the definitions of the variables see page 185.
b. Variables 2, 11, 12 and 13 are given in absolute changes, the remaining variables in percentage changes.

Figure 13.4. Eight quarter simulation 1957:1–1958:4 (billions of Dfl., index number 1963 = 100 or per cent)

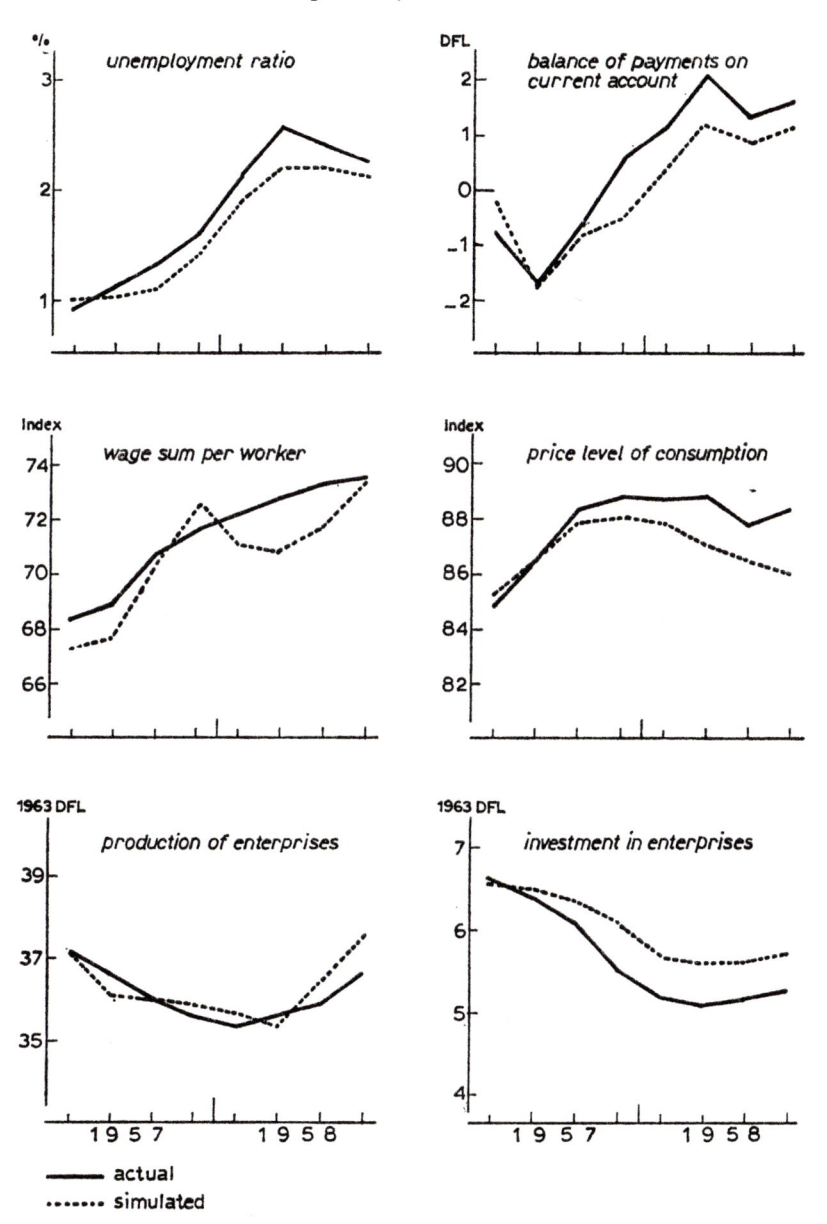

Table 13.5. Simulated annual data of selected variables[a] derived from eight quarter simulation 1959:1–1960:4

	Absolute level				Percentage or absolute change[b]			
	1959		1960		1959		1960	
	Actual	Simulated	Actual	Simulated	Actual	Simulated	Actual	Simulated
Employment	2715	2717	2806	2811	2.0	2.0	3.4	3.5
Unemployment ratio	1.9	1.8	1.2	1.1	−.4	−.5	−.7	−.7
Private consumption	24.92	25.18	26.43	26.34	4.4	5.5	6.1	4.6
Gross fixed investment	5.89	5.94	6.93	7.29	12.8	13.8	17.7	22.7
Exports of goods	13.87	14.17	15.86	15.92	12.1	14.6	14.4	12.3
Imports of goods	14.82	14.78	17.37	17.61	13.6	13.2	17.2	19.2
Production of enterprises	37.84	38.73	41.65	41.76	5.2	7.6	10.1	7.8
Price of consumption	89.6	89.2	91.8	92.2	1.3	.8	2.4	3.4
Wage sum per worker	74.7	75.6	80.8	80.7	2.4	3.5	8.1	6.8
Price of exports of goods	101.2	99.3	100.6	100.5	−.3	−2.2	−.7	1.3
Balance of payments on current account	1.78	1.87	1.25	1.08	.25	.34	−.53	−.79
Interest rate	4.2	4.0	4.2	3.9	−.2	−.4	0	−.1
Liquidity ratio	26.6	26.8	25.2	26.0	.1	.3	−1.4	−.8

a. For the definitions of the variables see page 185.
b. Variables 2, 11, 12 and 13 are given in absolute changes, the remaining variables in percentage changes.

Figure 13.5. Eight quarter simulation 1959:1–1960:4 (billions of Dfl., index number 1963 = 100 or per cent)

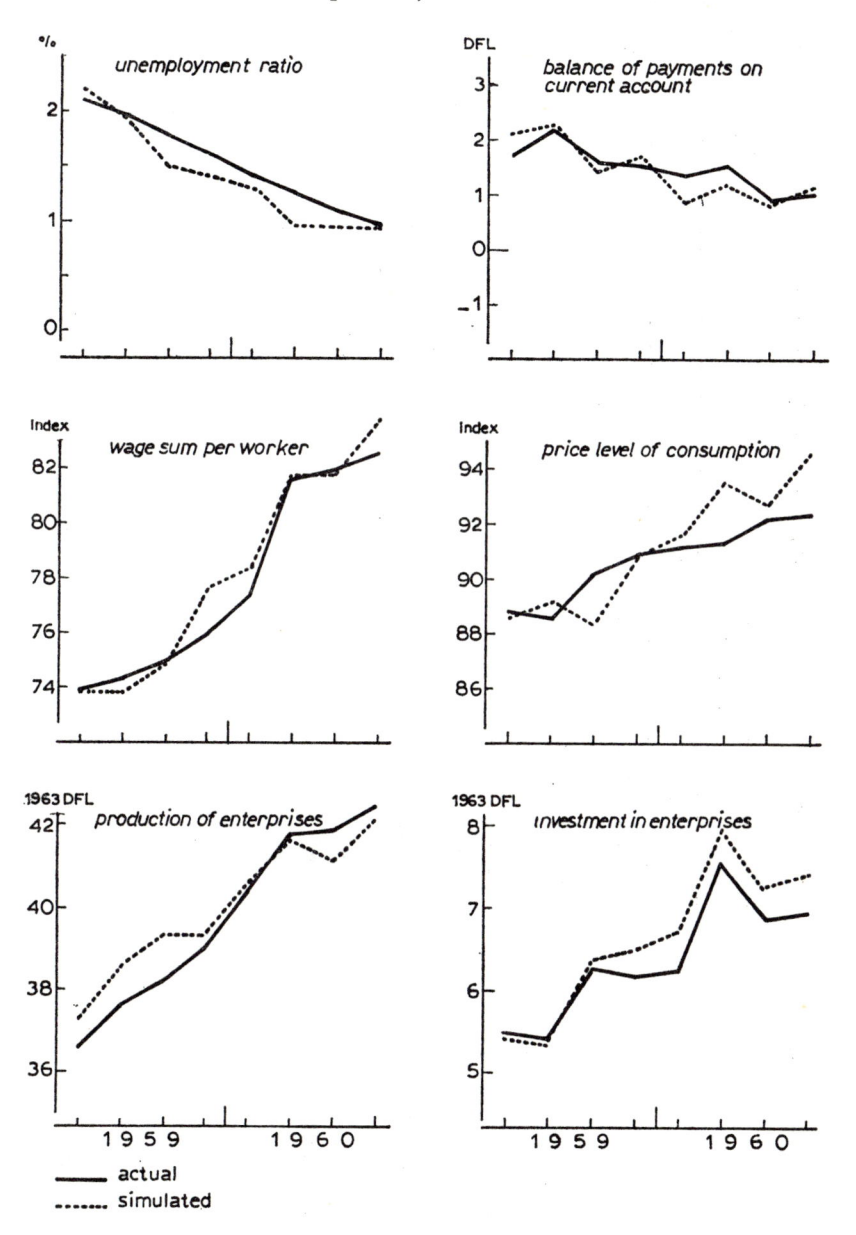

Table 13.6. Simulated annual data of selected variables[a] derived from eight quarter simulation 1961:1–1962:4

	Absolute level				Percentage or absolute change[b]			
	1961		1962		1961		1962	
	Actual	Simulated	Actual	Simulated	Actual	Simulated	Actual	Simulated
Employment	2872	2865	2960	2943	2.4	2.1	3.1	2.7
Unemployment ratio	.8	.9	.8	.9	-.4	-.2	0	0
Private consumption	27.86	27.95	29.57	30.13	5.4	5.8	6.1	7.8
Gross fixed investment	7.49	7.52	7.89	8.13	8.1	8.4	5.3	8.2
Exports of goods	16.32	16.15	17.47	17.53	2.9	1.8	7.1	8.5
Imports of goods	18.64	18.37	19.68	20.45	7.3	5.8	5.6	11.3
Production of enterprises	42.94	42.62	44.87	44.89	3.1	2.3	4.5	5.3
Price of consumption	93.9	93.7	96.3	96.4	2.3	2.0	2.6	3.0
Wage sum per worker	86.7	86.3	91.8	91.5	7.2	6.8	5.9	6.0
Price of exports of goods	98.4	99.3	97.8	98.7	-2.1	-1.2	-.7	-.6
Balance of payments on current account	.63	.73	.50	-.25	-.62	-.52	-.13	-.98
Interest rate	3.9	3.9	4.2	4.4	-.3	-.3	.3	.5
Liquidity ratio	25.1	25.4	24.6	23.7	-.1	.2	-.5	-1.7

a. For the definitions of the variables see page 185.
b. Variables 2, 11, 12 and 13 are given in absolute changes, the remaining variables in percentage changes.

Figure 13.6. Eight quarter simulation 1961:1–1962:4 (billions of Dfl., index number 1963 = 100 or per cent)

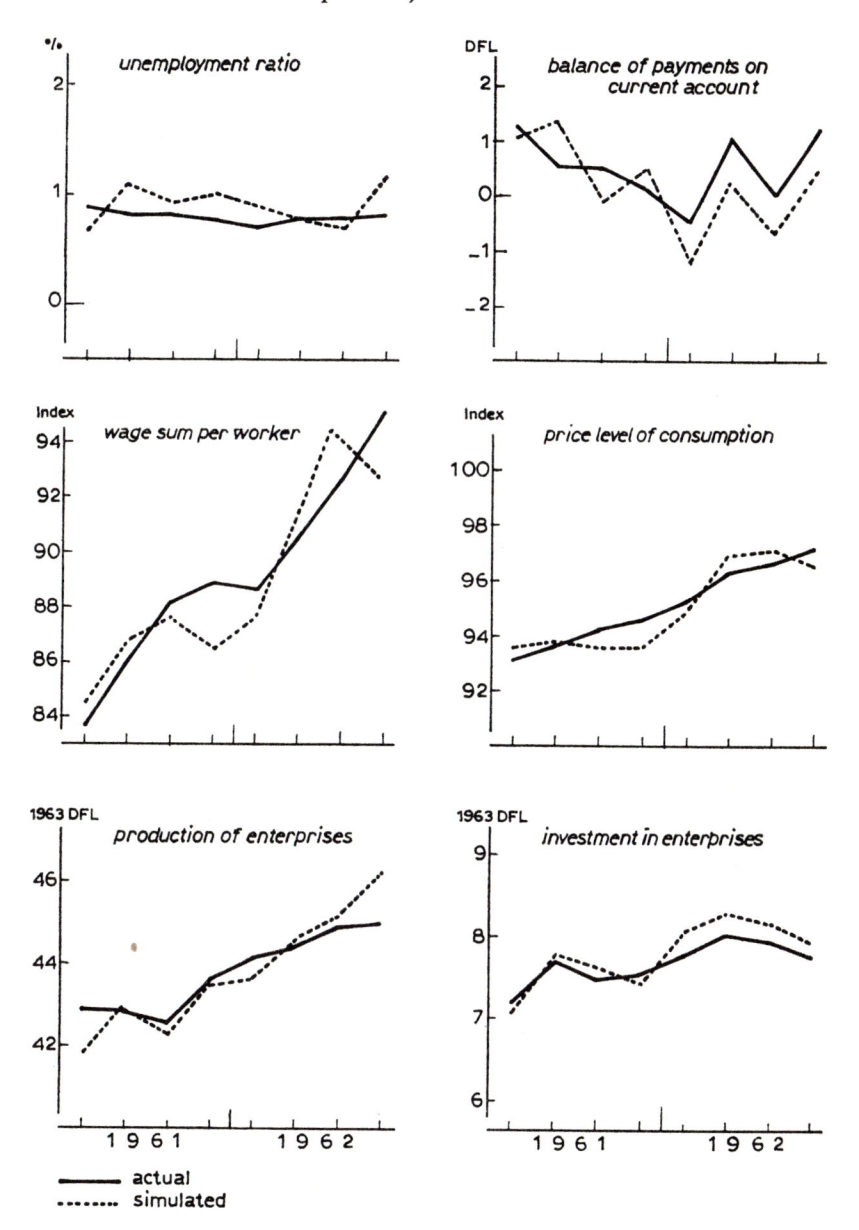

Table 13.7. Simulated annual data of selected variables [a] derived from eight quarter simulation 1963:1–1964:4

	Absolute level				Percentage or absolute change[b]			
	1963		1964		1963		1964	
	Actual	Simulated	Actual	Simulated	Actual	Simulated	Actual	Simulated
Employment	3027	3018	3111	3083	2.3	2.0	2.8	2.2
Unemployment ratio	.8	.9	.7	1.0	0	.1	−.1	.1
Private consumption	31.66	31.49	33.55	33.36	7.1	6.5	6.0	5.9
Gross fixed investment	7.89	7.60	9.14	8.41	0	−3.6	15.8	10.7
Exports of goods	18.59	19.30	20.96	20.99	6.4	10.5	12.8	8.8
Imports of goods	21.61	21.37	24.98	24.66	9.8	8.6	15.6	15.4
Production of enterprises	46.46	46.79	51.05	50.46	3.5	4.3	9.9	7.8
Price of consumption	100	100.2	106.7	108.0	3.8	4.1	6.8	7.7
Wage sum per worker	100	100.4	114.9	115.5	9.0	9.4	14.9	15.1
Price of exports of goods	100	99.7	102.1	102.1	2.3	1.9	2.1	2.5
Balance of payments on current account	.37	1.17	−.64	−.27	−.13	.67	−1.01	−1.44
Interest rate	4.2	4.1	5.1	4.3	0	−.1	.9	.2
Liquidity ratio	24.6	25.0	22.6	23.8	0	.4	−2.0	−1.2

a. For the definitions of the variables see page 185.
b. Variables 2, 11, 12 and 13 are given in absolute changes, the remaining variables in percentage changes.

Figure 13.7. Eight quarter simulation 1963:1–1964:4 (billions of Dfl., index number 1963 = 100 or per cent)

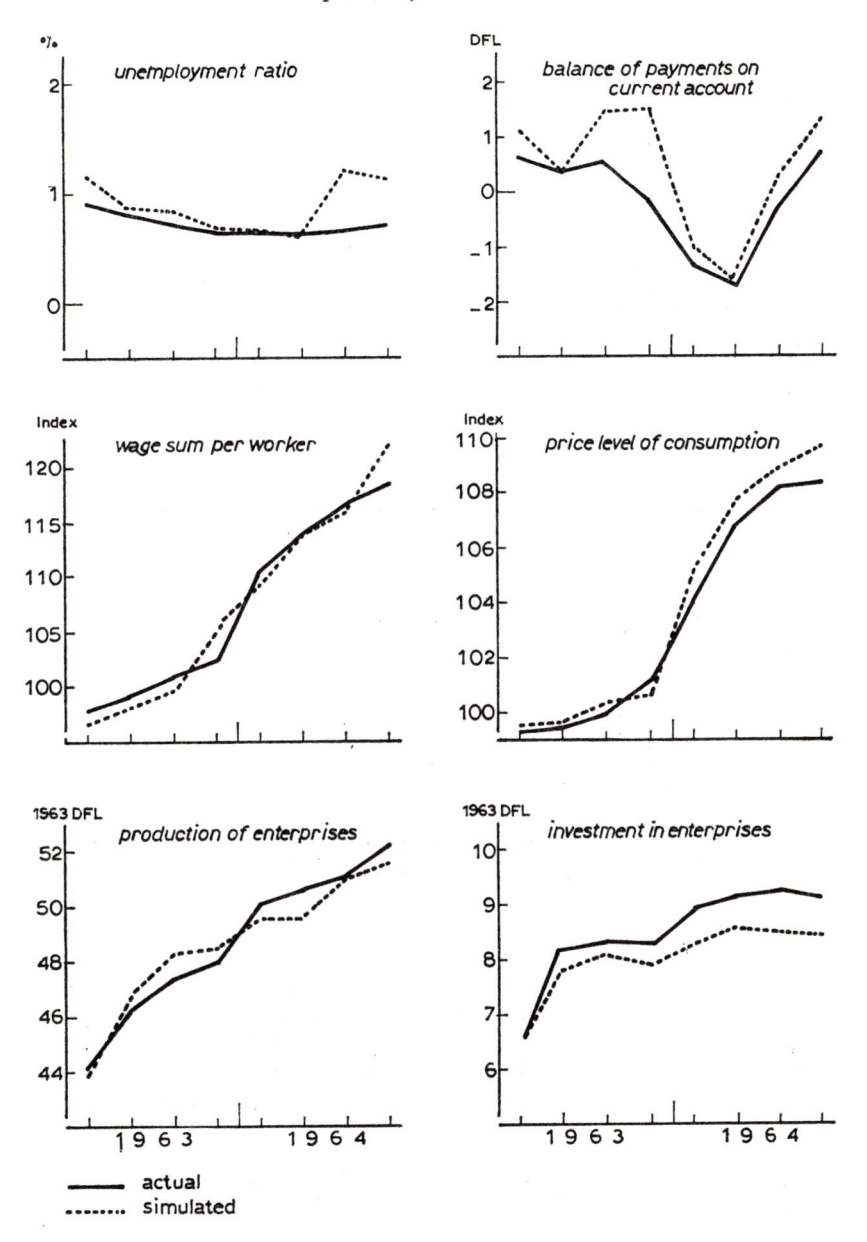

——— actual
········ simulated

Table 13.8. Simulated annual data of selected variables[a] derived from eight quarter simulation 1965:1–1966:4

	Absolute level				Percentage or absolute change[b]			
	1965		1966		1965		1966	
	Actual	Simulated	Actual	Simulated	Actual	Simulated	Actual	Simulated
Employment	3160	3156	3194	3190	1.6	1.4	1.1	1.1
Unemployment ratio	.8	.8	1.0	.8	.1	.1	.2	0
Private consumption	36.03	35.59	37.24	36.76	7.4	6.1	3.4	3.3
Gross fixed investment	9.47	9.44	10.45	10.15	3.6	3.9	10.3	7.5
Exports of goods	22.79	22.66	24.27	24.51	8.7	8.1	6.5	8.2
Imports of goods	26.50	26.43	28.17	28.08	6.1	5.8	6.3	6.2
Production of enterprises	54.10	53.21	55.69	55.54	6.0	4.2	2.9	4.4
Price of consumption	111.2	111.2	117.2	118.5	4.2	4.2	5.4	6.5
Wage sum per worker	127.8	128.8	141.8	143.6	11.2	12.0	11.0	11.5
Price of exports of goods	104.3	104.8	104.4	105.6	2.1	2.6	.1	.8
Balance of payments on current account	.07	.07	−.71	.23	.71	.71	−.78	.16
Interest rate	5.5	5.3	6.5	5.6	.4	.2	1.0	.3
Liquidity ratio	22.9	23.4	22.4	23.5	.3	.8	−.5	.1

a. For the definitions of the variables see page 185.
b. Variables 2, 11, 12 and 13 are given in absolute changes, the remaining variables in percentage changes.

Figure 13.8. Eight quarter simulation 1965:1–1966:4 (billions of Dfl., index number 1963 = 100 or per cent)

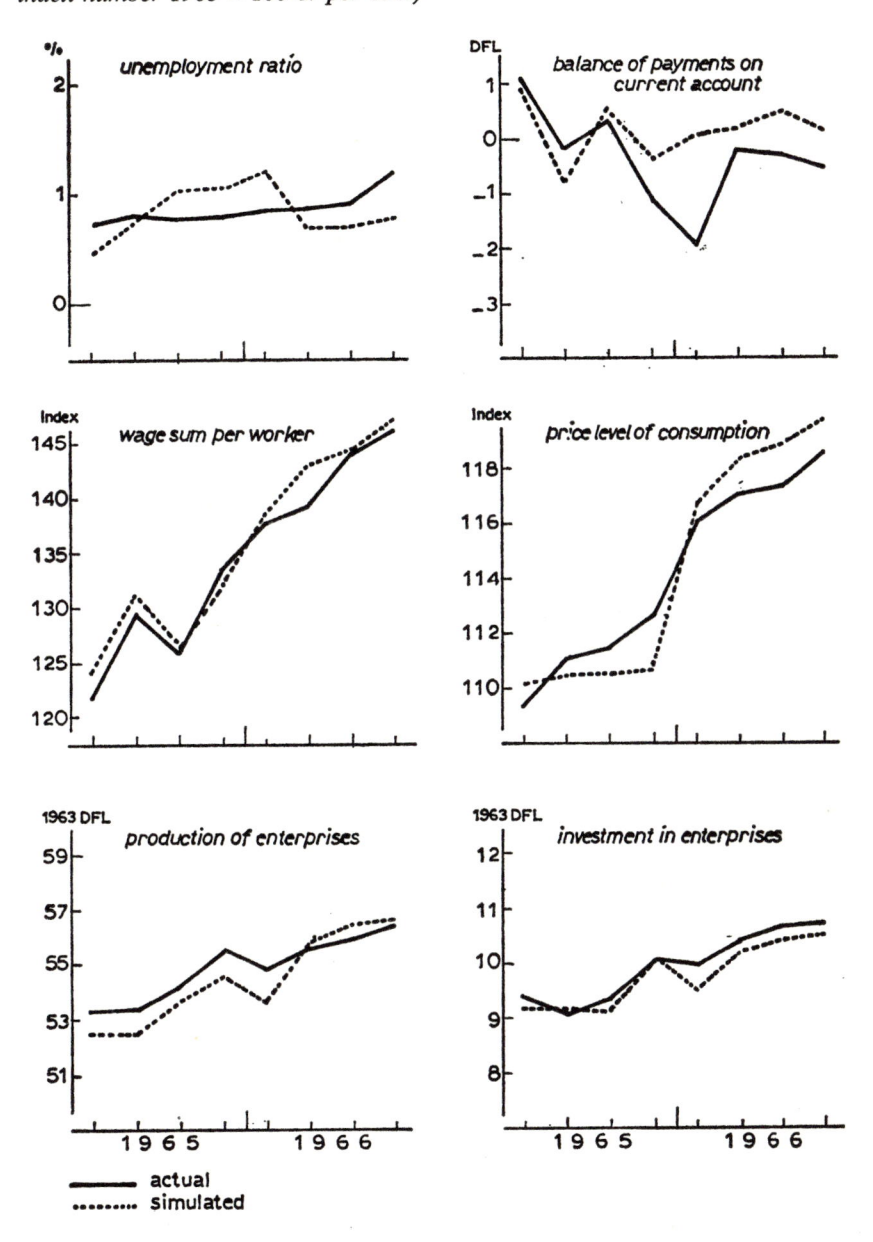

Table 13.9. Simulated annual data of selected variables[a] derived from eight quarter simulation 1967:1–1968:4

	Absolute level				Percentage or absolute change[b]			
	1967		1968		1967		1968	
	Actual	Simulated	Actual	Simulated	Actual	Simulated	Actual	Simulated
Employment	3181	3208	3231	3239	−.4	.4	1.6	1.0
Unemployment ratio	1.8	1.4	1.7	1.6	.8	.5	−.1	.2
Private consumption	39.16	38.46	41.87	40.00	5.2	3.3	6.9	4.0
Gross fixed investment	11.08	11.08	12.23	12.02	6.0	6.0	10.4	8.5
Exports of goods	26.09	25.87	29.94	29.57	7.5	6.6	14.8	14.3
Imports of goods	29.94	29.91	33.72	33.37	6.3	6.2	13.0	11.6
Production of enterprises	58.94	57.96	63.31	62.36	5.8	4.1	7.4	7.6
Price of consumption	121.3	121.4	124.1	125.7	3.5	3.6	2.3	3.5
Wage sum per worker	154.2	154.7	168.1	169.4	8.8	9.1	9.0	9.6
Price of exports of goods	103.6	103.1	102.5	101.8	−.8	−1.1	−1.0	−1.3
Balance of payments on current account	−.25	−.75	.27	.52	.46	−.04	.52	.89
Interest rate	6.1	6.4	6.4	6.2	−.4	−.9	.3	−.3
Liquidity ratio	23.1	23.3	24.2	24.3	.7	.9	1.1	1.0

a. For the definitions of the variables see page 185.
b. Variables 2, 11, 12 and 13 are given in absolute changes, the remaining variables in percentage changes.

Figure 13.9. Eight quarter simulation 1967:1–1968:4 billions of Dfl., index number 1963 = 100 or per cent)

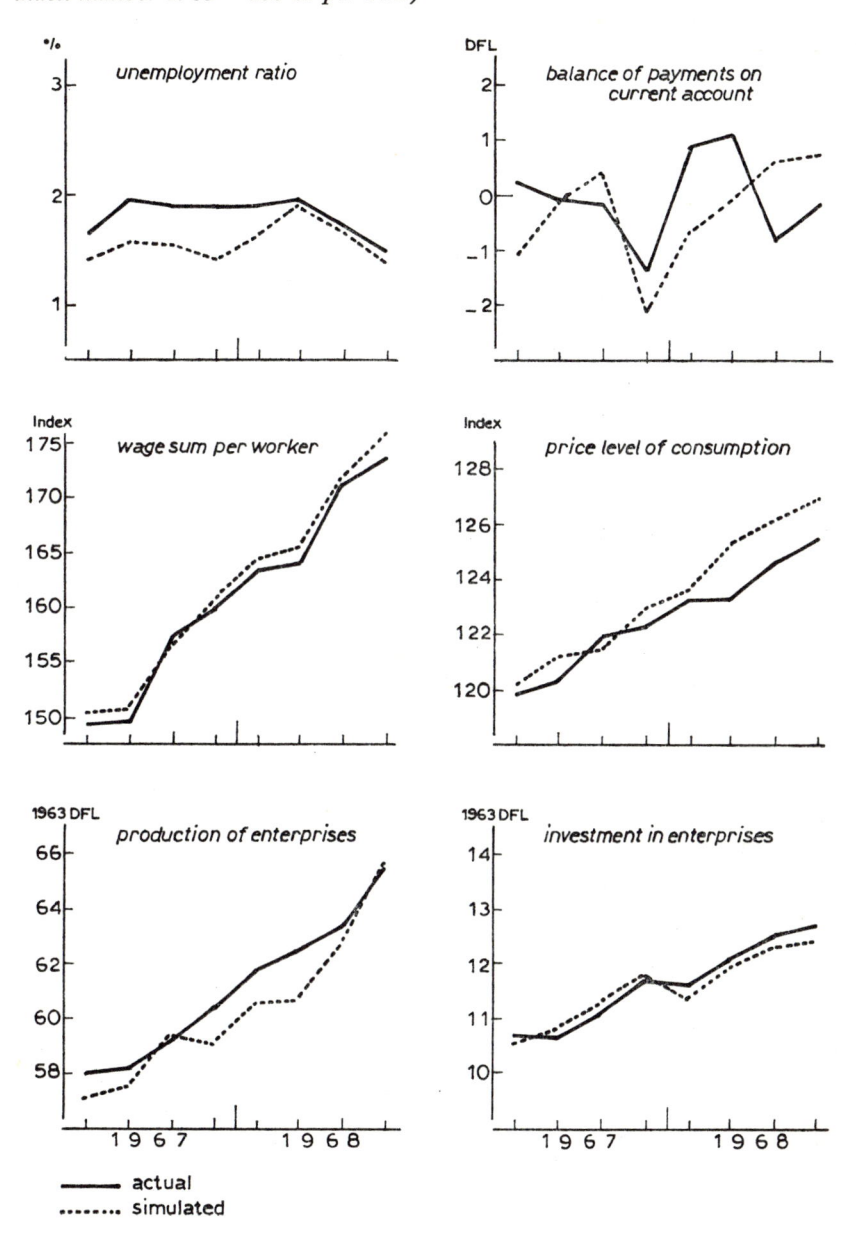

—— actual
······· simulated

ment ratio is therefore too small. This contributes to the overestimation of investment, as well as to wages and prices. Except for consumer prices turning points are picked up rather well by the model, although both the unemployment ratio and production are too volatile.

The inequality coefficient for the thirteen variables in table 13.5 is .21.

13.7. SIMULATION 1961:1–1962:4

On the average the labour market is not quite so tight as in reality. The price of labour is therefore slightly lower and so are consumer prices. Since user cost of capital are somewhat more underestimated the factor prices ratio is lowering employment and stimulating investment. Consequently the balance of payment is getting worse in 1962 and less liquidities are coming from abroad. The underestimated level of the liquidity ratio is reflected in an over-assessment of the interest rate.

The inequality coefficient is .35.

13.8. SIMULATION 1963:1–1964:4

Similar to the previous period the labour market is not so extremely tight in the simulation. Labour demand is underestimated, even in 1963 when production is above its real level. The narrow relationship between utilization rate and investment becomes again apparent in the underestimation of the latter. Since exports are too high and imports too low, the balance of payments on current account shows too large a surplus and too small a deficit in 1963 and 1964 respectively. This bears consequences for the liquidity ratio and the interest rate.

The inequality coefficient is .24.

13.9. SIMULATION 1965:1–1966:4

Although the simulation of the unemployment ratio is not so bad on the average its fluctuations within the eight quarter period are too large. Labour supply is largely responsible. Because imports are too high in 1966:1 the balance of payments simulation is extremely bad. On the average the balance of external trade is positive whereas there actually was a deficit. The interest rate is still rising but less than actual since the liquidity position was enlarged by liquidity creation via the current account.

The inequality coefficient is, .18.

13.10. SIMULATION 1967:1–1968:4

This simulation is completely beyond the sample period and shows shortcomings similar to simulations within the sample period. What is not shown, by the table or the figure, is that user cost of capital are overestimated which stimulates labour demand. As a consequence the unemployment ratio is too low which in its turn stimulates investment in the beginning of the period. Later on investment is lowered by the mentioned error in relative factor prices. Due to a wrong prediction of the consumption price a relatively large absolute error arises this time in the volume of private consumption.

The inequality coefficient of the selected variables in table 13.9. is .16.

13.11. SUMMARY

Within as well as beyond the sample period the nine eight-quarter simulations have yielded acceptable results, both in levels and in first differences. A general problem is, however, that the fluctuations of certain variables, especially the unemployment ratio, the production and the balance of payments on current account are too volatile. To a certain extent the root of these deficiencies is the simulation of the utilization rate of labour (approximately equal to one minus the unemployment ratio). An important reason for this error is the wholly inadequate quality of quarterly information on aggregate labour supply and its components.

The implicit annual simulations are characterized by low inequality coefficients which, with two exceptions, lie below .30. The average inequality coefficient of the short term annual model during the years 1953-1962, is .43. This is the inequality coefficient for ten variables, based on *perfect* knowledge of the predetermined variables, among them the lagged endogenous variables. For sixteen variables the inequality coefficient in the period 1949–1960, years within the sample period, was found to be .36; for two years beyond the sample period, 1961 and 1962, the coefficient was .29.[2] According to these results the errors to be attributed to the specification of the short term model (version 63-D) are on the average between 30 and 40 per cent of the normal rate of change of the variables.

Another model for comparison with the outcomes of the quarterly model is the cyclical growth model. For this model inequality coefficients are published for the years 1954–1963.[3] In contrast to the short-term annual model these coefficients are based on the same type of simulation experiments

2. See VERDOORN (1967).
3. See VAN DEN BELD (1968), p. 44.

as undertaken with our model. The coefficients result from a simulation of a time path of the endogenous variables with only the exogenous variables known, where the lagged endogenous variables are not predetermined but remain endogenous. The inequality coefficient per year for all variables in the cyclical growth model varies from .22 in 1954 to .58 in 1960, with an average of about .35. The predictive accuracy measured by the inequality coefficient is about the same as the short term annual model, but more satisfactory because the standard of accuracy imposed on the cyclical growth model is much higher than that on a short term model (cf. above).

Ultimately we have computed root mean square errors and inequality coefficients per variable for all the nine experiments. The results are given in table 13.10, where we give the variables upward from the lowest inequality coefficient. As might be expected from the foregoing analysis the unemployment ratio, the balance of payments and the monetary variables show a relatively unsatisfactory predictive record. Except for imports the root mean square errors of variables in our *simulations* are sometimes identical, but mostly even lower than the root mean square errors of the *residuals* of the comparable structural equations of the most recent version of the short term annual model.[4]

Table 13.10 Inequality coefficient and root mean square error of selected variables in nine eight-quarter simulations

	IC	RMSE		IC	RMSE
Wage sum per worker	.10	.9	Production of enterprises	.24	1.4
Price exports of goods	.20	1.1	Liquidity ratio	.28	.8
Imports of goods	.20	2.4	Unemployment ratio	.31	.2
Price of consumption	.21	.9	Employment	.32	.7
Exports of goods	.21	2.1	Balance of payments	.48	.46
Gross fixed investment	.23	2.8	Interest rate	.61	.3
Private consumption	.24	1.3			

4. See VERDOORN, POST and GOSLINGA (1970).

XIV. Medium-term simulations

14.1. INTRODUCTION

The simulation procedure described in the previous chapter is also applied for the testing of the 'growth' performance of the model. Actually the computer did four twenty-quarter runs. Again the 297 starting values of lagged endogenous variables must first be read in, together with 3300 values of 165 lagged and unlagged exogenous variables. The twenty-quarter simulation of the complete model then takes 34 seconds.

Once more both the level and the first difference aspects of the simulations are considered. These aspects are for thirteen selected variables mentioned in a table for each simulation period and speak plain language. Quarterly data have been transformed into annual data because we assume that the policymaker is not interested in the development between, say, the fourteenth and the fifteenth quarter.

Table 14.1. *Inequality coefficient and root mean square error of selected variables in simulation 1951:1 – 1955:4*

	IC	RMSE		*IC*	RMSE
Employment	.49	1.2	Price of consumption	.22	1.2
Unemployment ratio	.78	.6	Wage sum per worker	.10	.8
Private consumption	.34	1.6	Price exports of goods	.12	1.1
Gross fixed investment	.20	3.2	Balance of payments	.49	.56
Exports of goods	.16	1.9	Interest rate	.46	.2
Imports of goods	.35	5.5	Liquidity ratio	.25	1.2
Production of enterprises	.22	1.3			

Table 14.2. Simulated annual data of selected variables[a] derived from twenty quarter simulation 1951:1 – 1955:4

R = realisation P = simulation		Absolute level					Percentage or absolute change[b]				
		1951	1952	1953	1954	1955	1951	1952	1953	1954	1955
Employment	R	2395	2364	2416	2503	2581	1.7	−1.3	2.2	3.6	3.1
	P	2402	2352	2357	2443	2559	2.0	−2.1	.2	3.7	4.8
Unemployment ratio	R	2.4	3.5	2.6	1.9	1.3	.3	1.1	−.9	−.7	−.6
	P	2.2	3.4	3.5	2.3	1.0	.1	1.2	.1	−1.2	−1.3
Private consumption	R	18.45	18.59	19.69	20.75	22.08	−1.9	.8	5.9	5.4	6.4
	P	18.50	18.55	19.02	20.26	22.00	−1.6	.3	2.5	6.6	8.6
Gross fixed investment	R	3.71	3.34	3.69	4.50	5.55	−2.6	−10.0	10.5	22.0	23.3
	P	3.64	3.30	3.49	4.28	5.48	−4.6	−9.2	5.6	22.7	28.1
Exports of goods	R	6.78	7.38	8.27	9.37	10.35	13.4	8.9	12.1	13.3	10.5
	P	6.76	7.17	8.23	9.19	10.25	13.0	6.1	14.8	11.7	11.5
Imports of goods	R	8.26	7.36	8.81	10.99	11.87	−3.8	−10.9	19.7	24.7	8.0
	P	8.23	7.37	8.46	10.04	11.81	−4.2	−10.5	14.8	18.7	17.6
Production of enterprises	R	26.64	26.99	29.32	31.32	33.70	2.4	1.3	8.6	6.8	7.6
	P	26.90	26.63	29.04	31.37	34.07	3.4	−1.0	9.0	8.0	8.6
Price of consumption	R	75.5	75.5	75.2	78.7	80.5	10.6	−.1	−.3	4.7	2.3
	P	75.0	76.3	75.5	77.9	80.5	9.9	1.6	−1.0	3.2	3.3
Wage sum per worker	R	44.5	46.9	48.9	53.3	58.1	10.5	5.4	4.2	9.2	8.9
	P	44.3	47.2	48.6	52.9	57.8	10.0	6.6	2.9	9.0	9.2
Price of exports of goods	R	109.9	109.1	100.8	99.0	100.3	19.9	−.8	−7.6	−1.8	1.3
	P	111.7	110.3	102.0	98.5	100.1	21.9	−1.3	−7.5	−3.4	1.6
Balance of payments on current account	R	−.26	1.76	1.36	.23	.78	.86	2.02	−.40	−1.13	.55
	P	.03	1.71	1.83	1.07	.65	1.15	1.68	.12	−.76	−.42
Interest rate	R	4.0	4.0	3.3	3.2	3.1	.8	0	−.7	−.1	−.1
	P	3.8	3.7	3.3	2.9	2.8	.6	−.1	−.4	−.4	−.1
Liquidity ratio	R	20.5	25.8	26.8	25.9	24.9	−8.6	5.3	1.0	−.9	−1.0
	P	21.4	26.3	27.8	27.4	25.0	−7.7	4.9	1.5	−.4	−2.4

a. For the definitions of the variables see page 185.
b. Variables 2, 11, 12 and 13 are given in absolute changes, the remaining variables in percentage changes.

14.2. SIMULATION 1951:1 – 1955:4

This period includes both a recession (1951–52) and an upturn (1953–1955). Both in levels and in first differences the cyclical movements of the variables are captured very well. Nevertheless there are a few false turning points: the unemployment ratio in 1953, the production in 1952, the balance of payments in 1953 and 1955 and, of minor importance, the interest rate in 1952.

The simulation of employment, unemployment ratio, balance of payments and interest rate is less satisfactory. Although the RMSE of some variables seems high at first sight they are less striking when they are related to their average changes in the period considered.

14.3. SIMULATION 1955:1 – 1959:4

This period includes the top of a boom (1955–1956), a recession (1957–1958) and a, partial, recovery (1959). The model generates too mild a recession. Unemployment is not rising fast enough in 1957 since employment is too high in that year. Consequently investment is rising too much in 1957 and not sufficiently declining in the next year. Capacity utilization is also less stimulating for exports, while imports are too large. So the balance of payments does not improve substantially between 1956 and 1958 and the liquidity position therefore remains relatively tight. As a consequence the interest rate is .6 per cent higher in 1958. Finally, the performance of wages and prices is rather satisfactory. This is not so astonishing as our analysis has shown that wage policy has prevented wages to be dependent on the unemployment situation during this period. This has its influence on the simulation performance of prices as well.

Table 14.3. Inequality coefficient and root mean square error of selected variables in simulation 1955:1 – 1959:4

	IC	RMSE		IC	RMSE
Employment	.31	.7	Price of consumption	.23	.7
Unemployment ratio	.50	.3	Wage sum per worker	.18	1.4
Private consumption	.13	.6	Price exports of goods	.59	1.5
Gross fixed investment	.44	6.4	Balance of payments	.53	.64
Exports of goods	.16	1.9	Interest rate	.46	.3
Imports of goods	.42	3.8	Liquidity ratio	.67	1.4
Production of enterprises	.37	1.8			

Table 14.4. *Simulated annual data of selected variables[a] derived from twenty quarter simulation 1955:1 – 1959:4*

R = realisation P = simulation		Absolute level					Percentage or absolute change[b]				
		1955	1956	1957	1958	1959	1955	1956	1957	1958	1959
Employment	R	2581	2649	2686	2663	2715	3.1	2.6	1.4	−.9	2.0
	P	2580	2648	2717	2691	2721	3.1	2.6	2.6	−.9	1.1
Unemployment ratio	R	1.3	1.0	1.2	2.3	1.9	−.6	−.3	.2	1.1	−.4
	P	1.3	.9	.6	2.1	1.9	−.6	−.4	−.3	1.5	−.2
Private consumption	R	22.08	23.73	23.79	23.87	24.92	6.4	7.5	.3	.3	4.4
	P	22.01	23.74	23.99	24.15	25.00	6.1	7.9	1.1	.7	3.5
Gross fixed investment	R	5.55	6.07	6.16	5.22	5.89	23.3	9.4	1.5	−15.3	12.8
	P	5.38	5.82	6.56	5.91	6.32	19.7	8.2	12.7	−9.9	6.9
Exports of goods	R	10.35	10.66	11.24	12.37	13.87	10.5	3.0	5.4	10.1	12.1
	P	10.27	10.80	10.99	12.03	14.35	9.6	5.2	1.8	9.5	19.3
Imports of goods	R	11.87	13.47	13.88	13.05	14.82	8.0	13.5	3.0	−6.0	13.6
	P	11.93	13.20	13.90	13.48	14.95	8.6	10.7	5.3	−3.0	10.9
Production of enterprises	R	33.70	35.31	36.40	35.98	37.84	7.6	4.8	3.1	−1.2	5.2
	P	33.68	35.67	36.08	35.90	38.94	7.5	5.9	1.2	−.5	8.5
Price of consumption	R	80.5	82.5	87.1	88.5	89.6	2.3	2.4	5.7	1.6	1.3
	P	80.9	82.8	87.8	87.9	89.0	2.8	2.4	6.0	.1	1.3
Wage sum per worker	R	58.1	63.1	70.0	73.0	74.7	8.9	8.6	10.9	4.4	2.4
	P	58.5	64.0	70.8	72.5	75.8	9.6	9.4	10.6	2.5	4.5
Price of exports of goods	R	100.3	102.8	105.8	101.5	101.2	1.3	2.5	2.9	−4.0	−.3
	P	100.1	103.0	107.4	101.5	98.6	1.1	2.9	4.2	−5.5	−2.9
Balance of payments on current account	R	.78	−.75	−.59	1.53	1.78	.55	−1.53	.16	2.12	.25
	P	.56	−.37	−1.11	.68	1.76	.33	−.93	−.74	1.79	1.08
Interest rate	R	3.1	3.9	4.9	4.4	4.2	−.1	.8	1.0	−.5	−.2
	P	3.2	3.9	5.0	5.1	4.7	0	.7	1.1	.1	−.4
Liquidity ratio	R	24.9	23.0	22.4	26.5	26.6	−1.0	−1.9	−.6	4.1	.1
	P	23.7	23.3	22.1	24.5	26.3	−2.2	−.4	−1.2	2.4	1.8

a. For the definitions of the variables see page 185.
b. Variables 2, 11, 12 and 13 are given in absolute changes, the remaining variables in percentage changes.

14.4. SIMULATION 1959:1 – 1963:4

A high growth rate of production, a very low unemployment ratio and a deteriorating balance of payments are characteristic for this period. The model generates some false turning points, for instance: the rise in unemployment in 1962 and consequently a fall in investment in the same year, a rising surplus on the balance of payments in 1963 instead of a declining one and a rise in the price of exports in 1960 instead of a decrease. In general, the levels of the variables are simulated rather well except for the wage sum per worker which is underestimated in the years 1961–1963, due to an overestimation of the unemployment ratio in the years 1961 and 1962.

The table below shows very high inequality coefficients for the unemployment ratio, due to a large error in 1963, the export price level and the interest rate.

Table 14.5. *Inequality coefficient and root mean square error of selected variables in simulation 1959:1 – 1963:4*

	IC	RMSE		IC	RMSE
Employment	.33	.9	Price of consumption	.30	.8
Unemployment ratio	1.13	.5	Wage sum per worker	.26	1.8
Private consumption	.16	.9	Price exports of goods	1.00	1.5
Gross fixed investment	.49	5.2	Balance of payments	.60	.23
Exports of goods	.24	2.3	Interest rate	.80	.2
Imports of goods	.16	1.8	Liquidity ratio	.69	.5
Production of enterprises	.28	1.6			

14.5. SIMULATION 1963:1 – 1967:4

This period involves the top of a boom (1963–1965) and a moderate recession (1966–1967). The development of the economy is furthermore characterized by a number of structural changes, which are treated as exogenous in the simulation.[1] Similar to the eight quarter experiments, relatively serious deficiencies are the overestimation of the wage rate, the price level of consumption and consequently the underestimation of the consumption volume. Exports of goods are underassessed as well, with export prices too high and capacity utilization too low. The underestimation of expenditures bears consequences for imports and production. The balance

1. See also chapter XIII, page 186.

Table 14.6. Simulated annual data of selected variables[a] derived from twenty quarter simulation 1959:1 – 1963:4

R = realisation
P = simulation

		Absolute level					Percentage or absolute change[b]				
		1959	1960	1961	1962	1963	1959	1960	1961	1962	1963
Employment	R	2715	2806	2872	2960	3027	2.0	3.4	2.4	3.1	2.3
	P	2717	2811	2859	2915	3026	2.0	3.5	1.7	2.0	3.8
Unemployment ratio	R	1.9	1.2	.8	.8	.8	−.4	−.7	−.4	0	0
	P	1.8	1.1	1.1	1.4	.5	−.5	−.7	0	.3	−.9
Private consumption	R	24.92	26.43	27.86	29.57	31.66	4.4	6.1	5.4	6.1	7.1
	P	25.18	26.34	28.00	29.72	31.82	5.5	4.6	6.3	6.1	7.1
Gross fixed investment	R	5.89	6.93	7.49	7.89	7.89	12.8	17.7	8.1	5.3	0
	P	5.94	7.29	7.48	7.26	7.52	13.8	22.7	2.6	−2.9	3.6
Exports of goods	R	13.87	15.86	16.32	17.47	18.59	12.1	14.4	2.9	7.1	6.4
	P	14.17	15.92	16.18	17.94	19.00	14.6	12.3	1.6	10.9	5.9
Imports of goods	R	14.82	17.37	18.64	19.68	21.61	13.6	17.2	7.3	5.6	9.8
	P	14.78	17.61	18.33	19.62	21.58	13.2	19.2	4.1	7.0	10.0
Production of enterprises	R	37.84	41.65	42.94	44.87	46.46	5.2	10.1	3.1	4.5	3.5
	P	38.73	41.76	42.52	44.63	46.49	7.6	7.8	1.8	5.0	4.2
Price of consumption	R	89.6	91.8	93.9	96.3	100	1.3	2.4	2.3	2.6	3.8
	P	89.2	92.2	93.4	95.5	99.8	.8	3.4	1.3	2.2	4.6
Wage sum per worker	R	74.7	80.8	86.7	91.8	100	2.4	8.1	7.2	5.9	9.0
	P	75.6	80.7	84.6	87.5	96.5	3.5	6.8	4.8	3.5	10.2
Price of exports of goods	R	101.2	100.6	98.4	97.8	100	−.3	−.7	−2.1	−.7	2.3
	P	99.3	100.5	99.1	97.5	101.1	−2.2	1.3	−1.4	1.6	3.7
Balance of payments on current account	R	1.78	1.25	.63	.50	.37	.25	−.53	−.62	−.13	−.13
	P	1.87	1.08	.81	.79	.90	.34	−.79	−.27	−.02	.11
Interest rate	R	4.2	4.2	3.9	4.2	4.2	−.2	0	−.3	.3	0
	P	4.0	3.9	3.6	4.2	4.2	−.4	−.1	−.3	.6	0
Liquidity ratio	R	26.6	25.2	25.1	24.6	24.6	.1	−1.4	−.1	−.5	0
	P	26.8	26.0	25.5	24.5	25.0	.3	−.8	−.5	−1.0	.5

a. For the definitions of the variables see page 185.
b. Variables 2, 11, 12 and 13 are given in absolute changes, the remaining variables in percentage changes.

of payments simulation shows two false turning points. As the liquidity ratio is too large, the interest rate is underestimated by one per cent in 1967.

Although absolute errors may seem large for certain variables they become less striking when they are expressed as percentage changes. Table 14.7 shows in general inequality coefficients below .50, the exceptions are the balance of payments and the interest rate.

Table 14.7. *Inequality coefficient and root mean square error of selected variables in simulation 1963:1 – 1967:4*

	IC	RMSE		IC	RMSE
Employment	.25	.5	Price of consumption	.25	1.2
Unemployment ratio	.51	.2	Wage sum per worker	.13	1.4
Private consumption	.12	.7	Price exports of goods	.39	.7
Gross fixed investment	.44	4.0	Balance of payments	1.06	.73
Exports of goods	.14	3.8	Interest rate	.68	.4
Imports of goods	.26	1.3	Liquidity ratio	.46	.5
Production of enterprises	.26	1.6			

14.6. SUMMARY

The simulations described in the previous sections show that the model is able to generate medium-term growth. The forecasting records of the four twenty quarter simulations, measured by inequality coefficients, are in general satisfactory. The model's major difficulty is the simulation of the utilization rate of labour, or alternatively the unemployment ratio. Both the simulated levels and the changes in the unemployment ratio show sometimes serious discrepancies with reality and in general the fluctuations are too volatile. The quality of the labour supply function, estimated from inferior data, seems largely responsible for these errors. Other variables, however, show a more satisfactory simulation performance both in levels and in first differences. Similar to eight quarter experiments the simulated recessions are too mild.

Ranking the variables according to their average inequality coefficient in four medium-term simulations yields the order given in table 14.9.

It is interesting to compare the average inequality coefficients and root mean square errors of the eight quarter and twenty quarter simulations (tables 13.10 and 14.9). The ranking of the variables appears to be roughly the same: what is good/bad in the short term simulations is good/bad in

Table 14.8. Simulated annual data of selected variables[a] derived from twenty quarter simulation 1963:1 – 1967:4

R = realisation P = simulation		Absolute level					Percentage or absolute change[b]				
		1963	1964	1965	1966	1967	1963	1964	1965	1966	1967
Employment	R	3027	3111	3160	3194	3181	2.3	2.8	1.6	1.1	−.4
	P	3018	3083	3130	3181	3186	2.0	2.2	1.5	1.6	.2
Unemployment ratio	R	.8	.7	.8	1.0	1.8	0	−.1	.1	.2	.8
	P	.9	1.0	1.0	.8	1.5	.1	.1	0	−.2	.7
Private consumption	R	31.66	33.55	36.03	37.24	39.16	7.1	6.0	7.4	3.4	5.2
	P	31.49	33.36	35.44	36.82	38.48	6.5	5.9	6.2	3.9	4.5
Gross fixed investment	R	7.89	9.14	9.47	10.45	11.08	0	15.8	3.6	10.3	6.0
	P	7.60	8.41	8.91	10.16	11.24	−3.6	10.7	5.9	14.0	10.6
Exports of goods	R	18.59	20.96	22.79	24.27	26.09	6.4	12.8	8.7	6.5	7.5
	P	19.30	20.99	23.35	24.97	25.42	10.5	8.8	11.2	6.9	1.8
Imports of goods	R	21.61	24.98	26.50	28.17	29.94	9.8	15.6	6.1	6.3	6.3
	P	21.37	24.66	26.07	28.28	29.67	8.6	15.4	5.7	8.5	4.9
Production of enterprises	R	46.46	51.05	54.10	55.69	58.94	3.5	9.9	6.0	2.9	5.8
	P	46.79	50.46	53.58	55.67	57.59	4.3	7.8	6.2	4.1	3.3
Price of consumption	R	100	106.7	111.2	117.2	121.3	3.8	6.8	4.2	5.4	3.5
	P	100.2	108.0	112.0	119.9	126.3	4.1	7.7	3.7	7.0	5.4
Wage sum per worker	R	100	114.9	127.8	141.8	154.2	9.0	14.9	11.2	11.0	8.8
	P	100.4	115.5	128.8	144.4	161.4	9.4	15.1	11.5	12.1	11.8
Price of exports of goods	R	100	102.1	104.3	104.4	103.6	2.3	2.1	2.1	.1	−.8
	P	99.7	102.1	103.4	104.7	104.2	1.9	2.5	1.3	1.2	−.5
Balance of payments on current account	R	.37	−.64	.07	−.71	−.25	−.13	−1.01	.71	−.78	.46
	P	1.17	−.27	.82	.25	−.57	.67	−1.44	1.09	−.57	−.82
Interest rate	R	4.2	5.1	5.5	6.5	6.1	0	.9	.4	1.0	−.4
	P	4.1	4.4	4.4	4.9	4.9	−.1	.3	0	.5	0
Liquidity ratio	R	24.6	22.6	22.9	22.4	23.1	0	−2.0	.3	−.5	.7
	P	25.0	23.8	24.3	23.6	23.9	.4	−1.2	.5	−.7	.3

a. For the definitions of the variables see page 185.
b. Variables 2, 11, 12 and 13 are given in absolute changes, the remaining variables in percentage changes.

Table 14.9. Inequality coefficient and average root mean square error of selected variables in four medium-term simulations.

	IC	RMSE		IC	RMSE
Wage sum per worker	.16	1.4	Liquidity ratio	.34	.9
Private consumption	.19	1.0	Employment	.37	.9
Price of consumption	.24	1.0	Gross fixed investment	.38	4.9
Price exports of goods	.26	1.3	Interest rate	.60	.3
Imports of goods	.27	3.2	Balance of payments	.62	.57
Production of enterprises	.28	1.6	Unemployment ratio	.75	.4
Exports of goods	.31	3.1			

medium term simulations. On the whole the quality of the eight quarter experiments is better. This is what one would expect because the chance that the simulation errors in a certain quarter influence the simulations in subsequent quarters is increasing with the length of the simulation period. Table 14.10 expresses the average eight quarter root mean square errors as a decimal fraction of the average twenty quarter root mean square errors. Since the average rate of change is approximately equal for both types of simulations this ratio indicates as well the ratio of inequality coefficients. With two exceptions, short term simulations are better than medium term simulations but the differences are surprisingly small.

Table 14.10. Ratio of average eight-quarter to average twenty-quarter root mean square errors

Wage sum per worker	.64	Production of enterprises	.88
Price exports of goods	.85	Liquidity ratio	.89
Imports of goods	.75	Unemployment ratio	.50
Price of consumption	.90	Employment	.78
Exports of goods	.68	Balance of payments	.81
Gross fixed investment	.57	Interest rate	1.00
Private consumption	1.30		

XV. Policy and other simulations

15.1 INTRODUCTION

This final chapter describes the model's solution during the period 1963:1 – 1967:4 under circumstances different from the original solution. These types of solutions are usually called simulations among which the policy simulations are of course of special interest.

The results of such experiments may be useful from several points of view, among which the tracing of dubious simulation results to particular equations and their possible revision are particularly important for the model builder.[1] This, however, is a time consuming and ambitious task which we have reserved for the near future possibly leading to an enlarged insight into "Economic Policy in a Near-Full Employment Economy". Such an analysis should for instance include the calculation of multipliers for a great number of policies and dynamic stability tests of the model when exposed to exogenous shocks.[2]

So, although the analysis of policy simulations is a complicated and difficult task we nevertheless don't want to finish this book without giving an insight into the effects of a number of circumstances different from the original simulation during the period 1963:1 – 1967:4. These circumstances involve sustained changes in three government policies and in wages, as well as a sustained change in world imports of goods from 1963:1 onwards. More specifically we consider the effects of a sustained increase in
1. direct taxes of Dfl. 500 mln, half of which on wage and the other half on non-wage income;

---

1. See for instance TAUBMAN and FROMM (1967).
2. For a list of tests to which a new econometric model should be subjected, see GORDON (1970), p. 491.

2. indirect taxes of Dfl. 500 mln;
3. autonomous expenditures of Dfl. 500 mln;
4. wages in enterprises of 1%, and in
5. world imports of goods of 1%.

In the following sections we present the effects of these various policy alternatives and world imports on a number of variables, among which the targets of economic policy. These variables are: the wage sum per worker, the price of private consumption, the volume of private consumption, the price of gross fixed investment, the volume of gross fixed investment (excluding housing), the volume of exports of goods, the volume of imports of goods, the volume of production of enterprises, employment, non-wage income, the balance of payments on current account, the unemployment ratio, the interest rate and the liquidity ratio.

It should be kept in mind that the effects of the variants depend on the levels of the variables and on the cyclical position of the economy during the solution period. Especially important in this connection is the wage equation in use for these years.[3] The price of consumption variable in this equation has an elasticity coefficient above unity and is hardly lagged so that the system has an "explosive" nominal block which tends to set a wage-price spiral going in certain circumstances.

The results of the variants are given in the form of cumulated *annual* deviations from the control solution mentioned in Chapter XIV, table 14.4. Except for the interest rate, the liquidity ratio, the balance of payments on current account and the unemployment ratio they are presented as cumulated percentage deviations from the original solution.

All changes in the variables mentioned are in the positive direction but by changing signs the opposites of the variants, too, can be analysed. The effects of a policy mix can, within certain limits, be obtained by combining the effects of the desired set of variants.

Finally, it should be borne in mind that the variants only give a rough idea of the effects of the policy measures over a certain period of time because, apart from the quality of the model,
i. the policy measures cannot always be adequately translated in terms of autonomous changes in one or more variables of the model;
ii. the model does not consider more effects than endogenous variables included, and
iii. the model is of an aggregative character.

---

3. See Chapter VIII, section 8.12.

15.2 SHORT EVALUATION OF THE SIMULATIONS

The variants summarized in the tables 15.1–15.5 show fundamental differences in their effects on the selected variables. These differences are related to the time structure of the effects as well as to the intensity of reactions. As said before it is beyond the scope of this study to analyse and to explain all the effects which take place over time and to combine them into an appropriate policy mix for a given situation. Nevertheless we pay attention to some striking aspects of the policy and other simulations.

a. *Increase of direct taxes*

A sustained increase of Dfl. 500 million direct taxes (on cash basis) has a direct negative influence on disposable incomes and through this lowering effects on private consumption, investment and employment (table 15.1). The resulting decline in capacity utilization stimulates exports and restricts imports, the latter being directly influenced by the decrease in demand as

Table 15.1. *Cumulated effects of a sustained increase of direct taxes of Dfl. 500 mln in 1963*

Cumulated effect on:	Unit	1963	1964	1965	1966	1967
Wage sum per worker	%	.03	−.41	−.35	−.29	−.41
Price private consumption	%	−.04	−.35	−.29	−.21	−.30
Volume private consumption	%	−.76	−.86	−.52	−.43	−.48
Price gross fixed investment	%	.02	−.28	−.44	−.44	−.30
Volume gross fixed investment	%	−.50	−1.19	−.38	−.13	−.43
Volume exports of goods	%	.07	.62	.72	.62	.90
Volume imports of goods	%	−.50	−1.05	−.40	−.08	−.30
Volume production of enterprises	%	−.32	.01	.24	.16	.27
Employment	%	−.13	−.29	−.12	−.05	−.13
Non-wage income	%	−.79	−.36	−.09	−.20	−.18
Balance of payments on current account	Dfl	.14	.36	.21	.11	.22
Unemployment ratio	Δ	.09	.15	.05	.03	.07
Interest rate	Δ	−.01	−.05	−.11	−.15	−.14
Liquidity ratio	Δ	.05	.30	.30	.15	.15

% = cumulated deviation as percent of control solution.
Dfl = cumulated deviation in billions of guilders in current prices from the control solution.
Δ = cumulated absolute deviation from the control solution.

well. The result is an improvement of the current balance, an enlarging of liquid reserves and a lower interest rate. Although the negative effects on production are larger than on employment in the first year, which implies a decrease in labour productivity, wages are rising, though slightly, because employees shift their additional tax burden by claiming higher wages.

However, in the second and subsequent years wages are lower, as well as prices. The initial fall in production fully reflects itself in employment in the second year. More complete also is then the influence of real disposable non-wage income and capacity utilization on investment and therefore on imports, balance of payments and monetary variables. Monetary developments, however, are stimulating for investment in the third year, so that the relatively sharp second year effects are compensated somewhat later on. Finally, we draw attention to the rise in production and the fall in labour demand, which is explained by the rise in wages relative to the user costs of capital, as well as by the fall in disposable non-wage income, both leading to a reduction in labour demand. In addition, the rise in unemployment itself tends to reduce labour demand.

b. *Increase of indirect taxes*

When indirect taxes on private consumption are raised by Dfl. 500 mln, the wage-price mechanism included in the model for the period under consideration becomes fully clear. Table 15.2 shows the results for the selected variables. The most striking effect of a raise of indirect taxes seems the self propelling inflation, fed by an active process of shifting the new tax burden to other groups of subjects. This inflationary process as such has therefore hardly consequences for *real* wages but the more for the rate of return on invested capital and thus for capital accumulation and employment. Apart from the first year, labour-productivity is stimulated but is fully concentrated in export industries since exports speed up favoured by lower capacity utilization and lower export prices because the user costs of capital (interest rate), which are of importance here, are decreasing.

c. *Increase of autonomous expenditure*

Table 15.3 shows effects of a sustained increase of Dfl. 500 mln of autonomous expenditure, either government consumption, government investment or investment in housing. Such a policy is favourable for employment, especially in the second year, at the cost of more inflation and a larger deficit on current account. The latter as a consequence of a decrease in exports and rising imports. Initially production and investment are stimu-

Table 15.2. Cumulated effects of a sustained increase of indirect taxes of Dfl. 500 mln in 1963

Cumulated effect on:	Unit	Cumulated effects in:				
		1963	1964	1965	1966	1967
Wage sum per worker	%	1.16	.86	1.95	1.89	1.61
Price private consumption	%	1.20	.86	2.06	1.96	1.85
Volume private consumption	%	−.64	−.92	−1.12	−1.04	−1.00
Price gross fixed investment	%	.16	−.02	−.09	.20	.30
Volume gross fixed investment	%	−.80	−2.12	−1.33	−.83	−.68
Volume exports of goods	%	−.08	1.06	1.42	2.00	2.42
Volume imports of goods	%	−.41	−1.40	−.94	−.70	−.37
Volume production of enterprises	%	−.43	.18	.26	.67	.75
Employment	%	−.25	−.59	−.57	−.48	−.41
Non-wage income	%	−3.06	−1.94	−1.21	−.74	−.60
Balance of payments on current account	Dfl	.12	.49	.47	.48	.45
Unemployment ratio	Δ	.16	.32	.30	.25	.22
Interest rate	Δ	−.01	−.11	−.17	−.28	−.27
Liquidity ratio	Δ	0	.20	.40	.30	.30

Table 15.3. Cumulated effects of a sustained increase of autonomous expenditures of Dfl. 500 mln in 1963

Cumulated effect on:	Unit	Cumulated effects in:				
		1963	1964	1965	1966	1967
Wage sum per worker	%	.42	.75	.55	.60	.83
Price private consumption	%	.19	.39	.20	.20	.36
Volume private consumption	%	.23	.38	.01	.06	.13
Price gross fixed investment	%	.04	.61	.55	.42	.56
Volume gross fixed investment	%	.86	1.06	.03	−.09	.17
Volume exports of goods	%	−.27	−1.06	−1.01	−1.19	−1.59
Volume imports of goods	%	1.07	1.51	.41	.23	.41
Volume production of enterprises	%	.73	−.01	−.11	−.20	−.40
Employment	%	.03	.39	.18	.17	.17
Non-wage income	%	1.59	.56	.46	.32	.28
Balance of payments on current account	Dfl	−.31	−.52	−.24	−.23	−.34
Unemployment ratio	Δ	−.19	−.18	−.09	−.10	−.09
Interest rate	Δ	.02	.09	.20	.23	.21
Liquidity ratio	Δ	−.20	−.50	−.40	−.20	−.20

% = cumulated deviation as percent of control solution
Dfl = cumulated deviation in billions of guilders in current prices from the control solution.
Δ = cumulated absolute deviation from the control solution.

lated, but later on the effects are less attractive from the point of view of growth. The reduced money supply through the balance of payments sets a rise in interest rates into action which, combined with a higher price of investment, leads to a rise in the user costs of capital. Higher wages do not counterbalance this effect so that the capacity effect on investment demand is reduced. Again, the signs for production and employment differ in the later years, when production is lower, but employment higher. In this case, this is mainly explained by the increased tensions on the labour market, which induce enterpreneurs to hoard labour.

d. *Increase of wages in enterprises*

A sustained wage increase of 1% raises the real wage rate since consumer prices are rising less (table 15.4). This is favourable for real consumption, but for investment as well as exports the consequences are unfavourable. On balance, there results some surplus capacity, partly also due to a decline in employment because labour becomes more expensive than capital. The surprising result is that the volume of exports is positively affected from the

Table 15.4. Cumulated effects of a sustained wage increase of 1% in 1963

Cumulated effect on:	Unit	Cumulated effects in:				
		1963	1964	1965	1966	1967
Wage sum per worker	%	1.28	1.31	1.24	1.21	1.13
Price private consumption	%	.28	.29	.26	.27	.23
Volume private consumption	%	.33	.27	.33	.42	.37
Price gross fixed investment	%	.17	.31	.32	.43	.47
Volume gross fixed investment	%	−.30	−.71	−.49	−.17	−.28
Volume exports of goods	%	−.16	.31	.48	.39	.41
Volume imports of goods	%	.13	−.07	.10	.36	.30
Volume production of enterprises	%	.02	.21	.32	.25	.19
Employment	%	−.08	−.22	−.16	−.04	−.03
Non-wage income	%	−.76	−.45	−.35	−.53	−.66
Balance of payments on current account	Dfl	−.04	.04	.02	−.07	−.06
Unemployment ratio	Δ	.07	.12	.07	.02	.02
Interest rate	Δ	0	−.01	−.01	−.01	0
Liquidity ratio	Δ	0	0	0	0	0

% = cumulated deviation as percent of control solution
Dfl = cumulated deviation in billions of guilders in current prices from the control solution.
Δ = cumulated absolute deviation from the control solution

second year onwards, when the excess capacity effect overcompensates the negative influence of the rise in wages. This seems to be true only in the historical context of the simulation period when competitive positions abroad were still rather good. Wage increases seem to have hardly any effect under these circumstances on the balance of payments and the monetary phenomena, but are unfavourable from a growth point of view.[4] Although investment is stimulated by the development of relative factor prices as well as by the growth of production, the lower capacity utilization and especially the lower rate of return on capital overcompensate these effects.

e. *Increase of world imports of goods*

When world imports of goods are assumed to have a 1% higher level during the simulation period exports are stimulated but considerably less than 1% (see table 15.5). One reason is that the additional world demand is assumed

Table 15.5. *Cumulated effects of a sustained increase in world imports of goods of 1% in 1963*

Cumulated effect on:	Unit	Cumulated effects in:				
		1963	1964	1965	1966	1967
Wage sum per worker	%	.07	.11	.04	.12	.11
Price private consumption	%	.03	.06	−.01	.03	.02
Volume private consumption	%	.03	.07	0	.07	.06
Price gross fixed investment	%	0	.09	.04	.03	.05
Volume gross fixed investment	%	.14	.20	.02	.12	.13
Volume exports of goods	%	.49	.29	.30	.37	.36
Volume imports of goods	%	.26	.33	.09	.28	.24
Volume production of enterprises	%	.12	0	.06	.09	.08
Employment	%	.04	.03	−.01	.03	.02
Non-wage income	%	.34	.18	.22	.36	.31
Balance of payments on current account	Dfl	.05	.02	.07	.06	.06
Unemployment ratio	Δ	−.03	−.02	0	−.01	−.01
Interest rate	Δ	0	−.01	−.01	−.02	−.03
Liquidity ratio	Δ	0	0	.10	.10	0

% = cumulated deviation as percent of control solution
Dfl = cumulated deviation in billions of guilders in current prices from the control solution
Δ = cumulated absolute deviation from the control solution

4. It is to be noted that government wages are exogenous in the model. The present variant, therefore, is restricted to a rise in wages in the enterprise sector only.

to influence only exports of manufactured goods, thus excluding agricultural products (and ships and airplanes) according to the relevant equation, and this effect is related to total exports in table 15.5. Moreover, in the over-full-employment situation of the simulation period 1963–'67 production cannot considerably be stimulated by the rise in world demand and the induced increase in domestic demand. Imports are then rising relatively fast so that the balance of payments effects are rather small and so are the effects on monetary phenomena.

15.3 CONCLUSIONS

The above presented simulations under alternative circumstances are to be considered as a first step to a more complete and more advanced analysis in this field. It is stressed that the outcomes of the simulations are only valid for the period considered, given the present structure of the model. This means that when for instance capital imports and exports had been considered as endogenous rather than exogenous variables, the policy and other simulations would have given outcomes different from those presented in the foregoing tables.

After all a further analysis of the results in tables 15.1–15.5 may show that the presented effects are not quite realistic or even unrealistic. This brings us to a final remark. The work on this model has learned us that very few things are certain and fixed in economic life and therefore in an econometric model. One can never be quite certain in having obtained a fully realistic and optimal result. Therefore there needs to be a continuous interaction between the estimation of the *individual* model equations and the simulations, both control and policy simulations, of the *complete* model. From this point of view the present version of the quarterly model is only a starting point and it goes without saying that a lot of work remains to be done in improving and completing the current set of relationships.

Appendices

APPENDIX A. MODEL EQUATIONS

1. $\ln L = .8 \ln L_{-1}$

$$+ .800 \left[\sum_{-1}^{-7} \gamma_1 \ln y - .8 \sum_{-2}^{-8} \gamma_1 \ln y \right]$$

$$+ .267 \left[\sum_{-1}^{-10} \gamma_2 (\ln p_k - \ln w) - .8 \sum_{-2}^{-11} \gamma_2 (\ln p_k - \ln w) \right]$$

$$+ .712 \left[\sum_{-3}^{-7} \gamma_3 \, q_L - .8 \sum_{-4}^{-8} \gamma_3 \, q_L \right]$$

$$+ .040 \left[\sum_{-3}^{-5} \gamma_4 \ln \frac{L_q}{V} - .8 \sum_{-4}^{-6} \gamma_4 \ln \frac{L_q}{V} \right]$$

$$+ .061 \left[\sum_{-4}^{-7} \gamma_5 \{ \ln(Z - T_L) - \ln p_{i-sa} \} \right.$$

$$\left. - .8 \sum_{-5}^{-8} \gamma_5 \{ \ln(Z - T_L) - \ln p_{i-sa} \} \right]$$

$$- .742 \left[\sum_{-2}^{-3} \gamma_6 \ln h_c - .8 \sum_{-3}^{-4} \gamma_6 \ln h_c \right]$$

$$- .043 \sum_{-3}^{-6} \gamma_7 \ln i_{-sa}$$

$$+ .030\ [L_{aut} - .8\ L_{aut-1}]$$
$$+ .265$$

2. $\ln P_S - \ln P_{S-4} = .4(\ln P_{S-1} - \ln P_{S-5})$

$$+ 1.000\ [(\ln P_{ST} - \ln P_{ST-4}) - .4(\ln P_{ST-1} - \ln P_{ST-5})]$$

$$- .083\ \left[\sum_{-2}^{-3} \gamma_6 (\ln P_{ST} - \ln P_{ST-4}) - .4 \sum_{-3}^{-4} \gamma_6 (\ln P_{ST} - \ln P_{ST-4})\right]$$

$$+ .071\ \left[\sum_{-1}^{-9} \gamma_8 \left\{\left(\ln \frac{w}{p_c} - \ln \frac{w_{-4}}{p_{c-4}}\right) - \sum_{-1}^{-4} \gamma_7 \left(\ln \frac{w}{p_c} - \ln \frac{w_{-4}}{p_{c-4}}\right)\right\}\right.$$

$$\left. - .4 \sum_{-2}^{-10} \gamma_8 \left\{\left(\ln \frac{w}{p_c} - \ln \frac{w_{-4}}{p_{c-4}}\right) - \sum_{-1}^{-4} \gamma_7 \left(\ln \frac{w}{p_c} - \ln \frac{w_{-4}}{p_{c-4}}\right)\right\}\right]$$

$$+ .208\ \left[\sum_{-1}^{-3} \gamma_4 (q_L - q_{L-4}) - .4 \sum_{-2}^{-4} \gamma_4 (q_L - q_{L-4})\right]$$

$$+ .162\ \left[\sum_{-4}^{-6} \gamma_4\, \Delta (q_L - q_{L-4}) - .4 \sum_{-5}^{-7} \gamma_4\, \Delta (q_L - q_{L-4})\right]$$

$$+ .012\ [P_{S\,aut} - .4\ P_{S\,aut-1}]$$

$$- .001$$

3. $\ln i_{-sa} = .8 \ln i_{-sa-1}$

$$+ .704\ \left[\sum_{-1}^{-5} \gamma_9\, \Delta \ln y - .8 \sum_{-2}^{-6} \gamma_9\, \Delta \ln y\right]$$

$$- .146\ \sum_{-5}^{-6} \gamma_{10} (\Delta \ln p_k - \Delta \ln w)$$

$$+ 6.384\ \left[\sum_{0}^{-2} \gamma_4\, q_L - .8 \sum_{-1}^{-3} \gamma_4\, q_L\right]$$

$$+ 2.103\ \left[\sum_{-2}^{-3} \gamma_6\, \Delta q_L - .8 \sum_{-3}^{-4} \gamma_6\, \Delta q_L\right]$$

$$+ .613 \left[\sum_{-3}^{-5} \gamma_4 \frac{L_q}{V} - .8 \sum_{-4}^{-6} \gamma_4 \frac{L_q}{V} \right]$$

$$+ .245 \left[\sum_{-1}^{-5} \gamma_{11} \{\ln(Z - T_Z) - \ln p_{i-sa}\} \right.$$

$$\left. - .8 \sum_{-2}^{-6} \gamma_{11} \{\ln(Z - T_Z) - \ln p_{i-sa}\} \right]$$

$$+ .012 \, [t - .8 \, t_{-1}]$$

$$- .722 \left[\sum_{-3}^{-4} \gamma_6 \, \Delta \ln h_c - .8 \sum_{-4}^{-5} \gamma_6 \, \Delta \ln h_c \right]$$

$$+ .026 \, [T_c - .8 \, T_{c-1}]$$

$$+ .079 \, [i_{aut} - .8 \, i_{aut-1}]$$

$$- .933$$

4. $\ln C = .5 \ln C_{-1}$

$$+ .837 \left[\sum_{0}^{-2} \gamma_{12} \, \varphi_{-1} \ln W_D - .5 \sum_{-1}^{-3} \gamma_{12} \, \varphi_{-1} \ln W_D \right]$$

$$+ .308 \left[\sum_{0}^{-3} \gamma_5 (1 - \varphi_{-1}) \ln Z_D - .5 \sum_{-1}^{-4} \gamma_5 (1 - \varphi_{-1}) \ln Z_D \right]$$

$$+ .334 \, \Delta \ln p_{c-1}$$

$$- .003 \left[\sum_{-3}^{-4} \gamma_6 \, r - .5 \sum_{-4}^{-5} \gamma_6 \, r \right]$$

$$+ .184 \left[\sum_{-1}^{-2} \gamma_6 \frac{L_q}{V} - .5 \sum_{-2}^{-3} \gamma_6 \frac{L_q}{V} \right]$$

$$+ 1.238 \left[\sum_{-2}^{-3} \gamma_6 \, \Delta \, q_L - .5 \sum_{-3}^{-4} \gamma_6 \, \Delta \, q_L \right]$$

$$+ .190 \, [C_{aut} - .5 \, C_{aut-1}]$$

$$+ .466$$

5. $\Delta n = .5 \Delta n_{-1}$

   $+ .506 \left[\sum_{-1}^{-3} \gamma_{14} \Delta v - .5 \sum_{-2}^{-4} \gamma_{14} \Delta v \right]$

   $+ .377 (n_d - n_{-1})_{-1}$

   $- .134 [\Delta v - .5 \Delta v_{-1}]$

   $+ .006 \left[\sum_{0}^{-1} \gamma_6 \Delta p_{mg-sa} - .5 \sum_{-1}^{-2} \gamma_6 \Delta p_{mg-sa} \right]$

   $- .312 [\Delta r_{-1} - .5 \Delta r_{-2}]$

   $+ .705 \, Dum_1$

   $+ 1.021 \, Dum_2$

   $+ .142$

6. $n_d = (.390 - .127 \, t/100) \sum_{-1}^{-4} \gamma_{13} v$

7. $\ln b_{f-sa} = .4 \ln b_{f-sa-1}$

   $+ .930 \left[\sum_{0}^{-2} \gamma_{15} \ln m_w - .4 \sum_{-1}^{-3} \gamma_{15} \ln m_w \right]$

   $- 1.227 (\ln p_{bf-sa} - \ln p_{bgw})$

   $- .554 \left[\sum_{-3}^{-5} \gamma_4 \ln q_L - .4 \sum_{4}^{-6} \gamma_4 \ln q_L \right]$

   $+ .055 [b_{f\,eec} - .4 \, b_{f\,eec-1}]$

   $- .933$

8. $\ln b_{s-t} = .5 \ln b_{s-t-1}$

   $+ 1.126 [\ln y_w - .5 \ln y_{w-1}]$

   $- .284 \left(\sum_{0}^{-1} \gamma_6 \ln p_{bs-t} - \sum_{-1}^{-2} \gamma_6 \ln p_{bsw} \right)$

$$-1.628 \left[\sum_0^{-1} \gamma_6 \, \Delta \ln q_L - .5 \sum_{-1}^{-2} \gamma_6 \, \Delta \ln q_L \right]$$

$$-.024 \left[\sum_0^{-1} \gamma_6 \ln U_G - .5 \sum_{-1}^{-2} \gamma_6 \ln U_G \right]$$

$$+ .087 \, [b_{seec} - .5 \, b_{seec-1}]$$

$$+ .166 \, Dum_3$$

$$- 1.722$$

9. $\ln m_{g-sa} = .3 \ln m_{g-sa-1}$

$$+ 1.009 \, [\ln v_{mg} - .3 \ln v_{mg-1}]$$

$$+ .365 \, [\Delta \ln v_{mg-1} - .3 \, \Delta \ln v_{mg-2}]$$

$$+ .031 \, [\Delta n - .3 \, \Delta n_{-1}]$$

$$- .491 \, (\ln p_{mg-sa} - \ln p_{vmg})_{-1}$$

$$+ 1.684 \left[\sum_{-1}^{-3} \gamma_4 \, q_L - .3 \sum_{-2}^{-4} \gamma_4 \, q_L \right]$$

$$+ .850 \, [\Delta \ln p_{v-1} - .3 \, \Delta \ln p_{v-2}]$$

$$- 1.091$$

10. $\ln m_s = .5 \ln m_{s-1}$

$$+ .973 \, [\ln v_{ms} - .5 \ln v_{ms-1}]$$

$$+ .421 \, [\Delta \ln v_{ms-1} - .5 \, \Delta \ln v_{ms-2}]$$

$$- .477 \, (\Delta \ln p_{ms-1} - \Delta \ln p_{vms-2})$$

$$+ 2.155 \left[\sum_0^{-2} \gamma_4 \, \Delta q_L - .5 \sum_{-1}^{-3} \gamma_4 \, \Delta q_L \right]$$

$$+ .112 \, Dum_4$$

$$- .791$$

11.1. *1951:1 – 1954:3*

$$\ln w - \ln w_{-4} = .3(\ln w_{-1} - \ln w_{-5})$$
$$+ .549\ (\ln p_c - \ln p_{c-4})$$
$$+ .484 \left[\sum_{-1}^{-4} \gamma_{16} \{(\ln y - \ln L) - (\ln y_{-4} - \ln L_{-4})\} \right.$$
$$\left. - .3 \sum_{-2}^{-5} \gamma_{16} \{(\ln y - \ln L) - (\ln y_{-4} - \ln L_{-4})\} \right]$$
$$+ 1.441\ [\{(\ln h_w - \ln h_c) - (\ln h_{w-4} - \ln h_{c-4})\}$$
$$- .3\ \{(\ln h_{w-1} - \ln h_{c-1}) - (\ln h_{w-5} - \ln h_{c-5})\}]$$
$$+ 1.000\ [SPE - .3\ SPE_{-1}]$$
$$+ .541\ [TSPW - .3\ TSPW_{-1}]$$
$$+ .011$$

11.2. *1954:4 – 1959:2*

$$\ln w - \ln w_{-4} = .2(\ln w_{-1} - \ln w_{-5})$$
$$+ .739 \sum_{0}^{-1} \gamma_6 (\ln p_c - \ln p_{c-4})$$
$$+ .636 \left[\sum_{-1}^{-4} \gamma_{16} \{(\ln y - \ln L) - (\ln y_{-4} - \ln L_{-4})\} \right.$$
$$\left. - .2 \sum_{-2}^{-5} \gamma_{16} \{(\ln y - \ln L) - (\ln y_{-4} - \ln L_{-4})\} \right]$$
$$+ 1.000\ [SPE - .2\ SPE_{-1}]$$
$$+ .149\ [TSPW - .2\ TSPW_{-1}]$$
$$+ .049\ Dum_5$$
$$- .025\ Dum_6$$
$$+ .028$$

11.3. $\underline{1959:3 - 1962:4}$

$$\ln w - \ln w_{-4} = .900 \sum_{0}^{-1} \gamma_6 (\ln p_c - \ln p_{c-4})$$

$$+ .667 \sum_{-1}^{-4} \gamma_{16} \{(\ln y - \ln L) - (\ln y_{-4} - \ln L_{-4})\}$$

$$+ 2.854 \sum_{-1}^{-2} \gamma_6 \ln q_L$$

$$+ 1.000 \, SPE$$

$$+ .773 \, TSPW$$

$$+ .008 \, Dum_6$$

$$+ .042$$

11.4. $\underline{1963:1 - 1968:4}$

$$\ln w - \ln w_{-4} = 1.239 \sum_{0}^{-1} \gamma_6 (\ln p_c - \ln p_{c-4})$$

$$+ .378 \sum_{-1}^{-3} \gamma_{17} \{(\ln y - \ln L) - (\ln y_{-4} - \ln L_{-4})\}$$

$$+ .590 \sum_{0}^{-1} \gamma_6 \ln q_L$$

$$+ 1.000 \, SPE$$

$$+ .153 \, TSPW$$

$$+ .030$$

12. $\ln p_{c\,end} - \ln p_{c\,end-4} = .6(\ln p_{c\,end-1} - \ln p_{c\,end-5})$

$$+ .239 \left[\sum_{0}^{-1} \gamma_{18}(\ln w - \ln w_{-4}) - .6 \sum_{-1}^{-2} \gamma_{18}(\ln w - \ln w_{-4}) \right]$$

$$+ .014 \left[\sum_{-3}^{-5} \gamma_4(\ln p_k - \ln p_{k-4}) - .6 \sum_{-4}^{-6} \gamma_4(\ln p_k - \ln p_{k-4}) \right]$$

$$+ .194 \left[\sum_{0}^{-2} \gamma_{12} (\ln p_{mg-sa} - \ln p_{mg-sa_{-4}}) \right.$$
$$\left. - .6 \sum_{-1}^{-3} \gamma_{12} (\ln p_{mg-sa} - \ln p_{mg-sa_{-4}}) \right]$$
$$- .096 \left[\sum_{0}^{-2} \gamma_{17} \{ (\ln y - \ln L) - (\ln y - \ln L)_{-4} \} \right.$$
$$\left. - .6 \sum_{-1}^{-3} \gamma_{17} \{ (\ln y - \ln L) - (\ln y - \ln L)_{-4} \} \right]$$
$$+ .238 \left[\sum_{0}^{-2} \gamma_{4} (\ln q_{L} - \ln q_{L_{-4}}) - .6 \sum_{-1}^{-3} \gamma_{4} (\ln q_{L} - \ln q_{L_{-4}}) \right]$$
$$+ .209 \left[\sum_{0}^{-2} \gamma_{4} \ln q_{L} - .6 \sum_{-1}^{-3} \gamma_{4} \ln q_{L} \right]$$
$$+ .092 \left[\sum_{-2}^{-5} \gamma_{7} \{ (\ln c - \ln v) - (\ln c - \ln v)_{-4} \} \right.$$
$$\left. - .6 \sum_{-3}^{-6} \gamma_{7} \{ (\ln c - \ln v) - (\ln c - \ln v)_{-4} \} \right]$$
$$+ .008 \{ (n_{d} - n_{-1}) - (n_{d} - n_{-1})_{-4} \}$$
$$+ .006$$

13. $\ln p_{i-sa} - \ln p_{i-sa_{-4}} = .7 (\ln p_{i-sa_{-1}} - \ln p_{i-sa_{-5}})$
$$+ .144 \sum_{-1}^{-2} \gamma_{18} (\ln w - \ln w_{-4})$$
$$+ .031 \left[\sum_{-2}^{-3} \gamma_{6} (\ln p_{k} - \ln p_{k_{-4}}) - .7 \sum_{-3}^{-4} \gamma_{6} (\ln p_{k} - \ln p_{k_{-4}}) \right]$$
$$+ .144 \sum_{0}^{-1} \gamma_{6} (\ln p_{mg-sa} - \ln p_{mg-sa_{-4}})$$
$$- .058 \sum_{-1}^{-3} \gamma_{17} \{ (\ln y - \ln L) - (\ln y - \ln L)_{-4} \}$$
$$+ .972 \left[(\ln q_{L_{-2}} - \ln q_{L_{-6}}) - .7 (\ln q_{L_{-3}} - \ln q_{L_{-7}}) \right]$$

$$+ .065 \left[\sum_{-3}^{-5} \gamma_{12} \{(\ln i_{-sa} - \ln v) - (\ln i_{-sa} - \ln v)_{-4}\} \right.$$

$$\left. - .7 \sum_{-4}^{-6} \gamma_{12} \{(\ln i_{-sa} - \ln v) - (\ln i_{-sa} - \ln v)_{-4}\} \right]$$

$$- .001$$

14. $\ln p_x - \ln p_{x-4} = .7 (\ln p_{x-1} - \ln p_{x-5})$

$$+ .248 \left[\sum_{0}^{-1} \gamma_{18}(\ln w - \ln w_{-4}) - .7 \sum_{-1}^{-2} \gamma_{18}(\ln w - \ln w_{-4}) \right]$$

$$+ .236 \, (\ln p_{mg-sa} - \ln p_{mg-sa-4})$$

$$- .099 \left[\sum_{0}^{-2} \gamma_{17} \{(\ln y - \ln L) - (\ln y - \ln L)_{-4}\} \right.$$

$$\left. - .7 \sum_{-1}^{-3} \gamma_{17} \{(\ln y - \ln L) - (\ln y - \ln L)_{-4}\} \right]$$

$$+ .968 \left[\sum_{-1}^{-3} \gamma_{4}(\ln q_L - \ln q_{L-4}) - .7 \sum_{-2}^{-4} \gamma_{4}(\ln q_L - \ln q_{L-4}) \right]$$

$$+ .721 \left[\sum_{0}^{-2} \gamma_{4} \ln q_L - .7 \sum_{-1}^{-3} \gamma_{4} \ln q_L \right]$$

$$+ .093 \left[\sum_{-3}^{-5} \gamma_{4} \{(\ln x - \ln v) - (\ln x - \ln v)_{-4}\} \right.$$

$$\left. - .7 \sum_{-4}^{-6} \gamma_{4} \{(\ln x - \ln v) - (\ln x - \ln v)_{-4}\} \right]$$

$$+ .008$$

15. $\ln p_{bf-sa} - \ln p_{bf-sa-4} = .4(\ln p_{bf-sa-1} - \ln p_{bf-sa-5})$

$$+ .121 \sum_{0}^{-1} \gamma_{18}(\ln w - \ln w_{-4})$$

$$+ .100 \left[\sum_{-1}^{-2} \gamma_{6}(\ln p_k - \ln p_{k-4}) - .4 \sum_{-2}^{-3} \gamma_{6}(\ln p_k - \ln p_{k-4}) \right]$$

$$+ .283 \, (\ln p_{mg-sa} - \ln p_{mg-sa-4})$$

$$- .048 \sum_{0}^{-2} \gamma_{17} \{(\ln y - \ln L) - (\ln y - \ln L)_{-4}\}$$

$$+ 1.524 \, [(\ln q_{L-1} - \ln q_{L-5}) - .4(\ln q_{L-2} - \ln q_{L-6})]$$

$$+ 1.179 \left[\sum_{-1}^{-4} \gamma_7 \ln q_L - .4 \sum_{-2}^{-5} \gamma_7 \ln q_L \right]$$

$$+ .449 \left[\sum_{-2}^{-4} \gamma_4 \{(\ln b_{f-sa} - \ln v) - (\ln b_{f-sa} - \ln v)_{-4}\} \right.$$

$$\left. - .4 \sum_{-3}^{-5} \gamma_4 \{(\ln b_{f-sa} - \ln v) - (\ln b_{f-sa} - \ln v)_{-4}\} \right]$$

$$+ .260 \left[\sum_{-1}^{-4} \gamma_7 (\ln p_{bgw} - \ln p_{bgw-4}) - .4 \sum_{-2}^{-5} \gamma_7 (\ln p_{bgw} - \ln p_{bgw-4}) \right]$$

$$+ .210 \left[\sum_{-1}^{-3} \gamma_{19} \Delta(\ln m_w - \ln m_{w-4}) \right.$$

$$\left. - .4 \sum_{-2}^{-4} \gamma_{19} \Delta(\ln m_w - \ln m_{w-4}) \right]$$

$$- .012$$

16. $\ln p_{bs-t} - \ln p_{bs-t-4} = .300(\ln p_{bf-sa} - \ln p_{bf-sa-4})$

$\qquad + .300(\ln p_c - \ln p_{c-4})$

$\qquad + .400(\ln p_f - \ln p_{f-4})$

17.[a] $\Delta T_W = [\pi_W] \left\{ (1 - [v_W]) \Delta W_T + [v_W] \left(.60 \sum_{-1}^{-4} \gamma_7 \Delta W_T \right. \right.$

$\qquad \left. \left. + .40 \sum_{-6}^{-10} \gamma_{20} \sum_{0}^{-3} \gamma_7 \Delta W_T \right) \right\} + \Delta T_{W \, aut}$

18.[a] $\Delta T_Z = [\pi_Z] \left\{ (1 - [v_Z]) \sum_{-2}^{-8} \gamma_{21} \sum_{0}^{-3} \gamma_7 \Delta Z + [v_Z] \left(.60 \sum_{-1}^{-4} \gamma_7 \Delta Z \right. \right.$

$\qquad \left. \left. + .40 \sum_{-6}^{-10} \gamma_{20} \sum_{0}^{-3} \gamma_7 \Delta Z \right) \right\} + \Delta T_{Z \, aut}$

a. *Coefficients* between square brackets are changing over time.

19. $\quad \Delta T_K = [\pi_K] \Delta(V - CHR) + \Delta T_{K\,aut}$

20. $\quad r = .8\, r_{-1} - 7.565\, \dfrac{L_q}{V} + .525 \sum\limits_{-1}^{-10} \gamma_2 \left[\left(r - \sum\limits_{0}^{-3} \gamma_7\, 100\, \Delta \ln p_c \right) \right.$

$\qquad \left. - .8 \left(r_{-1} - \sum\limits_{-1}^{-4} \gamma_7\, 100\, \Delta \ln p_c \right) \right]$

$\qquad + .090 \left[\sum\limits_{0}^{-3} \gamma_7\, 100\, \Delta \ln p_c - .8 \sum\limits_{-1}^{-4} \gamma_7\, 100\, \Delta \ln p_c \right]$

$\qquad + .267\, [r_k - .8\, r_{k-1}]$

$\qquad + 5.590 \left[\dfrac{q_{L-2}}{\sum\limits_{-3}^{-6} \gamma_7\, q_L} - .8\, \dfrac{q_{L-3}}{\sum\limits_{-4}^{-7} \gamma_7\, q_L} \right]$

$\qquad + .285$

21. $\quad \dfrac{L_q}{V} = .3 \left(\dfrac{L_q}{V} \right)_{-1} + .364 \sum\limits_{0}^{-2} \gamma_4\, \dfrac{E_L + E_K}{V}$

$\qquad + .014 \sum\limits_{-1}^{-10} \gamma_2 \left[\left(r - \sum\limits_{0}^{-3} \gamma_7\, 100\, \Delta \ln p_c \right) \right.$

$\qquad \left. - .3 \left(r_{-1} - \sum\limits_{-1}^{-4} \gamma_7\, 100\, \Delta \ln p_c \right) \right]$

$\qquad - .016 \left[\left(r_{-1} - \sum\limits_{-1}^{-4} \gamma_7\, 100\, \Delta \ln p_c \right) - .3 \left(r_{-2} - \sum\limits_{-2}^{-5} \gamma_7\, 100\, \Delta \ln p_c \right) \right]$

$\qquad + .008\, [r_{k-1} - .3\, r_{k-2}]$

$\qquad - .007 \left[\sum\limits_{-1}^{-8} \gamma_{22}\, C_{rr} - .3 \sum\limits_{-2}^{-9} \gamma_{22}\, C_{rr} \right]$

$\qquad - .152 \left[\sum\limits_{0}^{-1} \gamma_6\, q_L - .3 \sum\limits_{-1}^{-2} \gamma_6\, q_L \right]$

$\qquad - .105 \left[\sum\limits_{-1}^{-4} \gamma_7\, 100\, \Delta \ln p_c - .3 \sum\limits_{-2}^{-5} \gamma_7\, 100\, \Delta \ln p_c \right]$

$\qquad + .267$

22. $\quad U = P_S - \exp \ln L - L_g - L_s$

23. $\quad U_p = \dfrac{U}{P_S} 100$

24. $\quad q_L = \dfrac{L}{P_S - L_g - L_s - .01} + .006$

25. $\quad \ln p_k = \ln p_{i-sa} + \ln A_r + \ln I_a - \ln 100$

26. $\quad \ln A_r = \ln r - \ln \{1 - (1 + .01\, r)^{-20}\} - \ln 7.488$

27. $\quad \ln p_i = \ln I - \ln i + \ln 100$

28. $\quad \ln I_{-sa} = \ln i_{-sa} + \ln p_{i-sa} - \ln 100$

29. $\quad I = \exp \ln I_{-sa} + i_{sa}$

30. $\quad i = \exp \ln i_{-sa} + i_{sa}$

31. $\quad \ln c = \ln C - \ln p_c + \ln 100$

32. $\quad \ln p_c = \ln p_{c\,end} + \ln p_{c\,aut} - \ln 100$

33. $\quad n = n_{-1} + .25\, \Delta n$

34. $\quad \Delta N = \Delta n \cdot p_{\Delta n}/100$

35. $\quad b_g = \exp \ln b_{f-sa} + b_{g\,aut}$

36. $\quad b_s = \exp \ln b_{s-t} + b_{s\,aut}$

37. $\quad B_{f-sa} = \exp \ln b_{f-sa} \cdot \exp \ln p_{bf-sa}/100$

38. $\quad B_g = B_{f-sa} + B_{g\,aut}$

39. $\quad B_{s-t} = \exp \ln b_{s-t} \cdot \exp \ln p_{bs-t}/100$

40. $$B_s = B_{s-t} + B_{s\,aut}$$

41. $$p_{bg} = \frac{B_g}{b_g} \cdot 100$$

42. $$p_{bs} = \frac{B_s}{b_s} \cdot 100$$

43. $$M_g = \exp\left(\ln m_{g-sa}\right) p_{mg-sa}/100 + M_{sa}$$

44. $$m_g = \frac{M_g}{p_{mg}} \cdot 100$$

45. $$M_s = m_s\, p_{ms}/100$$

46. $$E_L = B_g + B_s + B_p - M_g - M_s - M_p + D_s$$

47. $$\ln x = \ln X - \ln p_x + \ln 100$$

48. $$V = \exp \ln C + \exp \ln I_{-sa} + X + B_g$$

49. $$v = \exp \ln c + \exp \ln i_{-sa} + \exp \ln x + b_g$$

50. $$p_v = \frac{V}{v} \cdot 100$$

51. $$\ln v_{mg} = .420 \ln c + .170 \ln i_{-sa} + .080 \ln x + .300 \ln b_{f-sa} + .030 \ln b_{s-t}$$

52. $$\ln p_{vmg} = .420 \ln p_{c\,end} + .170 \ln p_{i-sa} + .080 \ln p_x + .300 \ln p_{bf-sa} + .030 \ln p_{bs-t}$$

53.[a] $$\ln v_{ms} = [.430] \ln c + .045 \ln i_{-sa} + .065 \ln x + .160 \ln b_{f-sa} + [.300] \ln b_{s-t}$$

54.[a] $$\ln p_{vms} = [.430] \ln p_{c\,end} + .045 \ln p_{i-sa} + .065 \ln p_x + .160 \ln p_{bf-sa} + [.300] \ln p_{bs-t}$$

a. *Coefficients* between square brackets are not constant over time.

55. $V' = V + I_{sa} + \Delta N + B_s + B_p$

56. $Y = V' - M_g - M_s - B_p - R_g$

57. $y = v + i_{sa} + \Delta n + b_s - m_g - m_s - r_g$

58. $Y_{gnp} = Y + W_g + B_p - M_p + R_g + C_{gl} + F_g$

59. $y_{gnp} = y + w_g + b_p - m_p + r_g + c_{gl} + f_g$

60. $p_{gnp} = \dfrac{Y_{gnp}}{y_{gnp}} \cdot 100$

61. $p_y = \dfrac{Y}{y} \cdot 100$

62. $w_s = w + w_{aut}$

63.[a] $\ln W = \ln w_s + \ln L - \ln 14.0618$

64. $Z = Y - \exp \ln W - F - T_K + S$

65. $W_T = \exp \ln W + W_g$

66. $W_D = W_T - T_W - O_W$

67. $Z_D = Z - T_Z - O_Z$

68. $\varphi = \dfrac{W_D}{W_D + .25\, Z_D}$

---

a. The constant $-\ln 14.0618$ should be read as $-\ln 100 + \ln 7.111$, the latter expressing the wage sum per worker in Dfl. in 1963.

APPENDIX B. LIST OF SYMBOLS

In general, upper case symbols refer to values in current prices, lower case symbols to volumes in constant prices of 1963 and price indexes (1963 = 100).
Underlined variables are exogenous.

Symbol	Description
A_r	present value of an annuity of a Dfl. after 20 years at the current interest rate
$\underline{b_{feec}}$	EEC effect on exports of goods (1959:1 – 1961:2 = 1, elsewhere 0)
B_{f-sa}	exports of manufactured goods excluding ships and airplanes, in current prices
b_{f-sa}	do., in 1963 prices
B_g	exports of goods, in current prices
b_g	do., in 1963 prices
$\underline{B_{gaut}}$	exports of unprocessed agricultural products, ships and airplanes, in current prices
$\underline{b_{gaut}}$	do., in 1963 prices
B_p	factor incomes received from abroad, in current prices
$\underline{b_p}$	do., in 1963 prices
B_s	exports of services, in current prices
b_s	do., in 1963 prices
$\underline{B_{saut}}$	net receipts from transit trade, in current prices
$\underline{b_{saut}}$	do., in 1963 prices
$\underline{b_{seec}}$	EEC effect on exports of services (1951:1 – 1961:4 = 1, elsewhere 0)
B_{s-t}	exports of services excluding net receipts from transit trade, in current prices
b_{s-t}	do., in 1963 prices
C	private consumption, in current prices
c	do., in 1963 prices
$\underline{C_{aut}}$	effect of anticipatory purchases on private consumption in 1956:4, 1957:1 and 1965:4
$\underline{C_{gl}}$	investment for the government's own use, in current prices
$\underline{c_{gl}}$	do., in 1963 prices
CHR	rent component in private consumption, in current prices

Symbol	Description
C_{rr}	quantitative credit restrictions by the Central Bank during 1962:1 –1965:4
D_s	net transfer income from abroad
Dum_1	dummy variable for effects of Korean war and Suez crisis (1956) on inventory formation
Dum_2	dummy variable for influence of exceptional crops on inventory formation
Dum_3	dummy for the influence of Korean war and Suez crisis (1956) on export of services
Dum_4	dummy for the influence of Korean war and Suez Crisis (1956) on imports of services
Dum_5	dummy variable representing the effect of the introduction of a new national insurance system in 1957 on wages
Dum_6	dummy variable for delay in wage negotiations due to discussions on a new wage policy in 1959
E_K	balance of payments on capital account
E_L	balance of payments on current account
F	depreciation (enterprises), in current prices
F_g	depreciation (government), in current prices
f_g	do., in 1963 prices
h_c	contractual working hours, 1963 = 100
h_w	hours worked, 1963 = 100
I	gross fixed investment in enterprises, excluding housing, in current prices
i	do., in 1963 prices
I_a	investment allowances, 1963 = 100
i_{aut}	effect of anticipatory outlays on gross fixed investment in 1965:4
I_{sa}	gross investment in ships and airplanes, in current prices
i_{sa}	do., in 1963 prices
I_{-sa}	gross fixed investment in enterprises excluding housing, ships and airplanes, in current prices
i_{-sa}	do., in 1963 prices
L	employment in enterprises
L_{aut}	impact of cold winters on employment in 1956:1 and 1963:1
L_g	government employment

Symbol	Description
L_s	self-employed working population
$\dfrac{L_q}{V}$	liquidity ratio, after correction for its decreasing trend
M_g	imports of goods, in current prices
m_g	do., in 1963 prices
m_{g-sa}	imports of goods excluding ships and airplanes, in 1963 prices
M_p	payments of factor incomes to abroad, in current prices
m_p	do., in 1963 prices
M_s	imports of services, in current prices
m_s	do., in 1963 prices
M_{sa}	imports of ships and airplanes, in current prices
m_w	world imports of goods, reweighted according to the geographical distribution of Dutch exports of goods, 1963 = 100
n	level of stocks, in 1963 prices
ΔN	inventory formation, in current prices
Δn	do., in 1963 prices
n_d	desired level of stocks, in 1963 prices
O_W	net income transfers (excluding direct taxes) with regard to wage income
O_Z	net income transfers (excluding direct taxes) with regard to non-wage income
p_{bf-sa}	price of exports of manufactured goods excluding ships and airplanes, 1963 = 100
p_{bg}	price of exports of goods, 1963 = 100
p_{bgw}	price of exports of goods of competitors (reweighted), 1963 = 100
p_{bs}	price of exports of services, 1963 = 100
p_{bs-t}	price of exports of services excluding transit trade, 1963 = 100
p_{bsw}	price of exports of services of competitors (reweighted), 1963 = 100
p_c	price of private consumption, 1963 = 100
p_{caut}	autonomous influences on the price of consumption (rents, indirect taxes, subsidies ect.), 1963 = 100
$p_{c\,end}$	price of private consumption excluding autonomous influences, 1963 = 100

Symbol	Description
p_f	ocean freight rates (weighted average of liner, tramp and tanker rates), 1963 = 100
p_i	price of gross fixed investment in enterprises excluding housing, 1963 = 100
p_{i-sa}	price of gross fixed investment in enterprises excluding housing, ships and airplanes, 1963 = 100
p_k	user cost of capital, 1963 = 100
p_{mg}	price of imports of goods, 1963 = 100
p_{mg-sa}	price of imports of goods excluding ships and airplanes, 1963 = 100
p_{ms}	price of imports of services, 1963 = 100
$p_{\Delta n}$	price of inventory formation, 1963 = 100
P_S	labour supply
P_{Saut}	cyclical variation in the labour participation of married women (four quarter changes)
P_{ST}	trend of working population
p_v	price of expenditures excluding governments wages, inventory formation, exports of services and factor incomes received from abroad, 1963 = 100
p_{vmg}	price of expenditures, reweighted according to the relative importance of expenditure categories for imports of goods, 1963 = 100 (equation 52)
p_{vms}	price of expenditures reweighted according to the relative importance of expenditure categories for imports of services, 1963 = 100 (equation 54)
p_x	price of autonomous expenditures, 1963 = 100
p_y	implicit price deflator of production of enterprises, 1963 = 100
p_{gnp}	implicit price deflator of gross national product, 1963 = 100
q_L	utilization rate of labour
r	long term interest rate
R_g	imputed rent on government buildings, in current prices
r_g	do., in 1963 prices
r_k	discount rate
SPE	four quarter change in social premiums paid by employers as percentage of the wage sum per worker
t	time trend
T_c	minimum temperature below 0° centigrade

Symbol	Description
T_K	indirect taxes (cash basis)
T_{Kaut}	autonomous indirect taxes
$TSPW$	four quarter change in autonomous income tax changes and social premiums paid by employees as percentage of the wage sum per worker
T_W	direct taxes on wage and transfer income (cash basis)
T_{Waut}	autonomous taxes on wage and transfer income (cash basis)
T_Z	direct taxes on non-wage income (cash basis)
T_{Zaut}	autonomous taxes on non-wage income (cash basis)
U	registered unemployment
U_G	unemployment ratio in Western Germany
U_p	unemployment ratio
V	total expenditures, less inventory formation, government wages, exports of services and factor incomes received from abroad, in current prices
v	do., in 1963 prices
V'	total expenditures excluding government wages, in current prices
v_{mg}	expenditures reweighted according to the relative importance of expenditure categories for imports of goods, in 1963 prices (equation 51)
v_{ms}	expenditures reweighted according to the relative importance of expenditure categories for imports of services, in 1963 prices (equation 53)
W	wage income in enterprises
w	wage sum per worker in enterprises excluding lump-sum payments, $1963 = 100$
w_{aut}	lump-sum payments
W_D	disposable wage and transfer income
W_g	government wages and salaries, in current prices
w_g	do., in 1963 prices
w_s	wage sum per worker in enterprises, $1963 = 100$
W_T	total wage sum
X	autonomous expenditures (government consumption, net government investment and investment in housing), in current prices
x	do., in 1963 prices

Symbol	Description
Y	production of enterprises, in current prices
y	do., in 1963 prices
Y_{gnp}	gross national product at market prices, in current prices
y_{gnp}	do., in 1963 prices
y_w	industrial production in OECD countries, reweighted according to the geographical distribution of Dutch exports of services, 1963 = 100.
Z	non-wage income (including corporate profits)
Z_D	disposable non-wage income
γ_1	.400, .300, .154, .075, .036, .022, .013
γ_2	.210, .170, .150, .120, .100, .080. .060, .050, .040, .020
γ_3	.140, .230, .260, .230, .140
γ_4	.330, .340, .330
γ_5	.100, .200, .300, .400
γ_6	.500, .500
γ_7	.250, .250, .250, .250
γ_8	.300, .210, .150, .110, .080, .060, .040, .030, .020
γ_9	.600, .240, .100, .040, .020
γ_{10}	.200, .800
γ_{11}	.100, .200, .250, .300, .150
γ_{12}	.700, .200, .100
γ_{13}	.400, .300, .200, .100
γ_{14}	.170, .330, .500
γ_{15}	.500, .330, .170
γ_{16}	.300, .450, .200, .050
γ_{17}	.600, .300, .100
γ_{18}	.800, .200
γ_{19}	.500, .300, .200
γ_{20}	.350, .300, .200, .100, .050
γ_{21}	.600, .950, .100, .100, −.450, −.250, −.050
γ_{22}	.400, .240, .150, .090, .060, .030, .020, .010
φ	estimated share of wage-earners consumption in total consumption
π_K	marginal indirect taxes quota
π_W	marginal tax quota of wage income
π_Z	marginal tax quota of non-wage income
v_W	share of income tax payments by individuals in total income tax
v_Z	share of income tax payments by self-employed in total income tax

APPENDIX C. DERIVATION OF QUARTERLY FIGURES FROM ANNUAL DATA

As has been mentioned in Chapter II a relatively small part of the required national accounts data is only yearly published. The same holds for a number of other variables needed for the construction of the model, especially population data. In these cases quarterly figures have been derived from their annual totals by a method designed for this purpose by BOOT, FEIBES and LISMAN (1967) which is in short repeated here.

Given are n annual totals $t_k (k=1, ..., n)$. Their quarterly figures x_i ($i=1, ..., 4n$) must be found. The requirement is that the sum of squares of the second differences of the subsequent quarterly figures is minimized:

(C.1) $$F = \sum_{i=1}^{4n-2} (x_{i+2} - 2x_{i+1} + x_i)^2$$

subject to n constraints

$$\sum_{i=4k-3}^{4k} x_i = t_k.$$

The problem is solved by considering the Lagrangean expression

(C.2) $$\frac{\delta F}{\delta x_i} - \lambda_i \frac{\partial \left(\sum_{1}^{4} x_i - t_1 \right)}{\partial x_i} - ... \lambda_n \frac{\partial \left(\sum_{4n-3}^{4n} x_i - t_n \right)}{\partial x_i} = 0$$

Together with the n constraints one has a system of $5n$ linear equations with $4n$ unknown quarterly figures and n, irrelevant, multiplicators.
In matrix notation

(C.3) $$\begin{bmatrix} C & -J' \\ J & 0 \end{bmatrix} \begin{bmatrix} x \\ \lambda \end{bmatrix} = \begin{bmatrix} 0 \\ t \end{bmatrix}$$

where J is the $(n, 4n)$ matrix

$$\begin{bmatrix} 1 & 1 & 1 & 1 & & & & & & & & \\ & & & & 1 & 1 & 1 & 1 & & & & \\ & & & & & & & & \cdot \cdot \cdot & & & \\ & & & & & & & & & 1 & 1 & 1 & 1 & \\ & & & & & & & & & & & & & 1 & 1 & 1 & 1 \end{bmatrix}$$

and C is the following $4n \times 4n$ band matrix

$$\begin{bmatrix} 2 & -4 & 2 & & & & & & & \\ -4 & 10 & -8 & 2 & & & & & & \\ 2 & -8 & 12 & -8 & 2 & & & & & \\ & 2 & -8 & 12 & -8 & 2 & & & & \\ & & & & \ddots & & & & & \\ & & & & & 2 & -8 & 12 & -8 & 2 \\ & & & & & & 2 & -8 & 12 & -8 & 2 \\ & & & & & & & 2 & -8 & 10 & -4 \\ & & & & & & & & 2 & -4 & 2 \end{bmatrix}$$

Furthermore we have the column vectors:

$$x_i, \ldots, x_{4n} \qquad \lambda_1, \ldots, \lambda_n \qquad \text{and } t_1, \ldots, t_n$$

The final result is

(C.4) $\qquad x = M't$

where M' is a $(4n, n)$ matrix. This matrix enables us to derive quarterly values from annual totals in a reasonable way. The quarterly figures obtained by this interpolation method are by definition not subject to seasonal fluctuations.

APPENDIX D. SEASONAL ADJUSTMENT OF THE DATA

Remember from chapter II that the parameters of the model equations have been estimated with seasonally adjusted data. The method of computation of the seasonal components in the original time series is developed by R.J.A. DEN HAAN and programmed for computer by D. BREKELMANS. We present the main computational steps here looking forward to a more elaborate publication on the matter.

Consider a time series Y_{ij}, containing three components: a trend cycle component D_{ij}, a seasonal component S_{ij} and a random component U_{ij}. This random component includes so-called extreme disturbances due to strikes, anticipation, extreme weather conditions, etc. We assume

(D.1) $\quad Y_{ij} = D_{ij} + S_{ij} + U_{ij}$

where the subscript ij indicates the i-th quarter of the j-th year and U_{ij}, except for its extremes, is postulated to be an independent stochastic component with zero expectation.

It is assumed that the process generating the seasonal component S_{ij} in this additive relationship is described by the following non-linear model:

(D.2) $\quad S_{ij} = s_{ij} k_{ij}$

(D.3) $\quad s_{ij} = a_{0i} + a_{1i} t$

(D.4) $\quad k_{ij} = b_0 + (1-b_0) D_{ij} / \bar{D}$

where S = seasonal component;
s = basic seasonal deviation, i.e. after adjustment for the trend cycle component;
t = time trend;
k = multiplicator;
D = trend cycle component;
$\bar{D}$ = average trend cycle component in a mid-year, when $t = 0$.

Herein the basic seasonal influence (s_{ij}) is assumed to be independent of the trend-cycle component but is allowed to change gradually over time due to, for instance, changes in social behaviour, changes in production methods etc. For $a_{1i} = 0$ we have a rigid basic seasonal influence. In addition, endogenous changes in the seasonal component are considered. These are represented by the term $(1-b_0) D_{ij}/\bar{D}$. For practical reasons, and following Wald's method of seasonal adjustment, it is postulated that in the mid-year

$k_{ij}=1$ and $t=0$.[1] The implication is that the relationship between the multiplicator and the trend-cycle component can be simplified to equation (D.4) since the average trend-cycle component is defined for that mid-year. We then have $D_{ij}=\bar{D}$ and so, according to equation (D.4), $k_{ij}=1$. This transformation changes the scale of measurement but bears no theoretical significance.[2] Most conveniently, however, the parameters in (D.4) sum to unity.

The estimation of the parameters a_{0i}, a_{1i} and b_0 can now be summarized by describing the following computational steps.

1. The original time series Y_{ij} is provisionally adjusted for seasonal variation by a simple procedure. A four-quarter centered moving average is used as estimator of the trend-cycle component ($\hat{D}_{ij}$). The parameters a_{0i} and a_{1i} are estimated for each quarter by the method of ordinary least squares in

(D.5) $\quad Y_{ij}-\hat{D}_{ij}=(a_{0i}+a_{1i}t)\hat{k}_{ij}+u_{ij}$

where a hat (^) over a variable indicates an estimated value.[3] The estimate for the multiplicator ($\hat{k}_{ij}$) is obtained by the *a priori* multiplicator formula

(D.6) $\quad \hat{k}_{it}=.25+.75(\hat{D}_{ij}/\bar{D})$

where the *a priori* value of b_0 (.25) is some average value found in many experiments.

Afterwards a small correction is necessary to impose the restriction

(D.7) $\quad \Sigma a_{0i}=\Sigma a_{1i}=0$.

The correction is of the type

(D.8) $\quad \hat{a}_{ij}=a_{ij}-|a_{ij}|\dfrac{\Sigma a_{ij}}{\Sigma|a_{ij}|}$.

With all parameters known a new series (Y'_{ij}), provisionally adjusted for seasonal variation, can be computed.

---

1. Wald's method is described in TINTNER (1952), pp. 227 and FERBER and VERDOORN (1962), pp. 328.
2. Experimentation has shown that a linear relationship between the multiplicator and the trend-cycle component suffices, except for unemployment series where a non-linear relationship is appropriate. A separate program has been developed for the adjustment of these time-series but is not reported here.
3. This is not an optimal procedure since a non-linear estimation method is required here.

2. In this series Y'_{ij}, in which also extreme values have been eliminated, a flexible and smooth trend-cycle component is estimated based on Spencer's 15-terms moving average.[4] The computed trend-cycle component is then adjusted for annual totals of the original time-series excluding the effect of extreme disturbances. Furthermore first order serial correlation in the estimated trend-cycle component is reduced by a specific program. We then arrive at the definite trend-cycle component (D'_{ij}).

3. The next step is the estimation of the parameters a_0 and a_1 for each quarter. For this purpose the multiplicator equation is repeatedly estimated with successive values for b_0 ranging from zero up to unity in steps of .125. Using the thus obtained successive estimates of the multiplicator series (k'_{ij}) we will find values for a_{0i} and a_{1i} for a given value of (k'_{ij}) by a regression of the type of equation (D.5).

4. Finally we chose the value for b_0 in the formula defining the multiplicator (k'_{ij}) for which the sum of the squared residuals is a minimum. With the selected values of a_{0i}, a_{1i} and b_0 known, the seasonal component S_{ij} can then be computed, which yields $Y^s_{ij} = Y_{ij} - S_{ij}$, where Y^s_{ij} is the seasonally adjusted time series.

---

4. See KENDALL and STUART (1966).

APPENDIX E. WEIGHTING SCHEMES FOR EXPORTS

One of the explanatory variables in the equation for the export volume of goods is world imports of goods reweighted according to the geographic composition of Netherland's exports of goods (m_w). The weights were computed as B_{gj}/B_g in the previous year, where B_{gj} is Dutch exports of goods to country j and B_g is total exports of goods, both in current prices. To give an impression of the relative importance of individual countries we mention the weighting scheme in 1965 in per cent:

Germany	28
France	9
Italy	5
Belgium-Luxembourg	15
EEC	57
United Kingdom	9
United States and Canada	4
Rest OECD	12
OECD	82
Non-OECD	18
World total	100

A variable appearing in the same equation is the price level of exports of goods of competitors (p_{bgw}). In order to assess the relative importance of competitors on a specific market a matrix of world imports and exports of goods was composed. From these matrices weights were computed for each competitor or group of competitors according to

$$(\text{E.1}) \quad \sum_{j=1}^{n} \frac{B_{gj}}{B_g} \cdot \frac{B_{gcj}}{M_{gj} - B_{gj}} \qquad (j \neq c)$$

where B_g = exports of goods of the Netherlands, in current prices
B_{gj} = exports of goods of the Netherlands to country j, in current prices
B_{gcj} = exports of goods of competitor c to country j, in current prices
M_{gj} = imports of goods of country j, in current prices

An impression of the relative importance of competitors on Dutch export markets can be obtained from the weighting scheme for 1965 (in per cent):

Germany	12.7
France	10.0
Italy	6.5
Belgium-Luxembourg	4.8
EEC	34.0
United Kingdom	8.3
United States and Canada	17.5
Rest OECD	16.1
OECD	75.9
Non-OECD	24.1
World total	100

One of the explanatory variables in the equation for the volume of exports of services is industrial production of OECD countries reweighted according to the geographical composition of Dutch exports of services (y_w). The weights were constant and computed as B_{sj}/B_s where B_{sj} is Dutch exports of services to country j and B_s is total exports of services, both in current prices. The weighting scheme below is computed as an average over the years 1962–1965.

Germany	32.7
France	6.4
Italy	1.1
Belgium-Luxembourg	9.5
EEC	50.7
United Kingdom	21.0
United States and Canada	13.9
Rest OECD	15.4
OECD	100

Similar to the equation for exports of goods the equation for exports of services involves the price level of exports of services of competitors as an explanatory variable. According to the procedure described already we find a weighting scheme for 1964 where the relative importance of competitors on Dutch export markets of services becomes clear.[1]

Germany	9.5
France	9.2
Italy	8.9
Belgium-Luxembourg	3.6
EEC	31.2
United Kingdom	14.1
United States and Canada	23.0
Rest OECD	31.7
OECD	100

1. Quarterly figures were obtained by interpolation of annual data. For the compilation of these see DRIEHUIS (1969).

APPENDIX F. WEIGHTING SCHEMES FOR IMPORTS

In the equations explaining the volumes of imports of goods and services respectively a reweighted demand variable appears. This variable is defined as total expenditures excluding government wages, inventory formation and factor incomes received from abroad and is reweighted according to the relative import content of remaining final demand components.

In principle it is possible to estimate total imports (m) as a function of a number of relevant expenditure categories, but the appearance of multicollinearity between explanatory variables will prevent the finding of appropriate parameters. Therefore we postulate total imports to be a function of a weighted expenditures variable

(F.1) $\quad m = f(\Sigma \gamma_j v_j)$

where v_j is expenditure component j and γ_j is a weighting factor.

The unknown weights γ_j must represent both the direct and the indirect imports incorporated in demand category v_j. The direct import content concerns the imports of final products that can be contributed directly to a specific final demand category. Indirect imports concern imports which are partly a direct input in the production process of an industry and partly an input of other industries via intermediate deliveries. Only to give an impression we mention that in 1970 direct imports made up about 40 per cent of total imports of services whereas for imports of goods this share was estimated at about 35 per cent.

The distribution of direct imports over the relevant expenditure items is no problem since it is directly available in input-output tables. The measurement of indirect imports has been carried out by using the input-output tables for the Netherlands.[1] The method used can be described as follows. Let M be the matrix of original import coefficients of a number of industries, i.e. imports of goods (or services) as a percentage of final deliveries of these industries (= matrix Y), then the cumulated import content can be computed as

(F.2) $\quad M(I-A)^{-1} Y$

where I is the unitary matrix and A is the matrix of intermediate deliveries as a fraction of final deliveries. In this way we arrive at cumulated indirect imports per final demand category in Dfl.

---

1. Input-output tables can be found in the publication of the Central Bureau of Statistics: '*The production structure of the Netherlands' economy*'.

When direct imports of goods or services incorporated in final demand component j are represented by the vector E, the total import content in Dfl. is defined as

(F.3) $\quad E + M(I-A)^{-1} Y$

Along these lines cumulated costs of imports of goods and imports of services have been computed for a great number of years. The computation for imports of goods was based on a 16×16 input-output table, whereas for imports of services a 5×5 table was used. As final demand categories we distinguish: private consumption, government consumption, investment in housing, gross fixed investment of enterprises, inventory formation, government investment, exports of goods and exports of services. With the thus obtained cumulated import contents we are able to compute for a number of years elasticity coefficients which can be used for the weighting of these final demand categories in the import equations.[2]

The weighting scheme for the expenditure (and domestic price) variable in the equation for imports of goods was rather stable. The equation reads:

(F.4) $\quad \ln v_{mg} = .420 \ln c + .170 \ln i_{-sa} + .080 \ln x + .300 \ln b_{f-sa}$
$\qquad + .030 \ln b_{s-t}$

The weighting scheme for the expenditure (and domestic price) variable in the equation for imports of services was unstable. The weight of private consumption was rising, in agreement with the increasing role of expenditures for tourism. The weight of exports of services, however, was declining since the relative importance of transportation services is diminishing. Therefore we adopt as expenditure variable:

(F.5) $\quad \ln v_{ms} = [.430] \ln c + .045 \ln i_{-sa} + .065 \ln x + .160 \ln b_{f-sa}$
$\qquad + [.300] \ln b_{s-t}$

where weights between square brackets are shifting over time. In 1951 private consumption has a weight of .350 and exports of services of .380, whereas in 1965 these weights are .560 and .170 respectively. The weights used in equation (F.5) are the weights in 1958.

---

2. See also BARKER and LECOMBER (1970).

APPENDIX G. METHOD OF SOLUTION OF THE MODEL

It is obvious that the overall model cannot be solved straightforwardly by the familiar methods of linear algebra. No linearity constraint whatsoever has been applied in specifying and estimating the separate equations of the model.

The solution of a non-linear model would still be possible with linear methods if the sole object would be to obtain a single solution. The non-linear equations could be linearized around initial estimates for the required solution, that is for the quarter covered by the forecast. If the results of the linearized version of the model differ too widely from the initial estimates, then repeated linearization is necessary.

However, the model is intended to produce successive quarterly simulations. The linearization method would be difficult and cumbersome to apply in this case, although possible from a technical point of view. VAN DER GIESSEN (1970) has suggested a much more practical and time-saving solution method for non-linear models. This so called method of successive approximation has been applied here.[1]

The method of successive approximation starts with initial estimates of a number of endogenous variables. These variables are chosen in such a way that a recursive model is obtained on inserting the initial estimates at the places where the variables appear as explanatory ones.

Using the recursive structure obtained in this way a first approximation is computed of all endogenous variables, i.e. including those for which the initial estimates are given. These initial estimates are then replaced by the first approximations. Substitution in the model produces new figures of all the endogenous variables. These are used for the third approximation round. This process has to be repeated until the difference between the successive approximations of all the endogenous variables does not exceed an acceptable (small) value.

The problem in this approach is the determination of the endogenous variables that have at least to be known and the sequence of solution in the (remaining) recursive model. To tackle this problem the 'structure' matrix of the model to be solved should be prepared. This matrix shows the interdependence of all endogenous variables. It is made to do so by inserting the i-th endogenous variable of the model before the i-th row and above the i-th column of a matrix. Next it is indicated for each row on which of the column variables the row variable depends. Indicating dependence with an

---

[1]. The exposition in this appendix leans heavily on VAN DER GIESSEN's (1970) publication.

asterisk in a field the 'structure' matrix of a seven equation model, for instance, may be written as follows:

	1	2	3	4	5	6	7	aux.
1		*	*					2
2						*		1
3				*	*			2
4		*			*			2
5						*		1
6							*	1
7		*						1

The variables to be given and the sequence of solution of the equations are determined with the aid of the structure matrix and an auxiliary vector indicating the number of dependents for each row in the matrix.

The endogenous variables for which the initial estimates are needed are the variables that yield the model non-recursive, as it were. The number of these 'essential' endogenous explanatory variables should be reduced to a minimum by substituting dependences. To find this minimum number a start is made with the substitution of endogenous variables that are exogenously determined. This kind of dependence does not appear in the seven equation sample. It does, however, appear in our model. This does not change the model but it reduces the number of (strictly) endogenous variables remaining. The next step is to substitute those endogenous variables that depend on one other endogenous variable only. These substitutions may possibly result in a variable becoming dependent on itself. As soon as this occurs, the variable should be assumed to be known. There is no point in delaying this assumption, otherwise more variables than necessary should have to be assumed to be known.

Assuming a variable to be known means a change in the 'structure' matrix. The process indicated before must then be repeated. After all the dependences on one variable have been dealt with in this way, the substitution of variables that are dependent on two, three or more variables is undertaken. Once again, variables should be assumed to be known as soon as the substitution indicates this. This will keep to a minimum the set of variables to be given.

Applied to the 'structure' matrix of the seven equation model the result is that variable 3 is assumed to be known, while the sequence of solution is 7, 2, 1, 6, 5, 4 and 3. Rearranging the 'structure' matrix in this order it is clear that the seven equation model is non-recursive because of the dependences on variable 3.

	7	2	1	6	5	4	3
7							*
2	*						
1		*					*
6	*						
5					*		
4					*	*	
3					*	*	

Applied to the present model consisting of 68 endogenous variables, the result of determining the recursive structure by computer is that the values of 4 endogenous variables must be given before the solution starts. These variables are[2]:

12   $p_{c\,end}$ = price of private consumption excluding autonomous influences, 1963 = 100
48   V = total expenditures, less inventory formation, government wages, exports of services and factor incomes received from abroad, in current prices
56   Y = production of enterprises, in current prices
57   y = production of enterprises, in 1963 prices

The sequence of solution for the 68 variables is found to be:

1,	2,	6,	13,	18,	22,	24,	3,
28,	29,	30,	27,	23,	32,	11,	62,
63,	65,	17,	66,	19,	12,	14,	15,
7,	16,	8,	35,	36,	37,	38,	39,
40,	41,	42,	47,	52,	54,	59,	64,
58,	60,	61,	67,	4,	31,	48,	49,
5,	33,	34,	50,	51,	9,	43,	44,
53,	10,	45,	55,	57,	56,	68,	46,
21,	20,	26,	25.				

2. Numbers correspond to the equations in Appendix A.

Bibliography

ABERT, J.C. (1969), *Economic Policy and Planning in the Netherlands, 1950–1965*, Yale University Press, New Haven and London.
ACKLEY, G. (1967), *Macro-economic Theory*, Collier-MacMillan, New York, (Student Edition, Second printing).
AGARWALA, R. and GOODSON, G.C. (1970), 'An Analysis of Consumer Goods' Prices in an Input-Output Framework', *Oxford Economic Papers*, Vol. 22, no. 1, pp. 57–72.
ALBECK, H. (1969), *Stabilisierungspolitik mit Entscheidungsmodellen. Das Beispiel der Niederländischen Lohn- und Finanzpolitik*, J.C.B. Mohr (Paul Siebeck), Tübingen.
ALLEN, R.G.D. (1967), *Macro-Economic Theory, A Mathematical Treatment*, MacMillan, London.
ALMON, S. (1965), 'The Distributed Lag between Capital Appropriations and Expenditures', *Econometrica*, Vol. 33, no. 1, pp. 178–196.
ANDERSON, W.H.L. (1967), 'Business Fixed Investment: A Marriage of Fact and Fancy' in Ferber, R., ed. *Determinants of Investment Behavior*, Colombia University Press for the National Bureau of Economic Research, New York.
ARCHIBALD, G.C. (1969), ,The Phillips Curve and the Distribution of Unemployment', *American Economic Review*, Vol. 59, no. 2, pp. 124–146.

BAKHOVEN, A.F. (1971), 'De Verklaring van het Renteniveau in Nederland', *Maandschrift Economie*, Jrg. 35, afl. 12, pp. 577–588.
BALASSA, B. (1967), *Trade Liberalization Among Industrial Countries, Objectives and Alternatives*, McGraw-Hill, New York.
BALL, R.J. and ST. CYR, E.B.A. (1966), 'Short-Term Employment Functions in British Manufacturing Industry', *Review of Economic Studies*, Vol. 33 (3), no. 95, pp. 179–207.
BALL, R.J. and DRAKE, P.S. (1963), 'Stock Adjustment Inventory Models of the United Kingdom Economy', *The Manchester School of Social and Economic Studies*, Vol. 31, no. 2, pp. 87–102.
BALL, R.J., EATON, J.D. and STEUER, M.D. (1966), 'The Relationship between U.K. Export Performance in Manufactures and the Internal Pressure of Demand', *Economic Journal*, Vol. 76, pp. 501–518.
BARKER, T.S. and LECOMBER, J.R.C. (1970), 'The Import Content of Final Expenditures in the United Kingdom 1954–1972', *Bulletin Oxford University Institute of Economics and Statistics*, Vol. 32, no. 1, pp. 1–17.

BARTEN, A. P. (1962), 'Note on Unbiased Estimation of the Squared Multiple Correlation Coefficient', *Statistica Neerlandica*, Vol. 16, no. 2, pp. 151–163.
BELD, C. A. VAN DEN (1964), 'National Accounting and Economic Policy Decisions (with special reference to the Netherlands)' in C. Clark and G. Stuvel eds. *Income Redistribution and the Statistical Foundations of Economic Policy*, Bowes and Bowes, London.
BELD, C. A. VAN DEN (1965), *Forecast and Realisation. The Forecasts by the Netherlands Central Planning Bureau, 1953–1963*, C.P.B. Monograph no. 10, Staatsdrukkerij, The Hague.
BELD, C. A. VAN DEN (1965a), 'Short-Term Planning Experience in the Netherlands' in *Quantative Planning of Economic Policy*, B.G. Hickmann ed., The Brookings Institution, Washington.
BELD, C. A. VAN DEN (1967), 'De Nederlandse Economie in het jaar 2000', in *De Nederlanders in het jaar 2000*. Prae-advies voor de Nederlandsche Maatschappij van Nijverheid en Handel.
BELD, C. A. VAN DEN (1968), 'An Experimental Medium-Term Macro-Model for the Dutch Economy', in *Mathematical Model Building in Economics and Industry*, C. Griffin and Company, London.
BELD, C. A. VAN DEN (1970), *The Central Planning Bureau at Work 1945-1970*, Central Planning Bureau, The Hague (mimeographed).
BELD, C. A. VAN DEN and MIDDELHOEK, A. J. (1971), 'Evaluation of Seaport Projects', Central Planning Bureau, The Hague, *Occasional Papers* no. 3/1971.
BELD, C. A. VAN DE, PAS, J. H. VAN DE and TJAN, H. S. (1965), *A Medium-Term Macro Model of the Netherlands*, Central Planning Bureau, The Hague, (mimeographed).
BERGSTRØM, A. R. (1962), 'A Model of Technical Progress, the Production Function and Cyclical Growth', *Economica*, Vol. 29, no. 116, pp. 357–370.
BISCHOFF, C. W. (1968), *Lags in Fiscal and Monetary Impacts on Investment in Producers' Durable Equipment*, Cowles Foundation Discussion Paper no. 250, Yale University.
BISCHOFF, C. W. (1969), 'Hypothesis Testing and Demand for Capital Goods', *Review of Economics and Statistics*, Vol. 51, no. 3, pp. 354–368.
BOOT, J. C. G., FEIBES, W. and LISMAN, J. H. C. (1967), 'Further Methods of Derivation of Quarterly Figures from Annual Data', *Applied Statistics*, Vol. 16, no. 1, pp. 65–75.
BRANSON, W. H. and KLEVORICK, A. K. (1969), 'Money Illusion and the Aggregate Consumption Function', *American Economic Review*, Vol. 59, nr. 5, pp. 832–849.
BRECHLING, F. P. R. (1965), 'The Relationship between Output and Employment in British Manufacturing Industries', *Review of Economic Studies*, Vol. 32 (3), no. 91, pp. 187–216.
BRECHLING, F. P. R. and O'BRIEN, P. (1967), 'Short-Run Employment Functions in Manufacturing Industries: An International Comparison', *Review of Economics and Statistics*, Vol. 49, no. 3, pp. 277–287.
BRISCOE, G., O'BRIEN, P. and SMYTH, D. J. (1970), 'The Measurement of Capacity Utilization in the United Kingdom', *The Manchester School of Social and Economic Studies*, Vol. 38, no. 2, pp. 91–118.
BROWN, M. (1966), *On the Theory and Measurement of Technological Change*, Cambridge University Press, Cambridge.
BROWN, T. M. (1952), 'Habit Persistence and Lags in Consumer Behavior', *Econometrica*, Vol. 20, no. 3, pp. 355–371.

CAGAN, P. (1956), 'The Monetary Dynamics of Hyper Inflation', in Friedman, ed., *Studies in the Quantitative Theory of Money*, University of Chicago Press, Chicago.

CHAMBERLAIN, E. (1933), *The Theory of Monopolistic Competition*, Harvard University Press, Cambridge.

CHENERY, H.B. (1952), 'Over-capacity and the Acceleration Principle', *Econometrica*, Vol. 20, no. 1, pp. 1–28.

CLARK, C. (1949), 'A System of Equations Explaining the United States Trade Cycle, 1921 to 1941', *Econometrica*, Vol. 17, no. 2, pp. 93–124.

COEN, R.M. (1968), 'Effects of Tax Policy on Investment in Manufacturing', *American Economic Review*, Vol. 58, no. 2, pp. 200–211.

COEN, R.M. and HICKMAN, B.G. (1970), 'Constrained Joint Estimation of Factor Demand and Production Functions', *Review of Economics and Statistics*, Vol. 52, no. 3, pp. 287–300.

COURCHENE, T.J. (1969), 'An Analysis of the Price-Inventory Nexus with Empirical Application to the Canadian Manufacturing Sector', *International Economic Review*, Vol. 10, no. 3, pp. 315–336.

CRAMER, J.S. (1969), *Empirical Econometrics*, North-Holland Publishing Company, Amsterdam.

DARLING, P.G. and LOVELL, M.C. (1965), 'Factors Influencing Investment in Inventories' in Duesenberry et al., *The Brookings Quarterly Econometric Model of the United States*, North-Holland Publishing Company, Amsterdam.

DENNISON, E.F. (1962), *The Sources of Economic Growth in the United States and the Alternatives Before Us*, Committee for Economic Development, New York.

DHRYMES, P.J. (1969), 'A Model of Short Run Labour Adjustment' in *The Brookings Model: Some Further Results*, North-Holland Publishing Company, Amsterdam.

DHRYMES, P.J. and KURZ, M. (1967), 'Investment, Dividend and External Finance Behavior of Firms' in *Determinants of Investment Behavior*, New York, pp. 427–467.

DICKS-MIREAUX, L.A. (1961), 'The Interrelationship between Cost and Price Changes, 1946–1959: a Study of Inflation in post-war Britain', *Oxford Economic Papers*, Vol. 13, pp. 267–292.

DICKS-MIREAUX, L.A. and DOW, J.C.R. (1959), 'The Determinants of Wage Inflation: United Kingdom, 1946–'56', *The Journal of the Royal Statistical Society*, Vol. 122, no. 2, pp. 145–174.

DOSSER, D., HAN, S.S. and HITIRIS, T. (1969), 'Trade Effects of Tax Harmonisation', *The Manchester School of Social and Economic Studies*, Vol. 37, no. 4, pp. 337–346.

DRIEHUIS, W. (1968), *Enige berekeningen omtrent het rendement van het geïnvesteerde vermogen*, Central Planning Bureau, The Hague, (mimeographed).

DRIEHUIS, W. (1969), 'Experiments in Explaining and Forecasting the Invisible Trade of the Netherlands, *Bulletin of the Oxford University Institute of Economics and Statistics*, Vol. 31, no. 4, pp. 335–351.

DRIEHUIS, W. (1970), *A Quarterly Model of the Netherlands' Economy*, Paper presented at the Second World Congress of the Econometric Society, Cambridge, Central Planning Bureau, The Hague (mimeographed).

DRIEHUIS, W. (1970a), 'An Econometric Analysis of Liner Freight Rates', *Weltwirtschaftliches Archiv*, Band 104, Heft 1, pp. 96–119.

DRIEHUIS, W. (1971), *Towards an Ocean Shipping Model*, Paper presented at the 4th IMF Siminar on Techniques of Commodity Price Forecasting, Hamburg.

DUESENBERRY, J.S. (1949), *Income, Saving and the Theory of Consumer Behavior*, Harvard University Press, Cambridge Mass.

DUESENBERRY, J.S. (1958), *Business Cycles and Economic Growth*, MacGraw Hill, New York.

DUESENBERRY, J.S., FROMM, G., KLEIN, L.R. and KUH, E., eds. (1965), *The Brookings Quarterly Econometric Model of the United States*, North-Holland Publishing Company, Amsterdam.

ECKSTEIN, O. (1964), 'A Theory of the Wage Price Process in Modern Industry', *Review of Economic Studies*, Vol. 31 (4), no. 88, pp. 267–286.
ECKSTEIN, O. and FROMM, G. (1968), 'The Price Equation', *American Economic Review*, Vol. 58, no. 5, pp. 1159–1183.
ECKSTEIN, O. and WILSON, T.A. (1962), 'The Determination of Money Wages in American Industry', *Quarterly Journal of Economics*, Vol. 76, pp. 379–414.
EISNER, R. (1964), 'Capital Expenditures, Profits and the Acceleration Principle' in *Models of Income Determination* (Conference on Research in Income and Wealth), Princeton University Press, Princeton.
EISNER, R. (1967), 'A Permanent Income Theory for Investment', *American Economic Review*, Vol. 57, no. 2, pp. 190–203.
EISNER, R. (1970), *Components of Capital Expenditures: Replacement and Modernization Versus Expansion*, Paper presented at the Second World Congress of the Econometric Society, Cambridge.
EVANS, M.K. (1969), *Macro-economic Activity*, Harper and Row, London.
EVANS, M.K. and KLEIN, L.R. (1967), *The Wharton Econometric Forecasting Model*, Economics Research Unit, University of Pennsylvania, Philadelphia.

FAIR, R.C. (1970), 'Labour Force Participation, Wage Rates and Money Illusion', *Review of Economics and Statistics*, Vol. 52, pp. 164–168.
FELDSTEIN, M.S. (1967), 'Specification of the Labour Input in the Aggregate Production Function', *Review of Economic Studies*, Vol. 34, no. 100, pp. 375–386.
FELDSTEIN, M.S. (1970), 'Inflation, Specification Bias and the Impact of Interest Rates', *Journal of Political Economy*, Vol. 78, no. 6, pp. 1325–1339.
FELDSTEIN, M.S. and ECKSTEIN, O. (1970), 'The Fundamental Determinants of the Interest Rate', *Review of Economics and Statistics*, Vol. 52, no. 4, pp. 363–375.
FELDSTEIN, M.S. and FOOT, D.K. (1971), 'The Other Half of Gross Investment: Replacement and Modernization Expenditures', *Review of Economics and Statistics*, Vol. 53, pp. 49–58.
FELLNER, W., GILBERT, M., HANSEN, B., KAHN, R., LUTZ, F. and WOLFF, P. DE (1961), *The Problem of Rising Prices*, OECD, Paris.
FERBER, R. (1953), *A Study of Aggregate Consumption Functions*, National Bureau of Economic Research, Inc. Technical Paper 8, New York.
FERBER, R. and VERDOORN, P.J. (1962), *Research Methods in Economics and Business*, MacMillan, New York.
FERGUSON, C.E. (1969), *The Neoclassical Theory of Production and Distribution*, Cambridge University Press, Cambridge.
FISHER, I. (1930), *The Theory of Interest*, MacMillan Company, New York.
FRIEDMAN, M. (1957), *A Theory of the Consumption Function* (National Bureau of Economic Research), Princeton University Press, Princeton N.J..
FRIEDMANN, M. (1970), 'A Theoretical Framework for Monetary Analysis', *Journal of Political Economy*, Vol. 78, no. 2, pp. 193–238.
FROMM, G. and TAUBMAN, P.J. (1968), *Policy Simulations with an Econometric Model*, North-Holland Publishing Company, Amsterdam.

GIESSEN, A.A. VAN DER, (1970), 'Solving Non-linear Systems by Computer; A New Method', *Statistica Neerlandica*, Vol. 24, no. 1, pp. 41–50.
GORDON, R.J. (1970), 'The Brookings Model in Action; A Review Article', *Journal of Political Economy*, Vol. 78, no. 3, pp. 489–525.
GRAY, H.P. (1971), 'On Measuring the Price Sensitivity of Invisible International Trade', *Bulletin Oxford University Institute of Economics and Statistics*, Vol. 33, no. 3, pp. 207–216.
GREENBERG, E. (1964), 'A Stock Adjustment Investment Model', *Econometrica*, Vol. 32, no. 3, pp. 339–357.
GREGORY, R.G. (1971), 'United States Imports and Internal Pressure of Demand', *American Economic Review*, Vol. 61, no. 1, pp. 38–47.
GRILICHES, Z. (1961), 'A Note on Serial Correlation Bias in Estimates of Distributed Lags', *Econometrica*, Vol. 29, no. 1, pp. 65–73.
GRILICHES, Z. (1967), 'Distributed Lags: A Survey', *Econometrica*, Vol. 35, no. 1, pp. 16–49.

HAAS, B. (1960), 'Wage Policy in Holland', *The Manchester School of Social and Economic Studies*, Vol. 28, no. 2, pp. 177–206.
HALEY, C.W. (1971), 'Taxes, the Cost of Capital, and the Firm's Investment Decisions', *Journal of Finance*, no. 4, pp. 901–917.
HALL, R.E. and JORGENSON, D.W. (1967), 'Tax Policy and Investment Behavior', *American Economic Review*, Vol. 57, no. 3, pp. 391–414.
HAMBURGER, M.J. (1967), 'Interest Rates and the Demand for Consumer Durable Goods', *American Economic Review*, Vol. 57, no. 5, pp. 1131–1153.
HARTOG, H. DEN and FALKE, H.G. (1970), 'An explanation of Investment Equipment by Enterprises in the Netherlands', *European Economic Review*, Vol. 1, no. 4, pp. 447–481.
HARTOG, H. DEN and FRAENKEL, M. (1972), *An Econometric Model of the Textile and Clothing Industries in the Netherlands*, Paper presented at the Ninth Meeting of Senior Economic Advisers to ECE Governments (to be published by the United Nations).
HENRY, G.B. (1970), 'Domestic Demand Pressure and Short-Run Export Fluctuations', *Yale Economic Essays*, Vol. 10, no. 1, pp. 43–81.
HESSEL, W. (1965), 'Quantitative Planning of Economic Policy in the Netherlands' in B.G. Hickmann ed. *Quantitative Planning of Economic Policy*, The Brookings Institution, Washington.
HICKMAN, B. (1957), 'Capacity, Capacity Utilization, and the Acceleration Principle', in *Problems of Capital Formation*. Studies in Income and Wealth, Vol. 19, Princeton University Press, Princeton.
HICKS, J.R. (1937), 'Mr. Keynes and the Classics; A suggested Interpretation', *Econometrica*, Vol. 37, pp. 147–159.
HICKS, J.R. (1946), *Value and Capital*, Second Edition, At the Clarendon Press, Oxford.
HILTON, K. assisted by DOLPHIN, H. (1970), 'Capital and Capacity Utilization in the United Kingdom: their Measurement and Reconciliation', *Bulletin Oxford University Institute of Economics and Statistics*, Vol. 32, no. 3, pp. 187–218.
HINES, A.G. (1964), 'Trade Unions and Wage Inflation in the United Kingdom 1893–1961', *Review of Economic Studies*, Vol. 31 (4), no. 88, pp. 211–252.
HOUTHAKKER, H.S. and MAGEE, S.P. (1969), 'Income and Price Elasticities in World Trade', *Review of Economics and Statistics*, Vol. 51, no. 2, pp. 111–125.
HUBBARD, N.S. (1968), 'Short-Run Changes in Labour Productivity in United States Manufacturing, 1954–'59', *Yale Economic Essays*, Vol. 8, no. 2, pp. 59–133.
HYMANS, S.H. and SHAPIRO, H.T. (1970), *The DHL III Quarterly Econometric Model of the U.S. Economy*, Ann Arbor, Michigan.

JONGMAN, C. D. (1960), *De Nederlandse Geldmarkt*, Stenfert Kroese, Leiden.
JORGENSON, D. W. (1963), 'Capital Theory and Investment Behavior', *American Economic Review*, Vol. 53, no. 2, pp. 247–259.
JORGENSON, D. W. (1965), 'Anticipations and Investment Behavior' in Duesenberry, et. al., *The Brookings Quarterly Econometric Model of the United States*, North-Holland Publishing Company, Amsterdam.
JORGENSON, D. W. (1966), 'Rational Distributed Lag Functions', *Econometrica*, Vol. 34, no. 1, pp. 135–149.
JORGENSON, D. W. and SIEBERT, C. D. (1968), A Comparison of Alternative Theories of Corporate Investment Behavior', *American Economic Review*, Vol. 58, no. 4, pp. 681–712.
JORGENSON, D. W. and STEPHENSON, J. A. (1967), 'Investment Behavior in United States Manufacturing 1947–1960', *Econometrica*, Vol. 35, no. 2, pp. 169–220.
JOHNSTON, J. (1963), *Econometric Methods*, MacGraw-Hill, New York, (International Student Edition).
JUNANKAR, P. N. (1970), 'The Relationship between Investment and Spare Capacity in the United Kingdom, 1957–1966', *Economica*, Vol. 37, no. 147, pp. 277–292.
KENDALL, M. G. and STUART, A. (1966), *The Advanced Theory of Statistics, Vol. 3*, C. Griffin and Company, London.
KEYNES, J. M.(1936), *The General Theory of Employment Interest and Money*, MacMillan and Co. Ltd., London.
KILLINGWORTH, M. R. (1970), A Critical Survey of 'Neoclassical Models of Labour', *Bulletin Oxford University Institute of Economics and Statistics*, Vol. 32, no. 2, pp. 133–165.
KIRSCHEN, E. S. (ed) (1964), *Economic Policy in Our Time, Vol. I*, North-Holland Publishing Company, Amsterdam.
KLEIN, L. R., BALL, R. J., HAZLEWOOD, A. and VANDOME, P. (1961), *An Econometric Model of the United Kingdom*, Oxford.
KLEIN, L. R. and PRESTON, R. S. (1967), 'Some New Results in the Measurement of Capacity Utilization', *American Economic Review*, Vol. 57, no. 1, pp. 34–58.
KOOYMAN, J. and MERKIES, A. H. Q. M. (1971), 'Possible Growth in the Netherlands up to 1985', in *Long-Term Planning*, Papers presented at the Seventh Meeting of Senior Economic Advisers to ECE Governments, United Nations, New York.
KOYCK, L. M. (1954), *Distributed Lags and Investment Analysis*, North-Holland Publishing Company, Amsterdam.
KRISHNAMURTY, K. (1961), *Industrial Utilization of Capacity*, American Statistical Association, Proceedings of the Business and Economic Statistics Section.
KUH, E. (1963), *Capital Stock Growth: A Micro-Econometric Approach*, North-Holland Publishing Company, Amsterdam.
KUH, E. (1967), 'A Productivity Theory of Wage Levels – An Alternative to the Phillips Curve', *Review of Economic Studies*, Vol. 34, no. 100, pp. 333–360.

LEEUW, F. DE and GRAMLICH, E. M. (1968), 'The Federal Reserve MIT Econometric Model', *Federal Reserve Bulletin*, pp. 11–40.
LIEBENBERG, M., HIRSCH, A. A. and POPKIN, J. (1966), *A Quarterly Econometric Model of the United States: A Progress Report*, U.S. Department of Commerce, Survey of Current Business.
LIPSEY, R. G. (1960), 'The Relationship Between Unemployment and the Rate of Change of Wage Rates in the U.K., 1862–1957: A Further Analysis', *Economica*, Vol. 27, no. 105, pp. 1–31.

LIPSEY, R.G. and PARKIN, J.M. (1970), 'Incomes Policy: A Re-Appraisal', *Economica*, Vol. 36, no. 146, pp. 115-138.

LOVELL, M. (1961), 'Manufacturers' Inventories, Sales Expectations, and the Acceleration Principle', *Econometrica*, Vol. 29, no. 3, pp. 293-314.

LUCAS, R.E. and RAPPING, L.A. (1969), 'Real Wages, Employment and Inflation', *Journal of Political Economy*, Vol. 77, no. 5, pp. 721-754.

LÜDEKE, D. (1969), *Ein Ökonometrisches Vierteljahres Modell für die Bundesrepublik Deutschland*, J.C.B. Mohr (Paul Siebeck), Tübingen.

MALINVAUD, E. (1966), *Statistical Methods of Econometrics*, North-Holland Publishing Company, Amsterdam.

MALKIEL, B.G. (1966), *The Term Structure of Interest Rates*, Princeton University Press, Princeton.

McCALLUM, B.T. (1970), 'The Effect of Demand on Prices in British Manufacturing: Another View', *Review of Economic Studies*, Vol. 37, no. 109, pp. 147-156.

MELTZER, A.H. (1963), 'The Demand for Money: The Evidence from the Time Series', *Journal of Political Economy*, Vol. 71, pp. 219-246.

MERKIES, A.H.Q.M. and PAS, J.H. VAN DE (1969), *Branches of Industry Medium Term Model*, Central Planning Bureau, The Hague (mimeographed).

MEYER, J. and KUH, E. (1957), *The Investment Decision*, Harvard University Press, Cambridge.

MUNDELL, R. (1963), 'Inflation and Real Interest', *Journal of Political Economy*, Vol. 71, pp. 280-283.

NADIRI, M.I. (1968), 'The Effects of Relative Prices and Capacity on the Demand for Labour in the U.S. Manufacturing Sector', *Review of Economic Studies*, July, pp. 273-288.

NADIRI, M.I. and ROSEN, S. (1969), 'Interrelated Factor Demand Functions', *American Economic Review*, Vol. 59, no. 4, pp. 457-471.

NEILD, R.R. (1963), *Pricing and Employment in the Trade Cycle*. A Study of British Manufacturing Industry, 1950 to 1961. National Institute of Economic and Social Research, Occasional Paper XXL.

NERLOVE, M. (1958), *Distributed Lags and Demand Analysis*, USDA, Agriculture Handbook N. 141, Washington.

NERLOVE, M. (1966), 'A Tabular Survey of Macro Econometric Models', *International Economic Review*, Vol. 7, pp. 127-175.

OFFICER, L.H. (1968), *An Econometric Model of Canada under the Fluctuating Exchange Rate*, Cambridge, Mass.

PAISH, F.W. (1962), *Studies in an Inflationary Economy. The United Kingdom 1948-1961*, MacMillan and Co., London.

PARKIN, J.M. (1970), 'Incomes Policy: Some Further Results on the Determination of the Rate of Change of Money Wages', *Economica*, Vol. 37, no. 148, pp. 386-401.

PERRY, G.L. (1966), *Unemployment, Money Wage Rates, and Inflation*, M.I.T. Press, Cambridge, Mass.

PHELPS, E.S. (1968), 'Money-Wage Dynamics and Labour-Market Equilibrium', *Journal of Political Economy*, Vol. 76, no. 4, pp. 678-754.

PHELPS BROWN, E.H. (1962), 'Wage Drift', *Economica*, Vol. 29, no. 116, pp. 339-356.

PHILLIPS, A.W. (1958), 'The Relation Between Unemployment and the Rate of Change of Money Wage Rates in the United Kingdom, 1861–1957', *Economica*, Vol. 25, no. 100, pp. 283–299.
PHILLIPS, A.W. (1961), 'A Simple Model of Employment, Money and Prices in a Growing Economy', *Economica*, Vol. 28, no. 112, pp. 360–370.
PIGOU, A.C. (1941), *Employment and Equilibrium*, MacMillan, London.
POWER, J.H. (1959), 'Price Expectations, Money Illusion and the Real-Balance Effect', *Journal of Political Economy*, Vol. 67, no. 2, pp. 131–143.

QUIRITANI, T. and MARU, J. (1970), *A Quarterly Econometric Model of Japan*, ISRI Technical Paper, no. 15.

RHOMBERG, R.R. and BOISSONNEAULT, L. (1965), 'The Foreign Sector' in Duesenberry et al., *The Brookings Econometric Quarterly Model of the United States*, North-Holland Publishing Company, Amsterdam.
RUSHDY, F. and LUND, P.J. (1967), 'The Effect of Demand on Prices in British Manufacturing Industry', *Review of Economic Studies*, Vol. 34, pp. 361–373.

SAMUELSON, P.A. (1948), *Foundations of Economic Analysis* (second edition), Harvard University Press, Cambridge.
SARGENT, T.J. (1969), 'Commodity Price Expectations and the Interest Rate', *Quarterly Journal of Economics*, Vol. 83, pp. 127–140.
SCHNEIDER, E. (1963), *Einführung in die Wirtschaftstheorie, II Teil*, MOHR, J.C.B. (Paul Siebeck), Tübingen.
SCHULTZE, C.L. and TYRON, J.L. (1965), 'Prices and Wages' in Duesenberry et. al., *The Brookings Quarterly Econometric Model of the United States*, North-Holland Publishing Company, Amsterdam.
SENGUPTA, J.K. (1965), 'Specification and Estimation of Structural Relations in Policy Models 'in HICKMAN, B.G. ed., *Quantitative Planning of Economic Policy*, Washington.
SIEBRAND, J.C. and HOOGLAND, J.G.D. (1969), *A World Trade Model in Relative First differences*, Central Planning Bureau, The Hague, (mimeographed).
SMITHIES, A. (1957), 'Economic Fluctuations and Growth', *Econometrica*, Vol. 25, no. 1, pp. 1–52.
SMYTH, D.J. and IRELAND, N.J. (1967), 'Short-Term Employment Functions in Australian Manufacturing', *Review of Economics and Statistics*, Vol. 49, no. 4, pp. 537–544.
SOLOW, R.M. (1957), 'Technical Change and the Aggregate Production Function', *Review of Economics and Statistics*, Vol. 39, no. 3, pp. 312–320.
SOLOW, R.M. (1960), 'On a Family of Lag Distributions', *Econometrica*, Vol. 28, no. 2, pp. 399–406.
STEVERS, TH.A. (1963), *Renteverschillen en renteniveau*, Nijgh and Van Ditmar, Rotterdam.
STREIT, M.E. (1970), 'Investment Reaction Patterns', *Weltwirtschaftliches Archiv*, Band 105, Heft 1, pp. 66–86.

TINBERGEN, J. (1936), 'An Economic Policy for 1936' in Klaassen, L.H., Koyck, L.M. and Witteveen, H.J. eds., *Jan Tinbergen Selected Papers*, North-Holland Publishing Company, Amsterdam, 1959. (Translation of the original 1936 article.)
TINTNER, G. (1952), *Econometrics*, Wiley, New York.
TOBIN, J. (1956), 'The Interest-Elasticity of Transactions Demand for Cash', *Review of Economics and Statistics*, Vol. 38, no. 3, pp. 241–247.
TYRNI, I. (1964), 'The Effect of Price Changes on Consumer Saving', *Review of Economic Studies*, Vol. 31 (2), no. 86, pp. 149–162.

VERDOORN, P.J. (1967), 'The Short-Term Model of the Central Planning Bureau and its Forecasting Performance (1953–1963)' in *Macro Economic Models for Planning and Policy-Making*, pp. 35–51. Edited by the Secretariat of the Economic Commission for Europe, Geneva.

VERDOORN, P.J. (1968), *Prolegomena of Consumption Functions*, Central Planning Bureau, The Hague, (mimeographed).

VERDOORN, P.J. and EIJK, C.J. VAN (1958), *Experimental Short-Term Forecasting Models*, Paper presented at the 20th European Meeting of the Econometric Society, Bilbao, Central Planning Bureau, The Hague, (mimeographed).

VERDOORN, P.J. and POST, J.J. (1964), 'Capacity and Short-Term Multipliers' in *Econometric Analysis for National Planning*, eds. Heart, P.E., Mills, G. and Whitaker, J.K., pp. 179–205, Butterworths, London.

VERDOORN, P.J., POST, J.J. and GOSLINGA, S.S. (1970), *The 1969 Re-estimation of the Annual Model*, Central Planning Bureau, The Hague.

WALLIS, K.F. (1969), 'Some Recent Developments in Applied Econometrics', *Journal of Economic Literature*, Vol. 7, no. 3, pp. 771–796.

WERF, D. VAN DER (1971), *De Westduitse economie in vijftien vergelijkingen*, Amsterdam.

WOLD, H.O.A. (1954), 'Causality and Econometrics', *Econometrica*, Vol. 22, no. 2, pp. 162–177.

ZELLNER, A., HUANG, D.S. and CHAU, L.C. (1965), 'Further Analysis of the Short-Run Consumption Function with Emphasis on the Role of Liquid Assets', *Econometrica*, Vol. 33, no. 3, pp. 571–581.

Index

Adaptive expectations
  hypothesis 17
Adjustment time 20
Almon distributed lag 19
Average lag(s)
  definition of 15
  tables of 40, 48, 64, 75, 84, 92, 95, 99, 102.
    115, 127, 146, 161, 169
Average growth rates 42

Balance of payments 85, 161–162, 164–166
  on current account 2, 180
  on capital account 85–86, 182, 225

Capacity utilization 49–52
Capital imports and exports 85–86, 182, 225
Capital stock 34, 36, 54
Capital utilization 30, 34–35, 49–52, 55–58
Central Bank (see Nederlandsche Bank, de)
Central Bureau of Statistics 7–8, 100
Central Economic Plan 2
Central Planning Bureau
  forecasting procedure of 1–2
  compilation of data by 8
  publications of 7–8, 179
Cobb Douglas production function 4, 27.
  41, 55, 104
Coefficient of determination 24
Comparison
  quaterly model with annual model 2–3
  short-term with medium-term
    simulations 217

Consistency
  of factor demand relationships 26
Consumption (private)
  average lags 75
  empirical results 74–76
  influence of:
    consumer prices 65–66
    income distribution 65–66, 71
    interest rate 73
    liquidity ratio 72
    money illusion 68–69
    non-wage income 65 ff
    Pigou effect 69
    price expectations 69
    utilization rate of labour 73
    wage income 65 ff
    wealth 72
Costs
  marginal 27, 130
  average 130
Cost minimization 28
Credit restriction 161–162, 168
Cyclical growth model 1, 92, 161, 205
Cyclical turning points 3, 186 ff, 210 ff

Demand model 5
Demographic factors 42
Discount rate 161, 164, 182
Distributed lag
  infinite 5, 14, 21
  finite 5, 14, 21
  geometrical 15
  rational 14

267

Domestic labour supply 42
Dynamic adjustment 12
Dynamic behaviour 7

Econometric model
  cyclical growth 1, 205
  short term annual 1, 205
  quarterly 1, 205
Eec effect 92, 93
Elasticity of substitution 29
Employment
  average lags 40
  empirical results 37–42
  influence of:
    labour time 25, 30, 41
    liquidity ratio 32
    production 25, 27
    rate of return 32
    technology 25, 35, 41
    user cost of capital 25, 28
    utilization rate of labour 25, 31
    wage rate 25, 28
Estimation procedure 21
Exchange rate policy 183
Expansion path function 29
Expectations 13
Exports of goods
  average lags 92
  empirical results 88–92
  influence of:
    autonomous factors 90
    capacity utilization 86–92
    EEC effect 92
    exports of competitors 86–87
    price substitution elasticity 90–91
    relative prices 86–88
    world demand 86–87
  weighting schemes for 89, 251
Exports of services
  average lags 95
  empirical results 92–95
  influence of:
    autonomous factors 93
    capacity utilization 86–92
    EEC effect 94
    exports of competitors 86–87
    relative prices 86–88
    world demand 86–87
  weighting schemes for 89, 252

Factor incomes
  received from abroad 86
  paid to abroad 86
Freight rates 145–146
Gradual adjustment of
  prices 20–21
Government
  consumption 148
  employees 51
  expenditures 147, 181
  investment 148
  liquidity creation 162–164
  revenue 147, 181

Heteroscedasticity 11
Humped curves of reaction 19
Imperfect competition 4, 27, 34, 88, 105–106, 129, 132–133
Imports of goods
  autonomous factors 97
  average lags 99
  empirical results 97–99
  influence of:
    demand 95
    capacity utilization 95
    domestic prices 96
    relative prices 95
  weighting schemes for 97[n], 253-254
Imports of services
  average lags 102
  empirical results 100–102
  influence of:
    capacity utilization 95
    demand 95
    relative prices 95
  weighting schemes for 101[n], 253-254
Inequality coefficient 185 ff
Incidental wage component (see wage drift)
Income distribution 66–71, 180
Input-cost ratio 29
Instrument variables 181–183
Instruments of economic policy
  exchange rate policy 183
  direct control 183
  government expenditure 181
  government revenue 182
  money and credit 182
  price policy 183
  wage policy 183

Interest rate
  average lags 161
  empirical results 158
  long-term 76, 81–82, 152 ff
  nominal 73, 156
  real 65, 73, 153–155, 156
  short-term 153–157, 166
  influence of:
    short term interest rate 153, 155, 157
    liquidity ratio 157
    normal interest rate 153, 155
    prices 157
    utilization rate of labour 154
Inventory formation
  average lags 84
  empirical results 82–83
  influence of:
    discrepancy actual/desired stocks 80
    interest rate 81
    price of imports 80
    sales 79
    utilization rate of labour 79
  planned 78–80
  precautionary motive for 79
  speculative 80
  speculative motive for 80
  transactions motive for 79
  unplanned 80
Investment allowances 40, 182
Investment in enterprises
  average lags 64
  empirical results 61–64
  for expansion 54 ff
  for replacement and modernization 50 ff
  influence of:
    capital utilization 55–58
    discrepancy desired-actual capital stock 54–55
    labour time 55
    liquidity ratio 57–58
    production 55, 58
    rate of return 57–58
    technology 55
    user costs of capital 55, 58
    utilization rate of labour 55, 58
    wage rate 55, 58
Iterations 19, 21, 38

Koyck distributed lag 16, 19, 21, 22

Labour costs
  unit 133–134
  standard unit 133–134
Labour demand
  see employment
Labour supply
  average lags 48
  border commuting 44
  domestic 42
  empirical results 45–48
  foreign migration 43
  influence of:
    participation married women 47–48
    real wages 42, 47–48
    relative wages 43–45
    utilization rate of labour 43–45
  medium term 42
Labour time
  actual 30, 52
  contractual 37, 40, 49, 52, 63
  overtime 108–109
Lag(s)
  distributed (see distributed lag)
  finite 5, 14, 21
  infinite 5, 14, 21
  institutional 13
  objective causes of 13
  single 14
  start of 21
  subjective causes of 13
  technological 13
Lag operator 15
Lagrange polynomials 19
Least squares
  generalized 22
  ordinary 12, 21
Liquidity ratio (see money supply)
  decreasing trend in 165

Macro Economic Outlook 2

Marginal costs
  of capital 27
  of labour 27
Marginal productivity theory 4
Ministry of Finance 8
Model
  dynamic version 226
  general character 3–5
  hypotheses 4

medium term elements 4
   non-linear solution 255–257
   static version 171 ff
   working of the 176–177
Monetary Policy 182
Money demand
   components of 154–155
      for precautionary motive 153
      for speculative motive 153
      for transactions motive 153
   decreasing trend in 165
Money illusion 42, 68–69
Money supply
   average lags 169
   empirical results 165
   influence of:
      balance of payments 162
      banking liquidity 161
      credit restrictions 162
      discount rate 164
      government liquidity creation 163
      interest rate 162
      prices 163
      utilization rate of labour 162
Multiplicator of Lagrange 28

National accounts 8
Nederlandsche Bank, de 8, 183
Neumann Ratio, Von 18, 24
Non-wage income 31, 57–58, 66–67, 150, 180
Notation 24

Partial adjustment model 17
Partial elasticity coefficients 11
Participation rates 42
Pascal distributed lags 16, 19
Perfect competition 34
Performance
   annual 185 ff
   comparison with other models 207–208
   first difference 185 ff
   level 185 ff
   of selected variables 185 ff
   quarterly 185 ff
Permanent income hypothesis 70–71
Phillips curve 128
Pigou effect 69

Policy simulations
   increase of autonomous expenditures 221
   increase of direct taxes 220
   increase of indirect taxes 221
   increase of wages 223
Polynomials 15
Precautionary motive
   for inventory formation 79
   for money demand 153
Premultiplication procedure 12
Price elasticity of:
   demand 27, 105, 130
   supply of capital 27, 130
   supply of labour 27, 105, 130
Price expectation 20–21, 65, 69
Price formation
   theory of 129–135
   average lags 146
   influence of:
      capital productivity 131
      final demand category/aggregate demand 132
      labour productivity 131
      import productivity 131
      price of imports 131
      user costs of capital 130
      utilization rate of labour 131
      wages 130
Price of autonomous expenditures
   average lags 146
   empirical results 140
   theory (see price formation)
Price of exports of manufactured goods
   average lags 146
   empirical results 142
   theory (see price formation)
Price of exports of services
   average lags 146
   empirical results 145
   theory (see price formation)
Price of fixed investment
   average lags 146
   empirical results 138
   theory (see price formation)
Price of private consumption 146
   average lags 146
   empirical results 135
   theory (see price formation)
Price policy 183

Product
  marginal 28
  average 28
Production factor
  quasi fixed 29
  rigid 29
Production function 26–27, 41
  (see Cobb Douglas)
Productivity
  capital 131
  import 131
  labour 110, 111, 131
  marginal capital 130
  marginal labour 130
Profit maximization 5, 26, 104, 130–131

Quarterly data, sources of 8–9
Quarterly model (see also Model)
  comparison with annual models 2–3
  general character 3–5
  working of 176–177

Rate of return 31, 57–58
Rational distributed lag function 14
Reaction coefficients 15
Recursive solution 12, 256 ff
Recursive system 12
Resources and expenditures account
  8, 178–179
Response
  long-run 15
  short-run 15
Returns to scale 27, 35
Root mean square error 185

Seasonal adjustment
  arguments in favour of 9
  multiplicator 10, 248
  objections against 10
  seasonal component 10, 248
  trend cycle component 10, 248
Seasonally adjusted series 9
Selection procedure 20–21
Self-employed working population 42, 51
Short-term annual model 1, 3, 64[n], 87[n], 95, 103, 205
Simulation(s)
  medium term (twenty-quarter) 209 ff
  other 224
  performance (see performance)

policy 220-223
  short-term (eight-quarter) 184 ff
Solution
  method of 255
  sequence of 257
Sources of data 7–9
Speculative motive 80
  for inventory formation 80
  for money demand 153
Standard error 22, 24
Standard forecasting period 3-4
Stocks
  actual 79–80
  desired 80–82
  discrepancy actual/desired 79–82, 135
Stocks-sales ratio 79, 82
Supply
  of capital 27, 34
  of labour 27, 34, 42 ff
  of imports 86, 131

Target variables 5, 180
Taxes
  institutional aspects 148–149
  on non-wage income 150
  on sales 151
  on wage income 149–150
Technological progress 27, 41
Time series, sources of 8–9
Tools 7
Transactions motive
  for inventory formation 79
  for money demand 153
Trending data 19

Unemployment
  frictional 51
  ratio 4, 180, 185 ff
User cost of capital 25, 28, 39–40, 55–58, 130
Utilization rate
  of capital 30, 34–35, 49–52, 55–58
  of labour 25–28, 32, 42–48, 51, 55–58, 68–69, 79, 106, 108, 131, 154, 162
  of labour time 49, 52
  of production 49, 52

Variables
  endogenous:
    classification of 177

list of 240
exogenous:
 classification of 179
 list of 240
 instrument 180–183
 target 180

Wage determination
 institutional factors 106–107
 sociological and
  psychological factors 111
 theory 104 ff
 trade unions 111ⁿ
Wage drift
 causes 107–109
 equation 109
Wage income 66–67, 149, 180
Wage policy 103, 183
 effects of 118–119, 122, 124, 128
 institutional aspects 115–117
Wages
 black 107
 contract 107–108
 government 147
 piece 107–108
 private 147
 time 107

Wage sum per worker
 average lags:
  sub-periods 127
  whole period 115
 empirical results:
  sub-periods 117 ff
  whole period 112
 influence of:
  autonomous taxes (shifting of) 111
  imperfect competition 111
  labour productivity 104–105, 110–111
  overtime 108, 111
  price of private consumption 109–110
  social premiums (shifting of) 111
  utilization rate of labour 106
 lump sum payments 113
Wealth 65, 72
Weighting schemes
 exports of goods 251
 exports of services 252
 imports of goods 253-254
 imports of services 253-254
Working hours 30–31
Working population
 trend of 42, 107